H                                    s

Pastime Guide

The guide is divided into 4 Country Colour Coded sections presenting you with three quite different types of holidays.

There are three sections titled:

### Bed and Breakfast

### Self Catering

### Farm and Country *Holidays.*

*It is as simple as that!*

Our advertisers all present a warm, welcoming invitation to stay with them.

We have paid particular attention to readers who require either a quiet, solitary holiday or a more active, historical sightseeing break.

Lastly, we hope the information provided in the following pages will help you to have a very happy holiday.

# Contents

Places of Interest England                          5

Places of Interest Scotland                        54

Places of Interest Wales                           73

Places of Interest Northern Ireland                78

Bed and Breakfast Accommodation                    83

Self Catering Accommodation                       129

Farm & Country Accommodation                      175

Colour Road Maps                                  202

Graphic Design: Sarah Pritchett.
Editing & Production: Louise Couper, Louise Stanton.
No part of "The Complete Holiday Accommodation Guide for the UK" may be published or
reproduced in any form without the prior consent of the publisher.©
Published by Pastime Publications Ltd., 8 St. Andrew Square, Edinburgh EH2 2PP.
Tel: 0131-556 1105  Fax: 0131-556 1129.
Printed & bound in Scotland.

Front Cover: The Old Forge at Totnes, Devon. See page 95.

# Places of Interest *England*

## AVON/SOMERSET

### Bath
The Roman Baths are one of Bath's most famous sights. Other attractions include the Pump Room and the 16th century Abbey, Georgian crescents and terraces, riverside gardens, fine shops, hotels, museums and flowers galore that have won Bath the "Britain in Bloom" award more times than any other British city. Amenities: theatre; excellent shopping; golf courses; horse racing; angling; sports centre; cinemas.

### Weston Supermare
Attractive family resort and ideal touring base. Long level promenade and spacious sandy beach. Main features include Tropicana - heated open air surf pool with thrilling chutes, renovated Winter Gardens and Knightstone Island leisure and entertainment com-plexes, Grand Pier, stage shows and films, lovely parks and woodland plus Ocean Earth undersea centre. Visit Cheddar Gorge and Caves, Wookey's wonders, wells Cathedral city, Bath Roman Spa, historic Bristol, roll-ing Mendip hills, all nearby.

### Avon Valley Railway
**Bitton station, Bristol. Tel: (0117) 9327296.**
Collection of locomotives and rolling stock including Stanier Black Five used to operate a standard gauge steam railway.

### Blaise Castle House Museum
**Henbury, Bristol. Tel: (0117) 9506789.**
Reconstruction of 18th and 19th century farm house kitchen. Victorian drawing room, home and rural crafts exhibits.

### Botanical Gardens
**Bath.**
Contains over 5,000 different varieties of plants from all over the world; also a lake and a children's pool.

### Bristol Zoological Gardens
**Bristol. Tel: (0117) 9738951.**
Comprehensive collection of animals including gorillas, okapi, nocturnal house, reptile house.

Gardens with lake.

### Dauphine Theatrical & Historical Costume Museum
**Bristol.**
Theatrical and historical costumes displayed in period scenes and shows.

### Dyrham Park
**Nr. Chippenham. Tel: (0117) 9372501**
Marvellous 17th century house with a naturalised formal garden and over 260 acres of ancient parkland with herd of fallow deer.

### Exploratory Hands-On Science Centre
**Bristol. Tel: (0117) 9252008.**
Exhibitions include lights, lasers, lenses and gyroscopes.

### International Helicopter Museum
**Weston-Super-Mare. Tel: (01934) 635227.**
Unique collection of helicopters and autogyros with background displays.

### Maritime Heritage Centre
**Bristol. Tel: (0117) 9260680.**
History of 200 years of shipbuilding in Bristol.

### Museum of Costume
**Bath. Tel: (01225) 461111.**
Displays of fashionable dress from 16th century to the present day.

### The Red Lodge
**Bristol. Tel: (0117) 9211360.**
Last surviving suite of 16th century rooms in Bristol.

### Roman Baths & Museum
**Bath. Tel: (01225) 461111.**
Great resort of Roman and Georgian England. Adjoining museum with Roman relics.

### St. Nicholas Church Museum
**Bristol. Tel: (0117) 9211365.**
Local history and church art.

### Sally Lunn's House
**Bath. Tel: (01225) 461634.**
The oldest house in Bath, with excavations

showing early medieval and Roman building.

### Stanton Drew Circles and Cove
**Nr. Chew Magna.**
One of the finest Neolithic monuments of its type in the country, consisting of stonecircles and burial chamber.

### Victoria Art Gallery
**Bath. Tel: (01225) 461111.**
18th century and modern painting, etchings, ceramics, coins of Bath mint, glass and watches on display.

# BEDFORDSHIRE

### Ampthill
One of Bedfordshire's finest historic towns 8 miles south of Bedford. A cross marks the spot where the 15th century castle stood; Catherine of Aragon was sent there while Henry VIII arranged the annulment of their marriage.

### Bedford
This ancient county town dates back to before Saxon times. It is known as the home of the author John Bunyan, whose life story is portrayed in the Bunyan Museum and the 16th century Moot Hall at Elstow. The Great River Ouse, which flows through the town, has been cherished since Victorian times and offers attractive gardens, water meadows and riverside walks. The town has a suspension bridge, a bandstand and many fine buildings. The Bedford River Festival is held every other year in May. The town also hosts a regatta in May.

### Leighton Buzzard
This market town, famous for sand, is situated on the Grand Union Canal and has a wide Georgian high street with mews shops, an ancient street market and a fine parish church, dating from 1277.

### Bedford Museum
**Castle Lane, Bedford. Tel: (01234) 353323.**
The museum is housed in a former brewery near the Great River Ouse. Exhibits include re-created interiors of farmhouse and cottage, local rocks and fossils, birds and mammals from town and countryside, local archaeological finds and lacemaking.

### Bromham Mill
**Stagsden Road, Bromham.**

**Tel: (01234) 824330.**
Watermill and art gallery alongside Great River Ouse. Milling demos and guided tours.

### Cecil Higgins Art Gallery and Museum
**Castle Close, Bedford. Tel: (01234) 211222.**
Award-winning re-created Victorian Mansion, once the home of Cecil Higgins, includes bedroom with furniture designed by William Burges. Gallery contains outstanding collections of ceramics, glass and watercolours and prints.

### Elstow Moot Hall
**Elstow Green, Church End, Elstow.**
**Tel: (01234) 266889.**
Medieval Market Hall with exhibits from 17th century life, including beautiful period furniture.

### Leighton Buzzard Railway
**Page's Park Station, Leighton Buzzard.**
**Tel: (01525) 373888.**
Preserved industrial railway with steam locomotives from India and a French Cameroons diesel collection. This two-foot-gauge railway, built in 1919, covers 5.5 miles.

### Luton Hoo - The Wernher Collection
**Luton. Tel: (01582) 22955.**
Historic house built in 1767, exhibiting tapestries, porcelain, bronzes, ivories, jewellery by Fabergé and mementoes of the last Russian Imperial Family.

### The Mossman Collection
**Stockwood Park, Farley Hill Luton.**
**Tel: (01582) 38714.**
Over 70 historic vehicles depicting the history of horse-drawn transport from Roman times to World War II, including an example of a Royal Mail Coach.
The collection is housed within period gardens which include the Hamilton Finlay Sculpture garden. Craft demos are held in the park at weekends.

### Priory Country Park
**Barkers Lane, Bedford. Tel: (01234) 264213.**
228 acres of open country, lake and river walks. Wildlife conservation area, angling, sailing. Visitor Centre.

### Shuttleworth Collection
**Old Warden Aerodrome, Biggleswade.**
**Tel: (01767) 627288.**
Unique historic collection of aircraft from 1909

Bleriot to 1942 Spitfire, all in flying conditions. Flying displays and many other events held throughout the year.

### The Swiss Garden
**Biggleswade Rd, Old Warden.**
**Tel: (01243) 228671.**
A unique, ornamental 18th century example of an English garden complete with splendid shrubs, mature trees, islands, ponds and tiny bridges.

### Toddington Manor
**Toddington. Tel: (01525) 873924.**
Beautiful gardens and woods with lakes covering an area of 20 acres where rare breeds of livestock roam freely. Vintage tractors also on display.

### Whipsnade Wild Animal Park
**Dunstable. Tel: (01582) 872171.**
Over 2,000 animals including rare and endangered species, as well as chimps, bears, zebras, penguins and tigers, in a 600 acre setting of parkland. Park also boasts a Children's Farm, Runwild Playcentre and Great Whipsnade Railway. Daily events include Birds of the World, Sealion and Elephant Encounters.

### Woburn Abbey
**Woburn. Tel: (01525) 290666.**
Home of the Dukes of Bedford for over 300 years, the house was built in the mid 12th century and altered by Henry Holland, the Prince Regent's architect in the mid 18th century. Contains an extensive art collection including paintings by Canaletto, Rembrandt, Holbein and others. Set in a 3,000 acre deer park.

### Woburn Safari Park
**Woburn Park, Woburn. Tel: (01525) 290407.**
Drive-through safari park and Wild World Leisure area offering boating lake, pets corner, new walk-through aviary and parrot, sea lion and elephant show.

### Woodside Farm & Wildfowl Park
**Mancroft Road, Slip End. Tel: (01582) 841044.**
Six-acre park with farm shop, poultry centre, arts and crafts centre, wildfowl collection, rare breeds centre, farm animals, children's play area and coffee shop.

### Wrest Park House & Gardens
**Wrest Park, Silsoe. Tel: (01525) 860152.**
150 years of English gardens laid out in the early 18th century, including a painted pavilion, Chinese bridge, lake, classical temple and Louis XV style French Mansion.

# BUCKINGHAMSHIRE

### Aylesbury
Great changes have taken place in recent years and the centre of Aylesbury is now filled with shopping complexes, tall offices and busy ring roads. Until a couple of decades ago , Aylesbury's main features were its cobbled streets, narrow alleyways and Georgian houses. Some dignified early buildings remain in Church Street - the 18th century grammar school buildings are used as the county museum. At the end of Church Street is the parish Church of St. Mary's, a building that stands on the site of the original Saxon church.

### Claydon House
**Middle Claydon, nr Buckingham.**
**Tel: (01296) 730349/730693.**
The house, a perfect expression of Rococco decoration in a series of great rooms, is the remaining wing of an even more ambitious mansion whose building was abandoned midway. Mementoes of the Verney family's role in the Civil War and of frequent visitor Florence Nightingale are displayed.

### Hughenden Manor
**High Wycombe. Tel: (01494) 532580.**
Home of prime minister and statesman Benjamin Disraeli from 1847 to 1881. The surrounding park and woodland has lovely walks and the garden is a recreation of Mary Anne Disraeli's colourful design.

### Stowe Landscape Gardens
**Buckingham. Tel: (01280) 8222850.**
Created by the 18th century's greatest designers and known as Britain's largest work of art, the gardens are adorned with 32 temples and monuments.

### Waddesdon Manor
**Waddesdon, nr. Aylesbury. (01296) 651282.**
French renaissance-style château designed in the 1870s as a showcase for Baron Ferdinand de Rothschild's magnificent collection of furniture, porcelain and art. Set in parkland with colourful aviary.

# CAMBRIDGESHIRE

## Cambridge

The famous university town has been an important settlement from early times thanks to the river and the Roman road. The Saxon tower of St. Benet's Church, the mound built by William the Conqueror for his castle and several medieval churches survive. The Folk Museum and the University Museum of Archaeology and Anthropology both have displayed interesting artifacts from the towns past. The university's first college was Peterhouse, founded in 1284. The Fitzwilliam Museum, housed in magnificent mid-19th century buildings, has amongst other offerings an internationally renowned collection of European paintings, a varied display of ceramics and some fine furniture and antiquities. 20th century paintings and sculpture are exhibited in Kettle's Yard.

## Ely

Notable for the impressive medieval edifice of Ely Cathedral, the town is also known for Oliver Cromwell's House. This houses Ely's Tourist Information Centre and a gift shop as well as containing a large Civil War Exhibition. Ely Museum has displays showing the history of Ely and the surrounding Fens from the pre-historic period onwards.

## Huntingdon

The birthplace of Oliver Cromwell, popular as a National Hunt Racing venue, this market town is famous for being at the heart of John Major's Parliamentary constituency. The Cromwell Museum contains an interesting collection of personal items and portraits that once belonged to Cromwell and his family. Hichingbrooke House, on the outskirts of the town was the ancestral home of the Cromwell family.

## Anglesey Abbey & Garden
**Lode. Tel: (01223) 811200.**
The house, dating from 1600, is built on the site of an Augustinian Abbey and contains the famous Fairhaven Collection of paintings and furniture. Surrounded by 100 acre garden and arboretum with a wonderful display of hyacinths in spring and magnificent herbaceous borders and a dahlia garden in summer. A watermill in the grounds is in full working order.

## Burghley House
**Stamford. Tel: (01780) 52451.**
Built by William Cecil in 1585 and occupied by his descendants ever since. 16 state rooms on view featuring paintings, tapestries, silver fireplaces, porcelain, wood carvings by Grinling Gibbons and ceilings painted by Verrio.

## Chilford Hall Vineyard
**Chilford Hall, Balsham Rd, Linton.**
**Tel: (01223) 892641.**
Follow the wine making process from vine to bottle. Two tastings and souvenir glass at the end. Collection of sculptures on view, cafe and shop.

## Elton Hall
**Elton. Tel: (01832) 28046.**
Historic house with a fine collection of paintings by Gainsborough, Reynolds, and Constable. There is a restored rose garden, a sunken garden and arboretum.

## Ely Cathedral
**Ely. Tel: (01353) 667735.**
Set in the centre of the Fens, Ely Cathedral stands as a jewel of the Romanesque style. Described as "a medieval engineering masterpiece", the octagon with its lantern and perpendicular downwards thrust illuminates the night sky and can be seen for miles. It is known as the "Ship of the Fens". The cathedral also contains a stained glass museum with 80 panels on display and models of a modern workshop. Welney Wildfowl Trust are nearby with swans flying in for the winter by the thousands.

## Imperial War Museum
**Duxford Airfield, nr. Cambridge.**
**Tel: (01223) 835000.**
A former Battle of Britain station, Duxford Airfield is home to hundreds of aircraft, tanks and military vehicles. Special exhibitions, ride simulator, adventure playground, shops, restaurant and picnic area. Pleasure flying during summer weekends.

## Long Sutton Butterfly Park
**1 mile off A17 in Long Sutton.**
**Tel: (01406) 363833.**
Set in 12 acres, one of Britain's largest walk-through tropical houses with hundreds of butterflies flying freely in a beautiful setting. Outdoor gardens, farm animals, adventure

playground, picnic area, farm museum and insectarium.

## National Horse Racing Museum
**Highstreet, Newmarket. Tel: (01638) 667333.**
Housed in Regency subscription rooms, 5 permanent galleries display the story and development of horse racing.

## Peakirk Waterfowls Gardens Trust
**Peakirk. Tel: (01733) 25227.**
Flock of Chilean flamingos and some 122 species of duck, geese and swans in 20 acres of water gardens. A favourite with photographers. Refreshment room and shop. Nature Walk and elevated picnic area.

## Peckover House
**North Brink, Wisbech. Tel: (01945) 58346.**
Early 18th century merchant's house on north bank of River Nene. Fine plaster and wood rococo interior. Two acre Victorian garden with roses, herbaceous borders, orangery, summer houses and croquet lawn.

## Wildfowl and Wetlands Trust
**Welney Centre, Welney. Tel: (01353) 860711.**
Nature reserve with numerous hides and a large observatory overlooking some 900 acres of the Washes. Around 3,500 wild swans and many thousands of wildfowl in winter. Notable in summer for waders and other birds. Pleasant walks in the unique washland habitat.

## Wimpole Hall & Home Farm
**Arrington, Royston. Tel: (01223) 207257.**
18th century mansion set in landscaped park. Folly and Chines bridge. Plunge bath and yellow drawing room in house, work of John Soane. Farm built in 1794. Has rare breeds centre with sheep, goats, cattle, pigs and hens.

# CHANNEL ISLANDS

## Guernsey
The Bailiwick of Guernsey includes the offshore islands of Alderney, Herm, Sark, Brecqhou and Jethou which are all worth a visit.
The island is 9 miles long and boasts 27 beaches, numerous night clubs, discos and restaurants. Activities include fishing, sailing, riding, playing tennis, squash or bowls and even flying. Visitors should also see Castle Cornet, Candie Museum,

Victor Hugo's house in Hauteville and the excellent craft centres.

## Candie Gardens
**Candie Road, St. Peter Port.**
The upper garden, where the Guernsey Museum can be found, features a fine lawn with splendid views over St. Peter Port to the islands of Herm and Sark. The lower garden is a well-preserved example of a Victorian pleasure garden and contains many exotic plants and two 18th century glasshouses.

## Castle Cornet
**St. Peter Port. Tel: (01481) 726518.**
The beautifully restored Castle guards the port and fires a daily noonday cannon. It contains a Royal Guernsey Militia Museum, a Maritime Museum and the 201 RAF Squadron Museum. There is a museum shop and a refectory.

## Coach House Gallery
**Les Islets, St. Pierre du Bois.**
**Tel: (01481) 65339.**
The islands leading art gallery with exhibitions of local and mainland artists' work. Also includes a pottery workshop, picture framing workshop and etching studio.

## Fort Grey
**Rocquaine Bay, St. Pierre du Bois.**
**Tel: (01481) 65036.**
Built in 1804 to defend the island against Napoleonic invasion, this delightful fort is known to locals as The Cup and Saucer, for obvious reasons. It has been restored as a museum of shipwrecks.

## Guernsey Coppercraft
**Rocquaine, St. Pierre du Bois.**
**Tel: (01481) 65112.**
Visitors can see traditional copperware being produced and browse in the gift showrooms.

## Guernsey Folk Museum
**Saumarez Park, Castel. Tel: (01481) 55384.**
Superb granite buildings in a 19th century farm setting with large lake. The kitchen, parlour, nursery, bedrooms, dairy, wash house, cider barn, tool room all used authentically-styled costumes alongside artifacts from the Trust's collection. Early farm machinery and horse drawn ploughs are also on display. National Trust shop, cafe.

### Guernsey Museum & Art Gallery
**Candie Gardens, St. Peter Port.**
**Tel: (01481) 726518.**
The museum is based on an existing Victorian bandstand and the main exhibition tells the story of Guernsey from Neolithic times to the present day. There is also an audio-visual theatre and an art gallery.

### Oatlands Craft Centre
**Braye Road, St. Sampsons. Tel: (01481) 49478.**
Restored thatched buildings house pottery, glass works, bee centre, craft shops and jewellery workshop. These are surrounded by 7 acres of open land where visitors can see Guernsey shire horses, calves and lambs etc. Also The Oatlands Guernsey Kitchen.

### Jersey
The largest and southernmost of the Channel Islands, Jersey has a wealth of history: Neolithic tombs, magnificent castles, Napoleonic towers and fortifications from the German occupation of World War II. The island is warmed by the Gulf Stream and has the most number of hours of sunshine in the British Isles. It boasts some of the best beaches in Europe, with numerous coves, caves and cliffs. Visitors can spend time in the busy town of St. Helier or enjoy the country parishes with their pink granite houses, manors and churches.

### Elizabeth Castle
**St. Aubin's Bay, St. Helier.**
**Tel: (01534) 607944.**
The castle was begun in 1590 and named after Elizabeth 1. Situated in an islet in the bay it can only be reached by foot across the causeway or by amphibious vehicle. Audio-visual exhibitions, museum of Jersey Militia, shop and restaurant.

### La Hougue Bie
**Grouville. Tel: (01534) 853823.**
A forty foot prehistoric mound dominated this site, set in beautiful grounds in the heat of the countryside. Inside is a Neolithic tomb, dating back some five and a half thousand years and reached by a narrow, low passage. Two medieval chapels top the mound. A discover Centre helps visitors understand archaeology, geology and natural environment of the site.

### Howard Davis Park
**St. Helier.**

The park was donated to the island by TB Davis in memory of his son Howard who died in action during World War I. The grounds contain colourful displays of trees and plants that flourish in the mild climate.

### Jersey Butterfly Centre
**Haute Tombette, St. Mary.**
**Tel: (01534) 481707.**
In the grounds of a carnation nursery, visitors can walk through an enclosed area in which hundreds of rare and exotic butterflies live freely. There is a restaurant in the nearby 17th century farmhouse.

### Jersey Museum
**The Weighbridge, St. Helier.**
**Tel: (01534) 30511.**
The museum contains a recreation of the 250,000-year old La Cotte archaeological site. Victorian school room and original merchant's house. Interactive videos and touch screens. Cafe.

### Jersey Pottery
**Gorey Village, Grouville. Tel: (01534) 851119.**
The extensive grounds of the Pottery include beautiful gardens, pools, patios and fountains. Visitors are welcome to wander at will enjoying the delights of the Pottery Restaurant or watching the skilled potters creating pieces in the distinctive Jersey Pottery style.

### Jersey Zoo
**Les Augres Manor, Trinity.**
**Tel: (01534) 864666.**
The zoo, founded by Gerald Durrell, is the headquarters of the Jersey Wildlife Preservation trust and has an international reputation for saving animals from extinction. The 25 acres of parkland and water gardens provide a beautiful and natural setting for some of the worlds most precious creatures from the lowland gorilla to the toad.

### Mont Orgueil Castle
**Gorey. Tel: (01534) 853292.**
This medieval castle was built in the 13th century to protect Jersey from invasion. It overlooks the nearby French coast from its position above Gorey harbour. Tableaux and a small museum illustrate important events in the castles history.

# CHESHIRE

## Chester

This ancient Walled city, on England's north West frontier with Wales has been welcoming visitors since Roman times. It started as a Roman garrison, built in AD 79 and was then called Deva Castra. It is possible to sail back in time on a Roman galley by visiting the Roman Experience, where visitors also experience the sights, sounds and smells of Deva Castra. Chester has a wealth of superb historic buildings from every age including Chester Cathedral. This is built on the site of a 10th century church built to house the relics of St. Werburgh. This was replaced by a Norman Benedictine Abbey in the 13th and 14th centuries and restored in the 19th century. The Guildhall Museum traces the history of the Freemans and Guilds of Chester from the Middle Ages to the present day.

## Arley Hall & Gardens
**Gt. Budworth, nr. Northwich.**
**Tel: (01565) 777353.**

One of the finest gardens in England is the setting for Arley Hall, owned by the same family for 500 years. The 12 acre garden ranks as one of Britain's best.

## The Boat Museum
**Ellesmere Port. Tel: (0151) 3555017.**

Set within the historic dock complex, the museum has the world's largest floating collection of canal craft. With steam engines, workers' cottages, blacksmith's forge, stables, boat trips and large indoor exhibitions.

## Bridgemere Garden World
**Bridgemere, nr. Nantwich.**
**Tel: (01270) 520381.**

25 fascinating acres of gardens, plants, shops and glasshouses. More plants in more varieties than anywhere in Britain.

## Cheshire Candle Workshops
**Burwardsley, nr. Chester. Tel: (01829) 770401.**
Craft workshops creating individual hand carved candles. Located in the Peckforton Hills overlooking the Cheshire Plain. Glass sculpture.

## Chester Zoo
**Upton-by-Chester. Tel: (01244) 380280.**
The UK's largest zoo outside London, set in 100 acres of glorious gardens. Chimpanzee Island, Penguin Pool, Tropical House, Children's Farm. Free car and coach parking.

## Jodrell Bank
**Science Centre and Arboretum,**
**Lower Withington, nr. Macclesfiled.**
**Tel: (01477) 571339.**

Science is fun in the 'hands on' gallery and spacious exhibition. Explore the universe every 45 minutes in the Planetarium and the trails, maze and trees in the Arboretum. Marvel at the 76m Lovell Radio telescope.

## Tatton Park
**Knutsford.**

England's most complete country estate and the National Trusts most popular property. Magnificent mansion. Glorious 60 acre gardens. Home Farm, working as it did 50 years ago. Medieval Old Hall, Deer Park and Meres, 1,000 tranquil acres.

# CORNWALL & THE ISLES OF SCILLY

## Bodmin

Cornwall's county town is set in beautiful countryside and positioned almost equi-distant between the north and south coasts. The town, whose name means "Abode of the Monks" is the perfect place to stay if you want to explore Cornwall. A steam locomotive will haul visitors between Bodmin General Station and the main-line Bodmin Parkway Station.
Near the main Priory Car Park stands the Shire House which houses the Tourist Information Centre.

## Bude

Delightful town protected by miles of cliffs. Salt water swimming pool. Good surfing and sandy beaches in deep bay facing the Atlantic ocean. Also excellent shops within easy reach of the moors of Devon and Cornwall.

## Falmouth

Set in an area of great natural beauty, on the sheltered south coast of Cornwall, Falmouth has four fine beaches, public gardens with sub-tropical plants and a busy harbour guarded by the twin castles of Pendennis and St. Mawes. Pendennis was erected by Henry VIII and enlarged by Elizabeth I, while St. Mawes was a fort also built during Henry VIII's reign. The resort is full of yachts, dinghies, windsurfers and power boats all year long. There are boat races in every class, held several times a week. Sailing schools are available to teach anyone the skills and the marinas below Penryn and around Trefusis Point at Mylor provide berths.

### Fowey
Fowey has charm all of its own. It has one of the most attractive sailing centres in the south west and is a delightful holiday resort. The town has a long history revolving around the trade brought in by the river. Most of the amenities centre on the river. There is a yachting centre, where self drive boats can be hired and sea angling is extremely popular. There are also marvellous walks on the coastal footpath or inland along the Saints Way. The great house of Fowey was the home of the Treffrys for five centuries. A visit to the museum is a must.

### Hayle
The famed three miles of golden sand attracts tens of thousands of holidaymakers to Hayle. The bay is almost circled by the superb beaches and many paths wind their way through the Towans, which is Cornish for sand dunes. The natural sandhills face St.Ives across the bay and stretch around to Godrevy Lighthouse.
Hayle still has a working port where visitors can watch the boats being prepared for sea or the fishermen unloading the catches of crabs, mackerel or prime fish, fresh and ready for the market.

### Launceston
The gateway to Cornwall, this small market town is full of history. There are traces of its medieval past in the form of a Norman Castle, built for Robert of Mortain, brother of William I, as well as a splendid museum and many other attractions.

### Liskeard
Ancient stannery town to which miners used to bring their tin for weighting and taxation. There is a 15th century church with a 17th century carved pulpit. The Family Adventure Park is nearby featuring an extensive miniature railroad, Cornish Craft Centre, Go-Karting for all ages and a gallery displaying the original works of

Archibald Thorburn, celebrated wildlife artist. 2 miles south of St. Keyne Mill is the Paul Corin Musical Collection.

### Looe
18 miles from Plymouth, Looe makes an ideal touring centre. Along with its twin rivers and its fine, safe beaches the town offers strolls through twisty narrow streets past quaint old buildings and all manner of activities. There is golf, shark and deep sea fishing, swimming, picturesque walks, bowling, tennis and horse riding.

### Mevagissey
A genuine Cornish village, Mevagissy is a fishing port with a labyrinth of narrow streets, steep lanes and traditional Cornish cottages perched on the hillside overlooking the delightful inner and outer harbours. There are two safe, sandy beaches just a few minutes away.

### Newquay
This resort town is most famous for its beaches, of which there are 11 in all. These provide seven miles of broad golden sands, each beach with its own attractions. Favourites for the family are probably Towan, Great Western and Tolcarne which all join at low tide to form a mile long pleasure ground fronted by the blue Atlantic and backed by cliffs topped with the hotels and attractions of the town. Dominating the scene is Towan Island, which is connected to the clifftop by an elegantly curving bridge. At low tide it provides a sea water paddling pool as its base, where children can play to their hearts content.

### Penzance
This appealing market town is a major tourist centre for West Cornwall. It has charming shopping streets, gorgeous gardens, a superb esplanade and busy working harbour. There are plenty of historic buildings, particularly in picturesque Chapel Street where visitors can stop to browse in the antique shops. Also worth seeing are the gleaming colours of the Egyptian House with its coat of arms. One of the towns latest attractions is the National Lighthouse Centre with its unique collection from Trinity House. St. Michael's Mount stands across the bay from Penzance. Built upon the great granite crag which rises from the waters of Mount's Bay is a 14th century castle, home of the St. Aubyn family for over 300 years.

## Perranporth

The resort has a three mile soft sandy beach set between the sea and rolling grassy dunes. There are stunning natural cliffs and caves along this coast as well. Amenities include surfing, gliding, golf, tennis, bowls, pony trekking and fishing. There is a boating lake and park. There is plenty of accommodation and entertainments which include local theatre groups, discos, carnival and life saving demonstrations.

## Polperro

This pretty old fishing village is home to a Smugglers Museum and model village. Set amongst rugged coastal scenery, the village itself has typically narrow streets and quaint old houses. The nearest station is at Looe 4m east.

## St. Ives

The sands, the sea, the artists, the little cobbled streets and gorgeous harbour scene, all combine to delight holidaymakers. The town grew out of the harbour and became prosperous thanks to the success of its fishing trade. Much of the atmosphere is retained in the narrow alleyways and cottages at Downalong.

## Tintagel

Here can be found the ruins of a castle, dating from the 12th century, reputed to be King Arthur's birthplace. A small 14th century manor house, full of charm and interest, has been restored in the fashion of the Post Office it was for nearly 50 years. There are two beaches, rugged cliffs and beautiful coastal scenery. The nearest station is Bodmin Parkway 16m south.

## Truro

With its majestic spiralling cathedral and splendid architecture, Truro has the distinct air of an elegant and prosperous city. It is the administrative and ecclesiastical centre of Cornwall as well as providing the main road and rail links to the rest of the county.
The wide open modern shopping precincts contrast beautifully with the more historic parts of the city where narrow, winding streets and alleyways house a fascinating mix of boutiques and shops. The County Museum and Art Gallery, an impressive silver-grey granite building, is set between the beautiful Victoria Gardens and Victoria Square.

## Charlestown Shipwreck & Heritage Centre
**Charlestown, nr. St. Austell.**
**Tel: (01726) 69897.**
The centre is located in the historic working port of Charlestown and set within a century-old china clay building on the edge of the dock. Underground tunnels lead visitors into the audio-visual theatre, showing animated scenes of historic village life, telling of the port, the people and their trades. Treasures from shipwrecks, sunken cargo, including 200 year old bales of leather recovered from the famous Mary Rose, copper ingots belonging to the King of Portugal 1527 and much, much more.

## Cotehele
**St. Dominick, nr. Saltash. Tel: (01579) 351346.**
Enchanted and remote, perched high above the wooded banks of the Tamar, Cotehele was owned by the Edgcumbe family for nearly six centuries. One of the least-altered medieval houses in the country, it contains original furniture, armour and a remarkable set of tapestries. Steeply terraced garden, pools and working watermill. Art and craft gallery.

## Falmouth Maritime Museum
**Falmouth.**
Historic listed building with displays on the maritime history of south west Cornwall.

## Glendurgan
**Mawnan Smith, nr. Falmouth.**
**Tel: (01326) 250906.**
One of the finest sub-tropical gardens of the South West. Set in a wooded valley, running down to the Helford River. There are fine trees and rare and exotic plants. Children love the Giant's Stride and the great laurel maze (from 1833).

## Helston Folk Museum
**Helston. Tel: (01326) 564027.**
Displays covering the history of the town and the immediate surrounding area.

## Killiow Golf Park
**Kea, nr. Truro. Tel: (01872) 70246.**
9 hole par 3 golf course and all-weather driving range.

## Land's End
**Tel: (01736) 871220**

Spectacular cliffs with breathtaking vistas. Last Labyrinth Show - multi-sensory journey down through the tunnels of Land's End. Exhibitions, craft workshops and children's play area.

## Lanhydrock
**Bodmin. Tel: (01208) 73320**

17th century house, rebuilt after a fire in 1881, set in 450 acres of wooded parkland. There are 49 rooms on display ranging from the richly furnished main rooms to the maid's bedrooms. The principal rooms all have beautifully worked plaster ceilings, including that of the Long Gallery which illustrates scenes from the Old Testament. The idyllic walk down to the River Fowey at Respryn Bridge and back through the woods should not be missed.

## Mount Edgcumbe Country Park
**Torpoint. Tel: (01753) 822236.**

In the grounds of restored 16th century mansion overlooking Plymouth Sound.

## Padstow Tropical Bird Gardens
**Padstow. Tel: (01841) 532262.**

Approximately 200 species of birds and butterfly display.

## Paradise Park
**Hayle. Tel: (01736) 757407.**

Came first in BBC Wildlife Magazine's 1995 "Zoo Conservation Awards for Excellence." The world's rarest and most beautiful birds, fascinating otters, penguin feeding, superb sub-tropical gardens. Also children's play area, wildlife quizzes and Fun Farm with donkeys, rabbits and goats.

## Polkyth Recreation Centre
**St. Austell. Tel: (01726) 61585.**

Sports hall, badminton courts, swimming pools, sauna and hydrotherapy pool.

## Prideaux Place
**Padstow. Tel: (01841) 532411.**

Stunning Elizabethan house with treasures. It has been home to the Prideaux family for over 400 years. Extensive grounds and deer park overlooking the Camel Estuary. Tea room and gift shop.

## The Royal Cornwall Museum
**Truro. Tel: (01872) 72205.**

Archaeology and art gallery, mummies and minerals, children's discovery trail, cafe and gift shop.

## Trelissick
**Feock, nr. Truro. Tel: (01872) 862090.**

This tranquil garden is famous for its panoramic views down Carrick Road towards Falmouth and the open the sea. Trelissick has an abundance of tender shrubs such as magnolias, camellias and rhododendrons. Circular walk through the riverside woodlands. Art and craft gallery, barn restaurant and shop.

## Trerice
**Nr. Newquay. Tel: (01637) 875404.**

A small Elizabethan manor house, hidden away among a network of narrow lanes. Dutch-style gabled façade. Inside are ornate fireplaces, elaborate plaster ceilings and a collection of the highest quality English furniture. Summer-flowering garden, orchard and museum tracing the history of the lawn mower.

## Tresco Abbey Gardens
**Tresco, Isles of Scilly. Tel: (01720) 422849.**

Large collection of sub-tropical flora. Valhalla Museum with displays of ships figureheads.

## World of Model Railways
**Mevagissy. Tel: (01726) 842457.**

Over 2,000 models on display. Some 50 trains controlled in automatic sequence running through finely detailed scenery. Model shop with items for the beginner to the more experienced enthusiast.

# CUMBRIA

## Ambleside

The town is situated at the head of Lake Windermere and is surrounded by some of the most beautiful scenery in the country. Ambleside is an ideal walking base and boating and other watersports are available from Waterhead or nearby Low Wood. Annual Rushbearing Festival at the end of July; 17th century Bridge House.

## Appleby

A very historic town, Appleby is the former county town of Westmorland. It has many recreational facilities: a heated swimming pool, squash courts, cricket pitch, playgrounds, pony trekking and a bowling green. Appleby also has one of the most impressive golf courses in the north, set against a magnificent backdrop of the northern Pennines.

## Carlisle

Historic Carlisle, the Great Border City, offers the visitor a rich blend of heritage with modern day facilities. The citys border history is in the award winning Tullie House Museum and Art Gallery. Explore the mighty sandstone Castle, and picturesque Cathedral, with its 14th century stained glass and 16th century carved Flemish altarpiece. See how cloth is woven for fashion houses at the Linton Tweeds Centre. Other amenities include quality shopping, entertainment at the Sands Centre. Venturing further afield there is the scenic rail journey between Carlisle and Settle, the dramatic Birdoswald Roman Fort on Hadrian's Wall and the Borderlands market towns of Brampton, Lanercost Priory and Longtown which are strongly linked with Arthurian legend.

## Grange-over-Sands

A sheltered resort with a long seafront promenade, Grange-over-Sands is the centrepiece of Cumbria's Riviera. It has a 12th century Cartmel Priory Church, the stately Holker Hall which houses the Lakeland Motor Museum. An official guide is still appointed to take parties along the highway, through the treacherous quicksands, tides and river beds where many a stagecoach lost its race in the dash from Morecombe to Grange.

## Furness Peninsula

Ulverston, with its market and town crier; Laurel & Hardy Museum; the ruins of imposing Furness Abbey; Dock Museum; South Lakes Wild Animal Park; Classic Bikes Motorcycle Museum and Piel Island's Norman castle accessible only by boat.

## Kendal

The "auld grey town" on the River Kent, historic Kendal has outstanding museums of lakeland life, enjoyable shopping, a ruined castle and of course the Mint Cake.

## Keswick

In the northern part of the Lake District, this compact market town combines the attractions of interesting shops, museums and an indoor leisure pool. Keswicks long interesting history is seen in the Stone Circle, Crossthwaite Church, the Moot Hall and the Market.

## Penrith

The birthplace of William Wordsworth's mother, Anne Cookson, daughter of a draper who lived in the Market Square. The shop, built on the site of their house, Arnison's is still a drapers.

## Windermere

Windermere, on the hillside and Bowness on the lakeside, is set within the Lake District National Park and offers visitors panoramic views of the lake and fells. There are woodland walks and many superb attractions in the vicinity. Numerous activities and water sports.

## The Lake District National Park

Dramatic mountain scenery - with massive crags and ridges, rugged fells and wooded valleys - as well as the labyrinth of lakes and rivers. The scenery provides a paradise for outdoor activities such as walking, climbing, riding, golf, cycling, birdwatching and watersports of every kind.

## Acorn Bank Garden

**Temple Sowerby, Penrith. Tel: (01768) 361893.**
Impressive 2.5 acre garden, best known for its herb garden and large collection of culinary and medicinal plants.

## Abbot Hall Art Gallery Museum of Lakeland Life and Industry

**Kendal. Tel: (01539) 722464.**
A magnificent collection of fine art and displays on the life and art of the Lake District. Free parking, coffee shop.

## Appleby Castle Conservation Centre

**Tel: (017683) 51402.**
Set on the river, this centre is the home for rare breeds of farm animals and a large collection of birds and waterfowl. There is an 11th century Norman Keep and displays of Nanking Cargo salvaged from the South China Sea. Cafe, gift shop, nursery garden and picnic areas.

## Brantwood

**Coniston. Tel: (01539) 725133.**

is a beautifully situated house with wonderful lake and mountain views. Within the house is a superb collection of Ruskin's drawings and watercolours.

## Brewery Arts Centre
**Kendal. Tel: (01539) 725133.**
Multi-arts complex housed in 150-year old listed brewery. Three major festivals a year of theatre, folk and jazz music. Popular music venue, The Malt Room, bars and restaurant with garden patio.

## Brockhole Visitor Centre
The Visitor Centre for the Lake District National Park has extensive landscaped gardens and grounds, with regular cruises and exhibitions. Situated between Ambleside and Windermere, Brockhole is a great family day out, with restaurant and tea rooms and an exciting children's adventure playground.

## Cars of the Stars
**Keswick. Tel: (017687) 73757.**
Not-to-be-missed collection of vehicles from TV and cinema including the Batmobile, Chitty Chitty Bang Bang, the James Bond Collections and Herbie the Love Bug.

## Cumberland Pencil Museum & Exhibition Centre
**Keswick. Tel: (01768) 773626.**
The museum traces the history of pencil making from the discovery of Borrowdale graphite in the 1500's through early cottage industry to modern high speed production methods.

## The Cumberland Toy & Model Museum
**Cockermouth. Tel: (01900) 827606.**
On display are mostly British toys from 1900 to the present. Visitors can operate Scaletrix, Lego etc. Free toy quiz.

## Dove Cottage
**Grasmere. Tel: (015394) 35544.**
Set back from the shores of Grasmere, Dove Cottage, which was Wordsworth's home during his most creative years, is beautifully preserved. The Wordsworth Museum has many manuscripts and fine art treasures on display. Tearoom, book and gift shop.

## Fell Foot Park
**Newby Bridge, nr. Ulverston.**
Bathing area, fishing, facilities for boat launch-ing, a picnic area and adventure playground in an 18 acre country park.

## Hayes Garden World
**Ambleside. Tel: (015394) 33434.**
Thousands of plants, flowers, shrubs, bushes and trees provide a breathtaking multitude of colours and shapes as far as the eye can see.

## Heron Corn Mill and Museum of Papermaking
**Beetham, nr. Milnthorpe. Tel: (015395) 63363.**
A water-driven 17th century Lowder Corn Mill, with milling demonstrations and cereal products on sale. The museum offers displays showing historic and modern methods of papermaking.

## Hutton-in-the-Forest
**Nr. Penrith. Tel: (017684) 84449.**
The main parts of this house date from the 17th, 18th and 19th century but it was based on the 13th century Pele Tower. It has been in Lord Inglewood's family since 1605 and houses collections of furniture, paintings and tapestries. There is a walled garden, a woodland walk and topiary terraces. Tearoom.

## The Lakeland Bird of Prey Centre
**Lowther, nr. Penrith. (01931) 712746.**
Large collection of hawks, eagles, owls, buzzards and falcons can be seen at close quarters. Delightful tea room and tea gardens. Cumbrian craft gallery.

## Levens Hall & World-Famous Topiary Garden
**Tel: (015395) 60321.**
The Elizabethan home of the Bagot where visitors will find fine Jacobean furniture, superb panelling, plasterwork and paintings. Award-winning topiary garden. Working steam collection, gift shop, plant centre and play area.

## Lingholm Gardens
**Nr. Keswick. Tel: (017687) 72003.**
Situated on the western shore of Derwentwater are 40 acres of beautiful gardens. Spectacular rhododendrons, azaleas and formal terraces with spring bulbs, blue poppies and magnolias and extensive woodlands. The tearoom has a verandah offering scenic views. Plant centre and free parking.

## Lowther Leisure and Wildlife Park
**Penrith. Tel: (01931) 712523.**

150 acres of beautiful parkland offering scenic miniature railway, adventure play areas, boating lake and sports.

## Muncaster Castle, Gardens and Owl Centre
Ravenglass. Tel: (01229) 717614.
Visitors can see majestic owls and beautiful gardens with stunning views of the Lakeland Fells. Cafe, gift shop, plant centre and free parking.

## Ravensglass and Eskdale Railway
Ravensglass. Tel: (01229) 717171
England's oldest narrow gauge steam railway takes the visitor on a seven-miles journey through unspoilt Lakeland. Railway Museum and Muncaster Water Mill.

## Rydal Mount
Nr. Ambleside. Tel: (015394) 33002.
William Wordsworth lived here from 1813 until his death in 1850 and it is the home of his direct descendants. There are 4.5 acres of gardens, landscaped by the poet and inside are family portraits, personal possessions and first editions.

## South Tynedale Railway
Alston. Tel: 901434) 381696.
Travel by the beautifully preserved steam and diesel locomotives through the South Tyne Valley. Also restored 19th century railway featuring original ticket office.

## Steam Yacht Gondola
Coniston Water. Tel: (015394) 41288.
The gondola was first launched in 1859 and provides the only scheduled steam powered passenger service in the Lake District. Luxurious upholstered heated saloons.

## Trotters & Friends Animal Farm
Nr. Keswick. Tel: (017687) 76239.
Watch the hatchlings make their arrival into the world, bottle feed the baby animals and cuddle the adorable rabbits. Reptile house with Monty the Python.

## Ullswater Steamers
Tel: (017684) 82229.
Motor Yachts Raven and Lady of the Lake run daily services between Glenridding, Howtown and Pooley. Both are over 100 years old but fitted to modern standards of comfort and safety.

## Windermere Steamboat Museum
Tel: (015394) 45565.
On display is one of the finest collections of steamboats in the world. There are trips on a steam launch as well as a lakeside picnic area, model boat pons and shop.

## Wordsworth House
Cockermouth. Tel (01900) 824805.
A fine example of a North Country Georgian town house, this was the birthplace of William Wordsworth in 1770. Rooms are furnished in the style of his time. There is a peaceful garden and visitors can walk down to the delightful banks of the Derwent.

# DERBYSHIRE

The Peak District is England's most southerly high-land country, with Britain's first national park at its heart. Rising to over 2000 feet (610m), most of the Peak National Park's 555 square miles are centrally situated in Derbyshire but include parts of Staffordshire, Cheshire, Yorkshire and Greater Manchester. It is doubtful whether any other area in Britain has such variety of scenery in such a relatively small area as the Peak District.

## Aeropark & Visitors Centre
East Midlands International Airport, Castle Donington, Derby. Tel: (01332) 852852.
12 acre aeropark has several static aircraft and comprehensive displays outlining history of the airport, civil aviation and science of flight.

## Arkwright's Cromford Mill
Cromford, Matlock. Tel: (01692) 824297.
Restoration of world's first successful water-powered cotton spinning mill built by Richard Arkwright 1771.

## Calke Abbey, Park and Gardens
Ticknell, Derby. Tel: (01332) 863822.
Built 1701-3 and largely unchanged in 100 years. Extensive natural history collections. 750 acre landscaped park, ponds, trees, woodlands. Walled gardens, pleasure gardens.

## Cathedral of All Saints
Derby. Tel: (01332) 34201.
Early 16th century tower, 18th century interior and wrought iron chancel gate by Robert Bakewell.

## Chatsworth House and Garden
**Bakewell. Tel: (01246) 582204.**
One of England's most beautiful houses, set on
the banks of the River Derwent. The house
contains fine collections of paintings, china,
furniture, sculpture and tapestries. The garden,
laid out by Capability Brown, is famous for its
cascade and spectacular fountains. Farmyard and
adventure playground. Special events during the
year such as angling fair and sheepdog trials.

## Chesterfield Museum and Art Gallery
**Chesterfield. Tel: (01246) 559727.**
The museum depicts the history of Chesterfield
from Roman times to the present day.

## Denby Pottery Visitors Centre
**Derby. Tel: (01773) 743641.**
"The Denby Experience". Guided factory tour,
audio-visual show, museum.

## Derby City Museum and Art Gallery
**Derby. Tel: (01332) 255586.**
Paintings by Joseph Wright, Royal Crown Derby
porcelain, natural history, local archaeology,
militaria and model theatre collection.

## Derby Industrial Museum
**Derby. Tel: (01332) 255308.**
The museum offers displays on the industries of
Derbyshire, Rolls-Royce aero engines, power
sources. The museum is built on the site of a
former silk mill which was apparently Britains
first factory.

## The Donington Collection
**Donington Park, Castle Donington, Derby.
Tel: (01332) 810048.**
The largest private collection of single seater
racing cars in the world, including the unique
Speedway Hall of Fame.

## Elvaston Castle Country Park
## and Estate Museum
**Elvaston, Thulston. Tel: (01332) 571342.**
200 acre country park with woodland, landscaped
parkland, lake, formal and old English gardens.
Estate Museum. Tea room and shop.

## Eyam Hall
**Eyam, Sheffield. Tel: (01433) 631976.**
17th century manor house in the centre of the
"plague village" of Eyam. It was built and is still
occupied by the Wright family. The house
contains a wealth of furniture, paintings and
tapestries. Very much a family home.

## Haddon Hall
**Nr. Bakewell. Tel:(01629) 812855.**
Medieval home built during 14th and 15th
centuries. Includes banqueting hall, long gallery
and chapel frescoes. Beautiful terraced rose
gardens. The legend of Dorothy Vernon's
elopement with John Manners nearly 400 years
ago adds to the romance of the place.

## Hardwick Hall
**Doe Lea, Chesterfield. Tel: (01246) 850430.**
The house was built between 1591-97 for Bess
Harwick. Inside, visitors will find needlework,
tapestries, portraits and furniture. There are
formal gardens, a walled courtyard and herb
garden. See also 18th century watermill.

## Kedleston Hall
**Kedleston, Derby. Tel: (01332) 842191.**
Robert Adam house from 1759-65, with 12th
century church set in park. Unique marble hall,
saloon, state rooms. Some Old Masters, Lord
Curzon's Indian Museum.

## Melbourne Crystal
**The Old Bakehouse, Melbourne.
Tel: (01332) 862811.**
Visitors are welcome to watch the craftsmen at
work blowing and cutting glass.

## Midland Railway Centre
**Ripley, Derby. Tel: (01773) 747674.**
Over 25 locomotives and over 80 items of
historic rolling stock of Midland and LMS origin.
Excursions by steam-hauled trains. Country park
and farm.

## The Opera House
A lavishly decorated Edwardian theatre built in
1903. It is home to the acclaimed Buxton
International Festival and to many other events
throughout the year.

## Pavilion Gardens
**Buxton.**
Pleasant walks in 23 acres of garden and
woodland centre on the Octagon, with its
conservatory and restaurant. There are also
several small lakes, a children's play area, an
indoor spa water swimming pool and various
other activities.

## Peak District Mining Museum
**Matlock. Tel: (01629) 583834.**
Exhibitions show 2500 years of lead mining,
with displays on geology, the mines and miners,

tools and engines. Climbing shafts suitable for children.

## Peak Rail plc
**Matlock. Tel: (01629) 580381.**
Working steam and diesel locomotives on display as well as loco restoration and shop. Peak Rail is a project to reopen 20 miles of railway between Matlock and Buxton as a steam railway.

## Peveril Castle
**Castleton, Sheffield. Tel: (01433) 20613.**
Ruined Norman castle from 11th century, built on hill above Castleton. The curtain wall is almost complete and there is a small but imposing keep.

## Pickford's House Museum
**Derby. Tel: (01332) 255363.**
The house was built by architect Joseph Pickford in 1769. Visitors can see a Georgian dining room and morning room and late Georgian kitchen, scullery and bedroom. Garden.

## Shipley Garden and Aquatic Centre
**North Shipley, nr. Heanor.**
**Tel: (01773) 713596.**
New complex for garden, home and leisure. Tropical, marine and cold water aquatics.

## Sudbury Hall
**Sudbury, Ashbourne. Tel: (01283) 585305.**
The Hall was one of Charles II houses. Worth seeing are the plasterwork, ceilings, carved staircase and overmantel. There is also a Museum of Childhood in what was once the servants' wing.

# DEVON

## Appledore
Unspoilt little fishing village, with mainly 18th century white cottages, networks of tiny cobbled streets and shops tucked away in unexpected places. Maritime Museum has many displays including a complete Victorian Devon Kitchen. Ferry service to Instow, boating and fishing trips.

## Barnstaple
Administrative centre of north Devon, which proudly claims to be the oldest borough in the kingdom. Pannier market. 13th century, 16 arch bridge crossing the Taw.

## Bideford

Busy riverside town on west bank of Torridge. It was Britain's third port during 16th century. Interesting shop and pannier market. 16th century, 24 arch bridge.

## Brixham
Tiers of charming fishermen's cottages interspersed with hotels, guest houses and inns rise steeply above each other above Brixham's busy harbour. Fishing remains the mainstay of life here. The harbour is filled with pleasure boats, modern yachts and trawlers.

## Combe Martin
Much of the Coastline here is owned by the National Trust. There is a bewildering variety of inlets, coves and cliffs, safe beaches and interesting old inns.

## Dartmoor
365 square miles of magnificent countryside. Granite tors, sweeping moorland, streams and wooded valleys with ancient stone circles, historic towns and charming villages.

## Dartmouth
A favourite port of call for sailing enthusiasts and visiting yachts, much of Dartmouth's activities are centred around ships, all culminating in the annual Dartmouth Royal Regatta. Everyone can enjoy the tranquil River Dart on a cruise up-stream to Totnes.

## Dawlish
A popular holiday town. The Lawn running through the town centre is an ideal place to sit and relax, admiring the colourful displays and the many species of waterfowl on Dawlish Water. Visitors can follow the stream down to Dawlish beach and take a stroll along to Boat Cove. From there are trips along the coast in passenger launches. Sea angling.

## Exmoor
The Exmoor National Park is in the northern part of Devon and West Somerset. It has acres of natural moorland and ancient oak woodlands and is the home of the Exmoor ponies and wild red deer.

## Exmouth
Situated where the River Exe meets the sea on

the glorious Devon coast, Exmouth is a West facing natural sun trap. Walking, birdwatching and other country pursuits. An ideal touring centre for east Devon.

## Ilfracombe
A beautiful natural harbour, pleasure gardens from the turn of the century, tunnels to the beach and plenty to do make Ilfracombe a perfect holiday resort. Shops, theatres, bars, cinemas, bingo and dancing. Sandy beaches nearby.

## Lynton
Perched high on cliffs where two rivers merge, above its twin town of Lynmouth, Lynton is a popular resort once frequented by Shelly, Coleridge and Wordsworth.

## Paignton
Paignton has 8 beaches, ranging from the long and golden to the intimate and wooded. Amenities: steam trains, open-top buses, pitch and putt, Punch and Judy shows and much more. Through Paignton's back door lies the incomparable Devon landscape of undulating hills, sea views, winding lanes, red soil farms, country pubs and villages.

## Plymouth
Located between the sea and the moor, between Devon and Cornwall, Plymouth is the hub in a merry-go-round of themed attractions, stately homes and historic houses, grand parks and gardens, beaches and coves. Fine range of accommodation, shops and restaurants and the superb entertainment and visitor attractions make it an ideal base for holidaymakers. Visitors can wander along the avenues of the modern city centre or the busy Elizabethan streets of the Barbican.

## Salcombe
A beautiful sailing and fishing centre. Superb climate. The town is a maze of streets, quayside walks and has fine beaches on both sides.

## Seaton
A pretty seaside town where the shingle beach extends for over a mile, bordered by an attractive promenade. At the Western end is Seaton Hole, a sheltered and sandy sunbathing spot.

## Torquay
The resort is situated in a outstanding area of natural beauty known as the English Riviera, where palm trees and other sub-tropical plants flourish. There are 10 miles of spectacular coastline, with 4 principal beaches and many small coves. Amenities: conference centre, 2 theatres, cinema, aquarium, model village, prehistoric caves, entertainment and leisure centres, night clubs, and golf courses. Events: Regatta Carnival, Boat Show, Illuminations.

## Totnes
The main street, with its closely-packed houses and shops dating from the 16th century can be quite an experience especially when the Totnes Elizabethans are going about their daily business in authentic period costume.

## Westward Ho!
Name taken from title of Charles Kingsley's famous novel. Kipling attended old United Services College here. Three miles of gently sloping sand with good surfing. Long pebbled ridge. Many picnic spots, golf course, swimming pool, riding, tennis.

## Arlington Court
**Nr. Barnstaple. Tel: (01271) 850296.**
The house was built in 1822 and contains a fascinating collection of model ships, costumes, pewter and furniture of the last century brought together by Rosalie Chichester. There are 12 hectares of park, grazed by Shetland ponies and Jacob's sheep. Garden with lakeside walks and carriage rides.

## The Big Sheep
**Nr. Bideford. Tel: (01237) 477916.**
A working farm, which combines traditional rural crafts such as cheesemaking and shearing, with hilarious novelties like sheep racing and duck trials.

## Buckfast Abbey
**Buckfastleigh. Tel: (01364) 642519.**
The Abbey is set in the beautiful valley of the river Dart on the edge of Dartmoor. The present Abbey took four monks 32 years to build and was completed in 1938. It contains many art treasures including stained glass windows. The monks who live there now are engaged in farming, beekeeping, winemaking and craftwork.

## Buckland Abbey
**Yelverton. Tel (01822) 855024.**
Originally a Cistercian monastery, then the home

of Sir Francis Drake. Exhibitions on medieval monastic life and the Armada. Box-hedged herb garden, Great Barn and estate walks.

## Castle Drogo
**Drewsteignton. Tel: (01647) 433306.**
This creation of Sir Edwin Lutyens was built between 1910 and 1930 for Julian Drewe. It stands more than 900ft overlooking the wooded gorge of the River Teign and has stunning views of Dartmoor. The house has a formal terraced garden and colourful herbaceous borders.

## Canonteign Falls
**Tel: (01647) 252434.**
A breathtaking combination of waterfalls, woodlands and lakes. Includes Lady Exmouth Falls, a sheer drop of 220ft.

## Clovelly
Historic unspoilt village. Cobbled streets lead towards tiny harbour, from where visitors can take a trip round the bay. Visitor Centre with audio-visual show explaining the development of Clovelly.

## Compton Castle
**Paignton. Tel: (01803) 872112.**
This fortified house was built at three periods: 1340, 1450 and 1520 by the Gilbert family. It was the home of Sir Humphrey Gilbert, coloniser of Newfoundland and half brother of Sir Walter Raleigh.

## Dartington Crystal
**Great Torrington. Tel: (01805) 624233.**
Visitors can watch skilled craftsmen blowing and shaping the famous crystal. There is a Visitor Centre, with displays on the history of glass and factory shopping.

## Dartmoor Wildlife Park
**Sparkwell, Plymouth.**
Over 100 species of animals and birds.

## Exeter Maritime Museum
**Exeter. Tel: (01392) 58075.**
Over 100 boats afloat and indoors. Working craft from many different countries and a unique collection of boats used for the Atlantic and Pacific rowed crossings.

## Exmoor Bird Gardens
**Bratton Fleming, nr. Barnstaple.**
**Tel: (015983) 352.**
Landscaped gardens with exotic birds, waterfowl and penguins. Tarzan-Land for children.

## Elizabethan House
**The Barbican, Plymouth. Tel: (01752) 253871.**
A typical Tudor sea captain's timber-framed house, featuring period furniture. National Trust Shop and Information Centre.

## Escot Aquatic Centre and Gardens
**Ottery St. Mary. Tel: (01404) 822188.**
8 acres of wetlands and waterfowl park, pet centre, wilderness walks with specimen trees and shrubs. Otters on display, wild boar living in the forest. Pet centre with tropical and coldwater fish as well as birds and small mammals. Victorian walled rose garden.

## Finch Foundry
**Stickepath, Okehampton. Tel: (01837) 840046.**
19th century water-powered forge which produced agricultural hand tools. Regular demonstrations of working water wheels, forge with huge tilt hammers and grindstone.

## Kents Cavern Showcases
**Nr. Torquay. Tel: (01803) 294059.**
Guided tour through huge 2m year old caves. Stalactites and stalagmites. Flint stones, bones of bears and mammoths.

## Killerton
**Broadclyst, Exeter. Tel: (01392) 881345.**
The house, set in a 6,500 acre estate, was rebuilt in 1778 to the design of John Johnson. Costume collection from 18th century to present day. 8 hectare hillside garden with rhododendrons, magnolias and rare trees.

## Knightshayes Court
**Tiverton. Tel: (01884) 254665.**
Striking Victorian gothic house with richly decorated interior, including Billiard Room and Smoking Room. Garden has formal terraces and borders, unusual topiary, a tranquil lily pool and the "Garden in the Wood" of rare trees and shrubs.

## Lydford Gorge
**Lydford.**
The gorge is 1.5 miles long, leading to the 90ft

White Lady Waterfall. Also whirlpools including Devil's Cauldron.

## Model Village
**Babbacombe, Torquay. Tel: (01803) 328669.**
Found within 4 acres of miniature landscaped gardens are hundreds of models and a model railway.

## Morwellham Quay Open Air Museum
**Nr. Tavistock. Tel: (01822) 832766.**
The museum illustrates the history of Morwellham as a port and its association with the mining industry of the area. Tramway into copper mine.

## National Shire Horse Centre
**Nr. Plymouth.**
**Tel: (01752) 880268.**
Shire horses, farm carts, children's adventure playground and craft centre. Horse parades.

## North Devon Leisure Centre
**Barnstaple. Tel: (01271) 73361.**
Swimming pool, bowls, squash, fitness and sun rooms. Snooker, skittle alley.

## Orchid Paradise
**Newton Abbot. Tel: (01626) 52233.**
Orchids in bloom, displayed in natural setting. Rain forest pool.

## Ottery Nurseries Garden Centre
**Ottery St. Mary. Tel: (01404) 815815.**
Family-run garden centre. Restaurant and free parking.

## Otterton Mill Centre and Working Museum
**Otterton, nr. Budleigh Salterton. Tel: (01395) 68521.**
Working watermill, craft workshops, art and craft exhibitions.

## Overbecks Garden
**Sharpitor, Salcombe. Tel: (01548) 842893.**
6 acre garden with many rare plants. Fine views of Salcombe Harbour.

## Paignton Zoo
**Nr Paignton. Tel: (01803) 527936.**
Over 60 endangered species including African lions and Sumatran tigers. Jungle Express

miniature railway and Jolly Jungle, children's play area.

## Plymouth Dome
**Plymouth. Tel: (01752) 668000.**
New purpose built interpretation centre showing visitors the history of Plymouth and its people.

## Rosemoor Garden
**Nr. Great Torrington. Tel: (01805) 624067.**
40 acres set in the Torridge Valley. Lady Anne's magnificent garden and arboretum, bamboos and ferns, one of the longest herbaceous borders in the country, fruit and vegetable garden. Trails for children, picnic centre. Visitors Centre with restaurant. Shop and plant centre.

## Rougemont House Museum
**Exeter. Tel: (01392) 265858.**
Elegant Regency House with costumes displayed in restored period rooms.

## Saltram
**Plympton, Plymouth. Tel: (01752) 336546.**
Tudor mansion, with Palladian facades and plasterwork by Robert Adam. Georgian painting collection, including ten by Sir Joshua Reynolds. Great kitchen, gallery of local art in the chapel and orangery in the garden.

## Seaton Tramway
**Seaton. Tel: (01297) 21702.**
Seaton and District Electric Tramway offers a unique journey through the Axe and Coly Valleys on 2'9" gauge open-top double-deck tramcars.

## Shaldon Wildlife Trust
**Shaldon, nr. Teignmouth. Tel: (01626) 872234.**
Collection of small mammals and exotic birds, reptiles and invertebrates.

## Totnes Castle
**Totnes. Tel: (01803) 864406.**
Norman motte-and-bailey castle with 13th century stone shell keep.

## Trago Mills
**Nr. Newton Abbot. Tel: (01626) 821111.**
3/4 mile miniature steam railway, large model railway layout and audio-visual displays.

## Watermouth Castle
**Between Ilfracombe and Combe Martin. Tel: (01271) 867474.**
Enter the castle to experience nostalgic displays,

brilliant sights and sounds, coloured waterfalls, haunted dungeons and fairy tales that come to life. More attractions are to be found in the landscaped gardens.

## The Woodland Leisure Park
**Nr. Dartmouth. Tel: (01803) 712598.**
60 acres of glorious woods and gardens. Attractions include commando course, toddler's play village, falconry displays, animal farm and deer park.

## Yelverton Paperweight Centre
**Yelverton. Tel: (01822) 854250.**
Exhibition of the Broughton Collection of 800 antique and modern glass paperweights.

# DORSET

## Bournemouth
Major seaside resort and conference centre with excellent accommodation and facilities for visitors. Seven miles of golden sandy beaches. Attractive public gardens, parks and elegant shopping centre. Year-round programme of entertainment. Facilities for most open air sports.

## Christchurch
The charming heritage town of Christchurch is ideally situated for touring Dorset and the New Forest. Visitors can wander through the quaint streets of the Old Town, dominated by the magnificent Priory Church and follow the riverside walk down to the picturesque quay. The open-air Shakespearean Productions and Priory Concerts, together with the Regent Centre and Balloon Theatre Productions ensure entertainment for all ages. Annual Regatta in mid-August. All kinds of water activities available at nearby beaches.

## Dorchester
The county town of Dorset, famous for its tree lined avenues. Excellent shopping centre, market with places to visit including the Dorset County Museum and the nearby Maiden Castle, an early Iron Age hill town and fortress.

## Poole
Poole has become a major holiday destination in recent years. The narrow streets of the old town, lined with interesting architecture, lead to the bustling quayside. The harbour, now considered

to be the largest natural harbour in the world, is filled with many colourful sails, from the many windsurfers, racing yachts and powerboats going out to sea. Golden stretch of beach at Sandbanks. Tower Park leisure complex, with Ice Trax, Splashdown, Mega Bowl, nightclub and cinemas.

## Swanage
Popular family resort, occupying delightful position on Isle of Purbeck. Safe, sandy beach. Many of cottages and buildings built of local limestone. Stonework and street furnishings brought from London in the 19th century are an intriguing feature of Swanage. Victorian castle and Great Globe at Durlston Country Park. Corfe Castle 1m south. Superb walking area and cycling centre.

## Weymouth
A quality resort set in a breathtaking Georgian bay with 17th century picturesque harbour, a few minutes' drive from unspoilt "Hardy" countryside and European award-winning coastline. A short walk away is the Lodmoor Country park which offers peace and tranquillity in the RSPB Nature Reserve plus a host of other attractions including Sealife Park and Tropical Jungle, Model World, mini-golf, Leisurama with giant slide, miniature railways, numerous recreation and picnic areas plus ample parking.

## Abbotsbury Sub-Tropical Gardens
**Abbotsbury. Tel: (01305) 871387.**
English Heritage Grade I garden with 20 acres of exotic trees, shrubs and herbaceous plants.

## Brewer's Quay Museum
**Weymouth. Tel: (01305) 777622.**
The museum contains collections reflecting the past of the town and the surrounding area and occupies the fine old Devenish and John Groves Brewery situated in Hope Square on the western side of the harbour. The Timewalk is a fascinating journey through 600 years of Weymouth and Melcombe Regis history including Black Death, Spanish Armada and Royal Patronage of King George III. Also The Brewery's Tale Exhibition and shopping village.

## Bridport Museum
**Bridport. Tel: (01308) 422116.**
This fine Tudor building houses a local history centre with displays covering Bridport and West

Dorset in particular. There are maps, photographs, parish registers, census returns, family histories and publications. Also costume, fine art, dolls and exhibitions on rural history. Gift shop.

## Cloud's Hill
**Bovington, nr. Wareham.**
TE Lawrence (Lawrence of Arabia) bought his cottage in 1925 and it contains his furniture and other relics.

## Corfe Castle
**Wareham. Tel: (01929) 481294.**
One of the most impressive ruins in England. An important medieval royal castle, it was besieged by Parliamentary forces in 1646.

## Christchurch Priory
**Christchurch. Tel: (01202) 485804.**
A medieval monastic church from 1094. Considered to be England's longest serving Parish church. Massive Norman nave and turret, 15th century tower, St. Michael's Loft, now a museum. Guided tours available.

## The Deep Sea Adventure
**Weymouth. Tel: (01305) 760690.**
The story of diving with full-size models of early diving apparatus, diving bells and equipment.

## The Dinosaur Museum
**Icen Way, Dorchester. Tel: (01305) 269880.**
The only museum in the country devoted solely to dinosaurs. Life-size dinosaur reconstructions, actual fossils and skeletons combined with audio-visual, hands-on and computer displays.

## Dorset County Museum
**Dorchester. Tel: (01305) 262735.**
Exhibits collected since 1845 by the Dorset Natural History and Archaeological Society. State of the art gallery on Thomas Hardy and Dorset's Famous Writers. Archaeology, geological fossils and dinosaur remains.

## Harbour Museum
**West Bay, Bridport. Tel: (01308) 420997.**
The museum is a converted salt house overlooking Bridport Harbour. Inside, displays tell the story of Bridport's world-famous rope and net industry and of West Bay itself, with objects dating from the 18th century onwards.

## Forde Abbey and Gardens
**Nr. Chard.**
30 acres of gardens with lakes, arboretum, bog gardens and herbaceous borders.

## Hardy's Cottage
**Higher Bockhampton, nr. Dorchester.**
**Tel: (01305) 262366.**
Thatched cottage where poet and novelist Thomas Hardy was born in 1840.

## Kingston Lacy
**Wimborne Minster. Tel: (01202) 883402.**
17th century house, designed for Sir Ralph Bankes by Sir Roger Pratt. Set in formal gardens and woodland walks, surrounded by a park of 103 hectares.

## Max Gate
**Dorchester. Tel: (01305) 262538.**
Victorian house designed by Thomas Hardy and his home from 1885 until his death in 1928.

## The Museum of East Dorset Life & Garden
**Wimborne. Tel: (01202) 882533.**
The museum is found inside a historic town house with an beautiful walled garden. A series of period rooms tell the story of the people of Wimborne and East Dorset along with a hands-on archaeology gallery. Garden Tea Room open in the summer. Gift shop.

## Natural World at The Poole Aquarium
**Poole. Tel: (01202) 686712.**
Aquarium traces evolution of freshwater and sea-water species to one of the largest collections of snakes in the country.

## The Red House Museum & Gardens
**Christchurch. Tel: (01202) 482860.**
Local history, geology, natural history and archaeology, reflecting the interesting archaeological and wild-life sites of the area. Outstanding display of costumes. Formal gardens with many varieties of herbs, secluded informal gardens with old fashioned roses, shrubs and trees. Gift shop, coffee shop.

## Russel-Cotes Art Gallery and Museum
**Bournemouth. Tel; (01202) 451800.**
A spectacular collection of Victorian and 20th century paintings housed in an extravagant Italianate-style seaside villa. Also sculpture and

furniture. The garden and beautifully restored art galleries are sites for contemporary art and craft commissions.

## Sea Life Centre
**Weymouth. Tel: (01305) 788255.**
Variety of displays showing different aspects of under-water marine life.

## The Shelley Rooms
**Bournemouth. Tel: (01202) 303571.**
The rooms are in a part of Boscombe Manor, which was once the home of Shelley's son, Percy Florence Shelley. The displays look at Shelley's life, work and friends, particularly in the last few months of his life (1822).

## Sherborne Old Castle
**Sherborne. Tel: (01935) 812730.**
Built in 12th century. Sir Walter Raleigh made minor alterations after 1592.

## Sherborne Museum
**Sherborne. Tel: (01935) 812252.**
The museum features local geology, social history and industrial and agricultural artifacts. Special displays on Sherborne silk and glass fibre, a model of a Norman castle 1870 doll's house and an ecclesiastical wall painting from around 1500.

## Studland Beach and Nature Reserve
**Studland Bay, Swanage. Tel: (01929) 450259.**
3 miles of wonderful golden sand stretching from Shell Bay to Old Harry Rocks. Safe bathing.

## Tolpuddle Martyrs Museum
**Tolpuddle. Tel: (01305) 848237.**
The museum and cottages were built in 1934 by the Trades Union Congress in memory of the six agricultural workers transported to Australia in 1834 after forming a trade union. The museum tells their story and also introduces the other historical sites in the village.

## The Tutankhamun Exhibition
**Dorchester. Tel: (01305) 269571.**
Tutankhamun's tomb, treasures and mummy are superbly recreated through sight, sound and smell. Explore the ante-chamber and burial chamber filled with wonderful treasures.

## Upton Country Park
**Poole.**
Formal gardens, meadows and woodland.

## Wareham Museum
**Wareham. Tel: (01929) 553448.**
The museum has a local emphasis, featuring Old Wareham, agricultural and other implements from the past. Also birds and butterflies of the area. Most notable is the Lawrence of Arabia collection of photographs and ephemera.

## Waterfront Museum
**Poole. Tel: (01202) 683138.**
Displays illustrating Poole's links with the sea from pre-historic times until early 20th century.

## A World of Toys
**Arne, nr. Wareham. Tel: (01929) 552018.**
A collection of antique and collector's toys, musical boxes and automata. Audio-visual displays.

# DURHAM AND COUNTY DURHAM

The Norman Cathedral and castle dominate the historic university town of Durham from their setting high above the River Wear. Both are classified as World Heritage Sites. The castle is now part of England's third oldest university. The wooded riverbanks provide a beautiful setting for walking, fishing or boat trips. The narrow, twisting medieval streets survive as part of the town's busy shopping centre.

## Auckland Castle
**Bishop Aukland. Tel: (01388) 601627.**
The official residence of the Bishop of Durham since Norman times. The magnificent private chapel was built from the ruins of the 12th century Banqueting Hall in 1665. Free public access to adjacent Bishop's Park. Deer Shelter from 18th century.

## Barnard Castle
**Tel: (01833) 638212.**
Ruined castle overlooking the River Tees. Remains include 14th century Great Hall, three storey keep and circular round tower. Also picturesque ruins of Egglestone Abbey. The greater part of the nave and chancel are still standing.

## Beamish -the North of England Open Air Museum
Costumed staff welcome visitors to the

turn-of-the-century town with shops, houses, a working pub and printer's workshop. There is a Railway Station, complete with goods yard, signal box and steam locomotives. Colliery Village, with pit cottages, colliery buildings and "drift" mine. Home Farm, with animals and farmhouse kitchen.

### Binchester Roman Fort
**Bishop Auckland. Tel: (01388) 663089.**
Remains of part of the Roman Fort "Vinovia", including an excellent military bath-house.

### Castle Eden Dene National Nature Reserve
**Stanhope Chase, Peterlee. Tel: (0191) 5860004.**
Picturesque wooded valley (dene). 550 acres of natural woodland with 12 miles of footpaths.

### Darlington Museum
**Darlington. Tel: (01325) 463795.**
Displays on local and natural history. Observation beehive in summer months.

### Darlington Railway Centre and Museum
**Darlington. Tel: (01325) 460532.**
Restored passenger station dating from 1842, housing a collection of exhibits relating to railways in the north east of England. Includes Stephenson's "Locomotion".

### Durham Castle
**Tel: (0191) 3743800.**
Norman Castle, built as a fortress for the protection of the cathedral. Contains original crypt chapel (1080), Great Hall (1284), 15th century kitchens, Bishop Cosin's 17th century black staircase. It has been the University College since 1832, the first college of Durham University.

### Durham Cathedral
**Tel: (0191) 3743863.**
Many consider Durham Cathedral to be the finest example of Norman church architecture in England. Tombs of St. Cuthbert and The Venerable Bede. The Treasury contains the altar plate and other treasures.

### Durham Heritage Centre
Medieval church housing exhibitions on Durham County and City.

### Durham Light Infantry Museum and Durham Art Gallery
**Tel: (0191) 3842214.**

A collection tracing 200 years of the DLI County Regiment, including medals and uniforms. The Art Gallery has a changing programme of exhibitions and events.

### Durham University Oriental Museum
**Tel: (0191) 374911.**
Exhibits on ancient Egypt, Eastern religion, Japanese arts and crafts, Chinese ceramics and jade and the development of writing.

### Escomb Church
**Bishop Aukland. Tel: (01388) 602861.**
Saxon church, dating from 7th century. Contains a Roman arch and stonework.

### Finchale Priory
**Tel: (0191) 3833828.**
13th century Benedictine Priory by the River Wear. Built around the tomb of St. Godric who lived here until he was 105 years old.

### Hamsterley Forest
**Bishop Auckland. Tel: (01388) 488312.**
Visitor Centre with exhibits on forestry and wildlife. Walks and forest drive. Forest Orienteering course and cycle routes. Park and picnic places.

### High Force Waterfall
**Barnard Castle. Tel: (01833) 640209.**
The most majestic of the waterfalls on the River Tees. The falls are only a short walk from picnic area, bus stop and car park.

### Killhope Leadmining Centre
**St. John's Chapel, Bishop Auckland.**
**Tel: (01388) 537505.**
Most complete lead mining site in great Britain. Includes crushing mill with 34ft water wheel, reconstruction of Victorian machinery and miners accommodation.

### Museum of Archaeology
**Tel: (0191) 3743623.**
Exhibitions on archaeology of Durham City and County Durham. Temporary exhibitions on aspects of archaeology.

### Prince Bishop River Cruiser
**Tel: (0191) 3869525.**
150 seat luxury cruiser. Observation deck, lower deck saloon, bar, cafe and commentary. Also rowing boats for hire.

## Raby Castle
**Staindrop, Darlington. Tel: (01833) 660202.**
Medieval castle in 200 acre park, home of Lord
Barnard's family for over 350 years. 600 year old
kitchen and carriage collection. Walled gardens
and deer park.

## Tanfield Railway
**Marley Hill, nr. Stanley.**
The oldest existing railway in the world,
originally opened in 1725. 2 miles of railway
between Sunniside and Causey Arch. Collection
of locomotives and carriages from the area. Also
steam-driven workshop based in a working steam
engine shed from 1854.

## Timothy Hackworth Victorian
## Railway Museum
**Soho Cottage, Shildon. Tel: (01388) 777999.**
Former home of Timothy Hackworth
(1786-1850) railway pioneer. Also other cottages
and railway buildings including coal drops
and stables.

## University of Durham Botanical Garden
Botanic garden set in countryside and mature
woodland. Plant collections from North America,
Himalayas and China as well as rain forest and
desert. Mediterranean conservatory.

## Vindorama Roman Museum and
## Bath House
**Ebchester. Tel: (01207) 562180.**
Roman fort, the excavated remains of the
Commandant's bath house and small museum of
artifacts.

## The Weardale Museum of
## High House Chapel
**Ireshopeburn. Tel: (01388) 537417.**
The museum was formerly the Manse to the
High House Chapel. Includes the Weardale
Room from the 1870s and Wesley Room, which
commemorates Wesley's journeys through
Weardale. Also displays of minerals, lead,
agriculture and railways.

# GLOUCESTERSHIRE

## Bourton-on-the-Water
Popular large village, known as "The Little
Venice of the Cotswolds" for the low bridges
which span the River Windrush. Many visitor
attractions and restaurants.

## Cheltenham
A beautiful spa town, with a wide range of
accommodation, attractions and fashionable
shopping. There are colourful gardens and parks,
tree-lined avenues, flowing fountains and superb
floral decorations. Visitors can enjoy the illumi-
nated Imperial Gardens in the evening, as a
prelude to sampling Cheltenham's selection of
restaurants, theatres and nightlife.

## Gloucester
Gloucester has been called the Inland Riviera and
its rapidly developing docks and marina are
certainly amongst Britain's most exciting visitor
developments. The city was settled by the
Romans and by the Saxons and it was here that
William the Conqueror commissioned the
Domesday Book. Gloucester Cathedral is a
powerful symbol of the city's exciting past. Most
of Gloucester's numerous visitor attractions are
in and around its centre but the international
centre for wildlife art - Nature in Art - two miles
away, is not to be missed.

## Batsford Park Arboretum
**Off A44, nr. Moreton-in-Marsh.**
One of the largest private collections of rare trees
making up a 50 acre arboretum. Bronze statues,
garden centre and nursery.

## Birdland
Risington Road, Bournton-on-the Water.
Bird garden on the banks of the River Windrush.
Penguins, waterfowl, tropical and sub-tropical
birds, many at liberty.

## Clearwell Caves
**Ancient Iron Mines, nr. Coleford,**
**Royal Forest of Dean.**
Superb caverns and tunnels stretching far under
the Forest of Dean. Worked for iron ore for over
2,000 years until 1945.

## Cotswold Farm Park
**Guiting Power, Cheltenham.**
**Tel: (01451) 850307.**
Comprehensive collection of rare breed British
farm animals. Pets Corner, adventure playground,
picnic area. Seasonal exhibitions including
lambing and shearing.

## Cotswold Motor Museum
**Bourton-on-the-Water. Tel: (01451) 21255.**
A collection of 30 motor vehicles along with

vintage advertising signs. Also exhibition on Village Life.

## Cotswold Woollen Weavers
**Filkins, nr. Lechdale. Tel: (01452) 528095.**
Working woollen mill showing traditional skills in 18th century buildings.

## Cotswolds Water Park
**5 miles south of Cirencester off A419. Tel: (01285) 861459.**
2,000 acres of lakes with facilities for angling, bird watching, windsurfing, sailing and other water sports.

## Gloucester Cathedral
**Westgate Street, Gloucester. Tel: (01452) 528095.**
Magnificent Abbey church (1089) and chapter house. Earliest perpendicular work and fan vaulting. Great East window commemorates Battle of Crecy 1346.

## Gloucester Ski Centre
**Robinswood Hill, Gloucester. Tel: (01452) 414300.**
240m & 200m nursery slopes. Full length ski lifts. Beginners to experts. Full tuition and equipment. Ski shop.

## Gloucestershire-Warwickshire Railway
**Toddington, nr. Winchcombe at intersection of B4632/A438. Tel: (01242) 621405.**
Restored GWR station. Mainline steam rides 8 miles round trip. Large rail complex, rolling stock under restoration.

## Hidcote Manor Garden
**Hidcote Bartrim, nr. Chipping Campden. Tel: (01386) 438333.**
A delightful series of small gardens to be found within the whole, separated by walls and different species of hedges.

## Keith Harding's World of Mechanical Music
**Oak House, Northleach.**
The museum contains antique clocks, musical boxes, automata and mechanical musical instruments. Gift shop.

## National Birds of Prey Centre
**Newent, off B4216. Tel: (01531) 820286.**
Western Europe's largest collection of birds of Prey. Breeding aviaries, hawk walk and regular flying demonstrations.

## Nature in Art
**Wallsworth Hall, Twigworth, Gloucester. Tel: (01452) 731422.**
The world's first museum dedicated solely to the exhibition of wildlife art from all periods, all nations and all media. It offers a unique experience, housed in a beautiful Georgian mansion.

## Newent Butterfly & Natural World Centre
**Birches Lane, Newent off B4215. Tel: (01531) 821800.**
Tropical butterfly house, nature exhibition, menagerie and water life. Spiders, snakes, rabbits, guinea-pigs, rare breed fowl, waterfowl, pheasants, peacocks, parakeets and other small birds.

## Pittville Pump Room
**Pittville, Cheltenham. Tel: (01242) 512740.**
A magnificent Regency building, set in its own park. Spa Waters. Displays of original costumes form Cheltenham's Regency heyday through to the 1960s.

## Prinknash Abbey Pottery
**Cranham, Gloucester. Tel: (01452) 812239.**
The Benedictine community welcome visitors to the Abbey church and grounds. These offer relaxation in a tranquil atmosphere with a breathtaking view of the Vale of Gloucester. Tour of the pottery viewing gallery.

## Tewkesbury Abbey
**Tel: (01684) 850959.**
Founded in 8th century. Refounded at the end of 11th century. Massive Norman tower. Musica Deo Sacra Festival 1st week in August.

## Westbury Court Garden
**Westbury-on-Severn on A48. Tel: (01452) 276 461.**
A formal water garden with canals and yew hedges, laid out between 1696 and 1705: the earliest of its kind remaining in England.

## The Wildfowl & Wetlands Trust
**Slimbridge off A38. Tel: (01453) 890065.**
Vast collection of wildfowl in 73 acres of grounds. Tropical house. Permanent exhibition.

# HAMPSHIRE

### Andover
The centre of this ancient and picturesque market town has many old buildings including the Guildhall and the hilltop church of St. Mary's. Nearby are the Andover Museum and Museum of the Iron Age, both housed in the same building. There are walks down by the River Anton, past the nature reserve of Anton Lakes to the public gardens and old mill on the edge of the town centre. Swimming and dry sports complex at Andover Leisure Centre.

### Fordingbridge
Small town dating back to the Middle Ages, most well known for the medieval 7-arch bridge over the River Avon. Early English parish church and Georgian houses in the town.

### Hayling Island
Hayling Island is joined to the mainland by a bridge and by ferry from Portsmouth. The south of the island has 5 miles of beach with safe bathing. Variety of accommodation, golf course and sports centre. Also water-based activities such as water-skiing and boardsailing.

### New Forest
Between the great sea port of Southampton and the rolling hills of Dorset lies the New Forest. Throughout this landscape there are picturesque villages, historic towns, local inns, magnificent woodlands, ponies and majestic deer. The Forest itself, with its abundant wildlife and unrivaled scenery, can take days to explore either on foot or perhaps on horseback. For rainy days there are indoor attractions such as Palace House, the home of Lord Montagu at Beaulieu or the Elizabethan splendour of Breamore House.

### Southampton
The port of Southampton has much to offer including parks and gardens, theatres, art galleries and museums. There are sporting activities, marinas and harbour trips. The New Forest is only 15 miles from the city centre.

### Romsey
The narrow streets and central market place of Romsey are dominated by the magnificent Norman Abbey. There are many fine historic buildings including the 13th century King John's House. Close to the town centre is the extensive park and house at Broadlands. There are delightful walks alongside the bubbling streams of the River Test. The more active can enjoy the swirling pools and giant flume of the Rapids public swimming pool.

### Breamore House
**A338 between Salisbury and Ringwood.**
**Tel: (01725) 512468.**
The house, built in 1583, has a splendid collection of pictures and furniture contributed to by 10 generations. The Countryside Museum is designed to explain the development of village life from a self-contained unit to the post-war period. There are examples of a farm worker's cottage, dairy, wheelwright's shop, blacksmith's forge, a farm brewery, cider barn, saddler's shop and cobbler's shed. The stables house a collection of horse-drawn vehicles including Red Rover, the London to Southampton stage coach. Saxon church, park.

### Broadlands
**Romsey. Tel: (01794) 517888.**
An elegant Palladian mansion in a beautiful landscaped setting on the banks of the River Test. Famous as the home of the late Lord Mountbatten, and equally well known as the country residence of Lord Palmerston, Prime Minister during Victoria's reign. The House contains art treasures and mementoes of the famous, the Mountbatten Exhibition allows visitors to relive Lord Mountbatten's life and times. Tea Room and Gift Shop.

### Exbury Gardens
**Nr. Southampton. Tel: (01703) 891203.**
Extensive landscaped woodland gardens overlooking Beaulieu River. World famous plant collection (rhododendrons, azaleas etc.) plus wonderful trees, Rock Garden, Cascades, Ponds, River Walk, Rose Garden, Water Garden, Heather Gardens, seasonal trails and themed walks. Lunches/cream teas. Plant Centre and Gift Shop.

### Finkley Down Farm Park
**Nr. Andover. Tel: (01264) 352195.**
Feed the goats, stroke the rabbits, see lots of baby animals being reared in a natural environment. Activities such as feeding and grooming. Playground, Gypsy Caravans, Barn of Bygones, picnic area and Rooster's Rest Tearoom.

## Gosport Ferry
**Gosport. Tel: (01705) 524551.**
Leisure cruises around Portsmouth Harbour and
the Solent. Luxury all weather vessel with
refreshment facilities.

## The Hawk Conservancy
**Off A303, nr. Andover. Tel: (01264) 772252.**
22 acres of woodland gardens, over 250 birds of
prey. Also Butterfly Garden, Children's Garden
and Toddler's Play Area. Visitors can hold the
birds and adults can fly a hawk.

## Highclere Castle
**South of Newbury, off A34 to Winchester.**
**Tel: (01635) 253210.**
This Victorian castle was created by Sir Charles
Barry, builder of the Houses of Parliament and is
the home of the Earl and Countess of Carnavon.
There are stunning interiors, which include
Napoleon's chair and a collection of old masters.
The 5th Earl of Carnavon discovered the tomb of
Tutankhamun and his Egyptian antiquities are on
display. Location of many TV and film
productions including The Secret Garden,
Inspector Morse and Jeeves and Wooster.

## Jane Austen's House
**Chawton, nr. Alton. Tel: (01420) 83262.**
This is the 17th century house where Jane Austen
lived and wrote or revised her six great novels
between 1809 and 1817. It contains mementoes,
copy letters, jewellery and patchwork quilt she
and her mother made. Pleasant garden.

## Longdown Dairy Farm
**Longdown, Ashurst, nr. Southampton.**
**Tel: (01703) 293326.**
Combination of working dairy unit and children's
farm. Play and picnic areas, computer quiz, video
room.

## Marwell Zoological Park
**Colden Common, Winchester.**
**Tel: (01426) 943163.**
Nearly 1000 animals and some are the rarest on
earth. Set in 100 acres of beautiful parkland.
Camel rides, Adventure Playground, Picnic sites,
restaurant and bar.

## Mottisfont Abbey Garden
**Tel: (01794) 340757.**
Tranquil garden by the River Test, owned by the

National Trust. Magnificent trees, walled
gardens, old-fashioned roses and the spring or
"font" from which the place takes its name. In
the Abbey, visitors can see the drawing room,
decorated by Rex Whistler and the Cellarium of
the Old Priory. Lunches and homemade teas.

## Museum of the Iron Age
**Andover. Tel: (01264) 366283.**
Exhibitions trace the development of the site of
nearby Danebury Hill Fort and life in the pre-
Roman Iron Age. Reconstructions and models
displayed alongside original material found by
excavation.

## National Motor Museum
**Beaulieu. Tel: (01590) 612345.**
One of the finest collections of cars and motor
cycles in the world. Visitors can also see Palace
House, Gardens, Beaulieu Abbey and Exhibitions
of Monastic Life.

## New Forest Butterfly Farm
**Longdown, Ashurst, nr. Southampton.**
**Tel: (01703) 292166.**
Indoor tropical jungle with butterflies and moths
from all over the world flying freely.
Insectarium, woodland walk, dragonfly ponds,
adventure playground, picnic area.

## Paultons Park
**Ower, nr. Romsey. Tel; (01703) 814455.**
Family leisure park. Leafy gardens, landscaped
with exotic bird aviaries and wildfowl ponds.
Runaway Train ride, Dinosaur Land, Rio
Grande miniature railway, the Romany Museum,
Kids Kingdom. Also restaurant, tearooms,
picnic areas.

## Porchester Castle
**Off A27, south of Porchester.**
Grand Medieval castle and 18th century French
prisoner-of-war camp set within a large 3rd
century Roman fort, stands overlooking
Portsmouth Harbour. Exhibition on the Castle's
2,000 year old history.

## Portsmouth Naval Heritage Trust
**HM Naval Base, Portsmouth.**
**Tel: (01705) 870999.**
Portsmouth Historic Dockyard: Home to the
Mary Rose, HMS Victory, HMS Warrior 1860
and the Royal Navy Museum.

### Queen Elizabeth Country Park
**Waterlooville. Tel: (01705) 595040.**
Superb park, occupying 1400 acres of woodland and downland. There are walks, picnic areas, barbecues, pony trekking, wildlife and wonderful views.

### Romsey Abbey
**Romsey. Tel: (01794)513125.**
The Abbey was founded around 907 and the present building, the third on the site, is from 1120-1240 (Norman/Early English). The treasures include two Saxon stone carved crucifixes and 16th century painted reredos. Burial place of Earl Mountbatten of Burma.

### Southampton City Art Gallery
**Tel: (01703) 632601.**
This gallery houses one of the finest 20th century British art collections outside London and shows a lively programme of temporary exhibitions. Gallery shop, Fountains Cafe.

### Southampton Maritime Museum
**Southampton. Tel: (01703) 224216.**
The museum occupies a late 14th century wool warehouse. Features the history of the port of Southampton, including a model of the docks at their peak in 1930s.

### Watercress Line
**Alresford Station. Tel: (01962) 733810.**
Preserved steam trains running through the rolling Hampshire countryside, between Alton and Alresford.

### Winchester - River Park Leisure Centre
**Winchester. Tel: (01962) 869525.**
Badminton, squash, Health and Fitness suite, swimming pools, flume, dance studio, tennis courts, course and classes.

### Winchester Cathedral
**Winchester. Tel: (01962) 866854.**
Building first started in 1079. There are still remains of Norman architecture in transepts and crypt. The nave was remodelled in the 14th century and is said to be the longest cathedral nave in the perpendicular Gothic style. Visitors can see the tombs of Jane Austen and Izaac Walton and hear how William Walker, the diver, saved the Cathedral in 1906. Shop and Refectory.

## HEREFORDSHIRE

### Hereford
This cathedral city lies in the heart of the Wye Valley, at the centre of some of the most superb touring country in Britain. Hereford offers the visitor a good range of tourist accommodation and restaurants, with attractions and sports facilities for all ages. Modern shopping blends harmoniously with historic buildings. The Cathedral dates from 11th century and contains many treasures. Livestock and general market on Wednesday.

### Leominster
Leominster was one of the great wool markets in England for 500 years. Its wool acquired a national reputation for its high quality, being referred to Leominster Ore. This prosperity has left a legacy of fine Georgian houses but the impression to the visitor is of a medieval market town. Numerous specialist antique shops.

### Ross-on-Wye
High on a sandstone cliff, overlooking a large loop in the beautiful River Wye, is the historic market town of Ross-on-Wye. There are Tudor timbered houses clustered around the striking 17th century Market Hall where the twice weekly markets are still held. Superb shopping facilities ranging from small craft shops to larger High Street chains.

### Berrington Hall
**Leominster. Tel: (01568) 615721.**
Elegant mansion in a park, landscaped by Capability Brown. The austere exterior belies the intricacy of the interior, with elaborate plasterwork and delicate gilt tracery. Fully equipped Victorian laundry, pretty tiled Georgian dairy. Restaurant.

### Brobury Gardens & Gallery
**Brobury. Tel: (01981) 500595.**
7 acres of semi-formal gardens on the banks of the River Wye. Views of the Black Mountains. The gallery has over 200,000 antique prints, collection of old and contemporary watercolours.

### The Button Museum
**Ross-on-Wye. Tel: (01989) 66089.**
Unique collection of buttons worn by ladies and gentlemen over the last 200 years.

### Croft Castle
**Yarpole, Leominster. Tel: (01586) 780246.**
Massive walls and castellated turrets date from 14th and 15th centuries; interior mainly 18th century, when fine Georgian-Gothic staircase and plasterwork ceiling were added. Ancient oaks and sweet chestnuts in the surrounding park, with trails leading to Croft Ambrey, an Iron Age fort.

### Eastnor Castle
**Nr. Ledbury. Tel: (01531) 631776.**
Magnificent Georgian castle, encircled by the Malvern Hills and surrounded by a deer park, arboretum and lake. Inside visitors will find tapestries, fine art and armour. The Italianate and Gothic decor has been restored.

### L'Escargot Anglais
**Credenhill Snail Farm**
**Credenhill, Hereford. Tel: (01432) 760218.**
LEA has become one of the foremost authorities on snail farming in the world. The farming is carried out both indoors and outdoors, among the glorious Herefordshire countryside. Kitchens prepare snails to gourmet tastes, with a wide range of high quality recipes.

### Goodrich Castle
**5 miles south of Ross-on-Wye off A40.**
The red sandstone of Goodrich has a Norman keep, dungeon, huge towers, battlements and endless little rooms and stairways to be explored. The castle suffered damage during the Civil War, from a locally-made cannon Roaring Meg.

### The Hill Court Gardens and Garden Centre
**Ross-on-Wye.**
Set in the grounds of a William & Mary mansion the two and a half acres of ornamental gardens include a yew walk, rose garden, water garden and herbaceous borders.

### Lewstone Mill
**Whitchurch, Ross-on-Wye.**
Newly opened in 1996. The garden at Lewstone Mill was started in 1987 by the present owners. The old water wheel has been respoked and is now in full working order. The mill stream flows through the lower part of this colourful garden via a series of pools and falls. Teas, plants on sale.

### The Lost Street Museum
**Palma Court, Brookend Street, Ross-on-Wye.**
This unique Edwardian Street has fully stocked, life-sized shops. Also probably the largest privately-owned collection of music boxes, toys, dolls, wirelesses, gramophones, motor cycles and costume.

### Queenswood Country Park & Arboretum
**Bodenham.**
The Hereford Countryside Centre includes exciting displays and a full programme of the events and information on the Park. 170 acres of woodland and over 500 varieties of trees.

### South Herefordshire Golf Club
**Upton Bishop, Ross-on-Wye.**
**Tel: (01989) 780535.**
Golf complex including course, floodlit driving range, teaching, restaurant and bar.

### Welsh Court
**Yatton.**
Welsh Court is a traditional Herefordshire three storey farmhouse which has been tastefully updated and the gardens developed from scratch. There is a stream running through the land to the south of the house, which has been harnessed to produce two major ponds. Herb garden.

### Wye Valley Farm Park
**Goodrich, Ross-on-Wye. Tel: (01600) 890296.**
Situated between Goodrich Castle and Symonds Yat Rock, the Farm Park is set amongst beautiful woodland and riverside walks. Cider press with video on cider making. Children's play area. Gift shop.

## HUMBERSIDE

### Bridlington
Ever since Edwardian times, Bridlington and the Wolds has been one of Yorkshire's most popular seaside resorts, attracting visitors from far and wide. The sweeping bay is perfect for yachts, rowing boats, speed boats, pleasure cruisers. There are long golden sands set against the breath-taking backdrop of the Flamborough Headland Heritage Coast with its huge chalk cliffs.

### Burton Agnes Hall
**Nr. Driffield. Tel: (01262) 490324.**
Elizabethan house with superb collections of

antique furniture, Impressionist and Modern paintings. Potager and Jungle gardens, herbaceous borders, maze, giant board games and children's corner. Cafe, ice cream parlour, shops and plant sales.

## Burton Constable Hall
**Nr. Hull. Tel: (01964) 562400.**
Ancestral home of the Constable family since 16th century. The 29 rooms contain furniture, paintings, and a unique collection of 18th century scientific instruments.

## Elsham Hall Country & Wildlife Park
**Brigg. Tel: (01625) 688698.**
Falconry Centre, Children's Zoo and Playground, Granary Restaurant and Theatre, Craft and Garden Centre. Special events and evening performances.

## Museum of Army Transport
**Flemingate, Beverley. Tel: (01482) 860445.**
The museum tells the story of army transport by road, rail and sea through acres of indoor displays. There is also a flight simulator and narrow gauge railway.

## National Fishing Heritage Centre
**Alexandra Dock, Grimsby.**
**Tel: (01472) 344868.**
This was the Industrial History Museum of the Year in 1994 and takes the visitor on an epic journey to the Arctic fishing grounds for a dramatic battle against the elements to bring home the catch.

## Park Rose Pottery Leisure Park
**Bridlington. Tel: (01262) 602823.**
Factory tour, Owl Sanctuary & Woodland Conservation Area, 12 acres of beautiful parkland, gift shops, seconds warehouse, licensed cafe, picnic areas and children's adventure playground.

## Sewerby Hall & Grounds
**Bridlington.**
Impressive mansion set in 50 acres of beautiful gardens and parkland with attractions such as golf, putting, bowls, a zoo, children's play areas and the Clock Tower Tavern.

# ISLE OF WIGHT

## Butterfly World & Fountain World
**Wooton. Tel: (01983) 883430.**
Butterfly World is a beautifully landscaped indoor garden with hundreds of exotic butterflies on wing. Fountains World meanwhile, has an elegant landscaped formal Italian garden and Japanese garden. See the huge Koi carp.

## Classic Boat Centre
**Seaclose Wharf, Newport. Tel: (01983) 533493.**
A collection of beautiful boats of historic interest with engines, equipment, memorabilia. Art & photographic displays. Cafe and shop.

## Isle of Wight Pearl Centre
**Nr. Brighstone. Tel: (01983) 740352.**
One of the largest and most lavish collections of pearl jewellery under one roof. Spacious showroom with designs using natural, cultured and simulated pearls.

## Isle of Wight Steam Railway
**Havenstreet. Tel: (01983) 882204.**
Vintage trains take visitors on a 10 mile round trip through unspoilt countryside. Museum of Island Rail History, gardens and picnic area. Shop and refreshments.

## Nunwell House & Gardens
**Brading. Tel: (01983) 407240.**
The guided tour of the house includes a visit to the room where King Charles I spent his last night of freedom. Military and Home Guard Museums. Enchanting gardens.

## Quay Arts
**Newport. Tel: (01983) 528825.**
Galleries, workshops and dance studio in an 18th century brewer's warehouse on the waterfront in the old docks area. Programme of exhibitions, antique & craft fairs, music and performances. Cafe and shop.

## Rare Breeds & Waterfowl Park
**St. Lawrence, nr. Ventnor. Tel: (01983) 852582.**
The rare animals and exotic waterfowl are to be seen within a 30 acre coastal setting. Over 1,000 animals, including otters, Falabella miniature horses, llamas, deer. Picnic sites, lakeside cafe and gift shop.

### Robin Hill Country Park
**Downend, nr. Arreton. Tel: (01983) 527352.**
88 acres of countryside, filled with fun and adventure. Toboggan Run, Treetop Trail, Wooden Panel Maze, Games Area, country walks and activity course.

### Tropical Bird Park
**St. Lawrence, nr. Ventnor. Tel: (01983) 853526.**
The walk-through aviaries are home to over 600 rare and exotic birds such as toucans, macaws, cockatoos and touracos. Walking along the woodland trail visitors can see storks, owls, eagles and vultures. Lake with ducks, swans and geese.

## KENT

### Bay Museum & Pines Gardens
**St. Margaret's Bay, nr. Deal.**
**Tel: (01304) 852764.**
The museum contains a fascinating collection of items concerning shipping and history of the coastline. Opposite it are the lush green Pines Gardens.

### Canterbury Cathedral
**Tel: (01227) 762862.**
Important features include Norman crypt, early Gothic quire, 15th century nave and Bell Harry tower.

### Canterbury Tales
**Tel: (01227) 454888.**
A recreation of life in 14th century England, illustrating Chaucer's Canterbury Tales with sights, sounds and smells,

### Cobham Hall and Gardens
**Cobham. Tel: (01474) 824319.**
The gardens, landscaped for the 4th Earl of Darnley by Humphry Repton in 1790 are gradually being restored. In the grounds are several important classical buildings.

### Dickens House Museum
**Seafront, Broadstairs.**
This lovely old house, once the home of Miss Mary Strong on whom Charles Dickens based his famous character Miss Betsy Trotwood, is a fascinating museum commemorating the novelist's association with Broadstairs.

### Gazen Salts Nature Reserve & Bird Observatory
**Sandwich Bay.**
The 12 acre reserve is located beside the meandering course of the River Stour near its exit to the sea at Pegwell Bay. 160 species of bird have been recorded here including turtle dove, sedge, reed warbler, kestrel, cormorant and snipe.

### The Guild Hall Museum
**Rochester. Tel: (01634) 848717.**
Visitors step through exhibits from Prehistoric and Roman times to the 16th century then on to Victorian and Edwardian times. Brass rubbing, coin minting, educational audio-visual displays.

### Great Maytham Hall
**Cranbrook. Tel: (01580) 241346.**
Beautiful Lutyens House and Garden; 18 acre parkland with bluebells; formal gardens with blue and silver border; walled garden inspired Frances Hodgson Burnett to write The Secret Garden.

### Hever Castle and Gardens
**Edenbridge. Tel: (01732) 865224.**
This 13th century moated castle is set in magnificent gardens and grounds. The Italian Garden contains superb statuary and fountains. Walled rose garden, herb garden, maze, topiary and 35 acre lake.

### Leeds Castle
**Maidstone. Tel: (01622) 765400.**
In the 9th century, the castle was the site of a manor of the Saxon royal family. It has been a Norman stronghold, a royal residence to six of England's medieval Queens, a palace to Henry VIII and a private home. Inside is a magnificent collection of medieval furnishings, paintings, tapestries and treasure. There are 500 acres of glorious parkland and gardens. Superb Spring displays of wood anemones, narcissi and cherry blossom give way to summer rhododendrons.

### Margate Museum
**Market Place, Margate.**
The museum is situated in the Old Police Station and Court Building. It has displays covering all aspects of local history from 1600 to the present time.

## Margate Caves

Great caverns hewn out over a thousand years ago by our ancestors and now a monument to the skill and ability of those forgotten times. First used as a refuge, then as a medieval dungeon and church, and finally as a smuggler's hideout.

## Minster Abbey
**Minster, nr. Ramsgate.**

One of England's oldest buildings. The Abbey was founded in the year 670 and the present buildings date back, in part, to the 11th century.

## The Royal Museum & Art Gallery
**Canterbury.**

The city's picture collection, decorative arts, exhibitions and the Buffs regimental gallery.

## Model Village
**West Cliff, Ramsgate.**

A delightful reproduction of England's most beautiful countryside in miniature.

## Mount Ephraim Gardens
**Hern Hill, nr. Faversham. Tel: (01227) 751496.**

Daffodils, rhododendrons, a fine herbaceous border, topiary, rose terrace all set in 8 acres with a small lake and woodland area. Water garden and Japanese rock garden with pools. Vineyard, many mature trees and wonderful views over Swale Estuary.

## Rochester Castle
**Rochester-upon-Medway. Tel: (01634) 418742.**

Strategically situated on the old Roman road of Watling Street, Rochester Castle is a Norman castle with an imposing 113 ft high keep.

## Scotney Castle Garden
**Lamberhurst, nr. Royal Tunbridge Wells. Tel: (01892) 891081.**

One of England's most romantic gardens, surrounding the ruins of a 14th century moated castle. Rhododendrons, azaleas, water lilies and wisteria flower in profusion. Woodland and estate walks. Shop.

## Sissinghurst Garden
**Sissinghurst, nr. Cranbrook. Tel: (01580) 712850.**

Five and a half acre garden created by Vita Sackville-West and her husband Sir Harold Nicolson. This series of small, romantic "outdoor rooms" is of international acclaim.

## Stour River Bus
**Sandwich. Tel: (01304) 613925.**

Regular motor boat trips between Sandwich Toll Bridge and Richborough Roman Ruins - two miles upstream along the river.

# LANCASHIRE

## Astley Hall
**Chorley. Tel: (01257) 26166.**

The hall has sumptuous interior decoration and fine furnishings and is situated next to a lake. Wooded parkland. Cafe.

## Camelot Theme Park & Rare Breeds Farm
**Charnock Richard, Chorley. Tel: (01257) 453044.**

There is a 13 acre Rare Breeds Farm, where visitors can see 120 animals and birds at close hand and discover how they were farmed in Medieval Britain. Also over 100 thrilling rides such as Excalibur and the Tower of Terror.

## Fairhaven Lake
**Lytham St. Annes.**

Water sports of all kinds can be enjoyed here including boating, sailing, wind surfing, rowing, canoeing and motor boating. Paddling pool and children's playground. Bowling, tennis, putting and crazy golf.

## Frontier Land Western Theme Park
**Morecombe. Tel: (01524) 410024.**

Over 30 great rides, live shows, animals in the Dude Ranch and the Fun House.

## Helicentre
**Blackpool Airport, Blackpool. Tel: (01253) 343082.**

There are Charter, Training and Pleasure Flights. Also North Pier Helicopter Rides will take visitors on a tour of Blackpool's famous attractions.

## Lowther Gardens
**Lytham St. Annes.**

A haven for peace and tranquillity. Visitors can stroll around the lovely Rose Gardens, enjoy refreshments in the cafe or try bowling, tennis, crazy golf or putting.

## Lytham Windmill
**East Beach, Lytham.**

Built in 1805, the windmill produced flour and

oatmeal until a serious fire in 1919. Rebuilt in 1921, the mill has now been extensively renovated and houses a permanent exhibition on its history.

### Rufford Old Hall
**Nr. Southport.**
A 16th century timber framed house owned by the National Trust. The magnificent Great Hall contains an immense moveable oak screen and there are collections of arms and armour, oak furniture and costumes. Beautiful 14 acre garden. Tea room and shop.

### Tarzan's Adventureland
**Hambleton, Poulton-le-Fylde, nr. Blackpool. Tel: (01253) 701381.**
Exhilarating adventure trails for kids, climbing nets and slides. Adventure golf, animal train, water dome and gardens. Shop and restaurant. Toddler play areas.

### Toy and Teddy Bear Museum
**Lytham St. Annes. Tel: (01253) 713705.**
The museum is housed in one of St. Annes famous Porritt built Victorian buildings. There are toys from the past and childhood memorabilia, including model trains, cars, games, books, an extensive collection of dolls and dolls houses, children's costumes and photographs.

### Waves
**Blackburn. Tel: (01254) 51111.**
Flume ride, whirlpool spa, wave machine, beach style cafe, tropical atmosphere.

### The Wildfowl & Wetlands Trust
**Martin Mere, Burscough. Tel: (01704) 895181.**
There are over 1,000 tame ducks, geese, swans and flamingos in the beautiful waterfowl gardens. Play area, Visitor Centre with gallery, gift shop and coffee shop. Picnic area and nature trail.

### Williamson Park
**Lancaster. Tel: (01524) 33318.**
40 acres of parkland with lake and play area. Tropical Butterfly House, with exotic species flying free; Conservation Garden with wildlife pools; Mini Beast House and Free Flying Foreign Bird enclosure. The Ashton Memorial is an Edwardian Folly situated at the heart of the park. Tea room and souvenir shop.

### The World of Coronation Street
**Blackpool. Tel: (01253) 299555.**
Visitors can see famous sets, pop into the Rovers for a pint, and watch video presentations of the series.

# LINCOLNSHIRE

### Lincoln
Apart from the magnificent cathedral city of Lincoln and the holiday resorts of the coast, it is worth exploring the rolling hills of the Wolds, the mysterious fens and the ancient market towns. The poet Alfred Lord Tennyson, was born in the village of Somersby in the Wolds. The influence of Lincolnshire countryside remained a constant theme thoughout his poetry. Visitors are recommended to get off the beaten track and enjoy the rich history of Lincolnshire's towns and buildings as well of its varied countryside.

### Belton House, Park & Gardens
**Belton, Grantham. Tel: (01476) 66116.**
Belton House is a lovely example of Restoration country house architecture. It was built in 1685-88 for the Brownlows, originally lawyers who came here in Elizabethan times and alterations were made by James Wyatt in 1777. There are formal gardens, with orangery by Wyatville, a landscaped park, boat trips, miniature railway and adventure playground.

### Bolingbroke Castle
**Spilsby, Lincoln. Tel: (01529) 461499.**
Remains of the castle where Henry IV was born. Interpretation panels with artists impressions and text.

### Boston Guildhall Museum
**Boston. Tel: (01205) 365954.**
Visitors can see the cells where the Pilgrim Fathers were imprisoned in 1607 and the courtroom where they came to trial. Museum shop, maritime exhibits, pictures and farm tools.

### Burghley House
**Stamford. Tel: (01780) 52451.**
The home of the Cecil family for over 400 years, Burghley House is acknowledged to be the largest and grandest house of the first Elizabethan age. It was built between 1565 and 1587, for the First Lord Burghley, Lord High Treasurer to Queen Elizabeth I. Inside the house is an immense collection of art treasures.

There are 18 state rooms filled with fine paintings, furniture and wood carvings by Grinling Gibbons.

## Doddington Hall
**Doddington, Lincoln. Tel: (01522) 694308.**
Elizabethan mansion, Gatehouse and 5 acres of walled gardens. Good furniture, pictures, porcelain and textiles. Restaurant and gift shop.

## Grimsthorpe Castle, Park & Gardens
**Grimsthorpe, Bourne. Tel: (01778) 591205.**
The castle is an example of early 13th century architecture, the Tudor period and Sir John Vanburgh's last major work. It has been the home of Willoughby de Eresby family since 1576. Collection of mainly 18th century portraits and furniture. 3,000 acres of park landscaped by Capability Brown with lakes and ancient woods.

## Harlaxton Manor Gardens
**Grantham. Tel: (01476) 592101.**
This magnificent chateau, with Italian colonnade, French style terraces, Dutch ornamental canal and conservatory. 110 acres of gardens and grounds currently under restoration. Nature trails, tea room and picnic areas.

## Lincoln Castle
**Lincoln. Tel: (01522) 511068.**
A Medieval castle including towers and ramparts, with Magna Carta exhibition and Prison Chapel experience. Reconstructed Westgate. On the south side of the cathedral are the remains of the medieval palace of the Bishops of Lincoln, including shell of 12th century ceremonial hall, residential wing and Bishop Alnwick's 15th century entrance tower.

## Lincolnshire Aviation Heritage Centre
**East Kirkby, Spilsby. Tel: (01790) 763207.**
Part of wartime bomber airfield including a restored control tower. Displays military vehicles, air raid shelter, the Barnes Wallis original bouncing bomb and AVRO Lancaster Bomber.

## Long Sutton Butterfly and Falconry Park
**Long Sutton, Spalding. Tel: (01406) 363833.**
Large walk-through tropical butterfly house with insectarium, ant room, adventure playground, farm animals, pets corner and conservation area.

## Museum of Lincolnshire Life
**Lincoln. Tel: (01522) 528448.**
Agricultural, industrial & social history of Lincolnshire with exhibits ranging from a teapot to First World War tank.

## Rutland Water
**Tel: (01780) 86321.**
Largest man-made lake in Europe. Fishing, sailing, wind surfing, nature reserve. Normanton Church Water Museum. Adventure playground. Cycle hire. Pleasure cruiser.

## Skegness Natureland Seal Sanctuary
**The Promenade, Skegness.**
**Tel: (01754) 764345.**
Performing seals, baby seals and penguins. Crocodile, snakes, terrapins and scorpions. Free flight tropical birds and butterflies.

## Spalding Tropical Forest
**Pinchbeck, Spalding. Tel: (01775) 710882.**
Glass house enclosing a tropical environment. Over 100 species of orchids and flowering climbers, tropical and sub tropical plants in natural settings. Water Garden Centre. Advice on all aspects of gardening. Coffee shop, picnic area, adventure play area and gift shop.

## Tallington Lakes Leisure Parks
**Tallington, nr. Stamford.**
Leisure park with 200 acres of water. There is camping, caravaning, water skiing, wind surfing, dinghy sailing, jet skiing, a dry ski slope and fishing. Also woods, with an adventure playground, a health club and country club.

## Wingham Bird Park
**Between Wingham and Ash on B257.**
**Tel: (01227) 720836.**
The park and aviary contain a huge variety of rare birds; the centre is a breeding haven for endangered species. Pretty landscaping, animal corner and picnic spot.

## Woolsthorpe Manor
**Colsterworth, Grantham. Tel: (01476) 860338.**
Small 17th century house which was the birthplace of Sir Isaac Newton. Apple tree under which he was struck with the theory of gravity.

# NORFOLK

## Great Yarmouth

Great Yarmouth was once one of Britain's wealthiest medieval towns and visitors can still see the massive flint and rubble walls studded with watchtowers. The Maritime Museum of East Anglia occupies a house built in 1860 as a home for shipwrecked sailors. Visitors should also see the Marina Centre and the Sealife Centre, where visitors can walk underwater. The almost tropical beach runs for miles and there is every kind of amusement to be found.

## King's Lynn

Medieval streets run down to the quays, merchant's houses with private warehouses and the guild halls present the prosperity of this town. There's plenty to see here: the Town Hall houses Tales of the Old Gaol House, the King's Lynn Arts Centre, which hosts an annual festival, three museums, two market places and Leisure Park, the largest sports and leisure complex in East Anglia.

## Norwich

A beautiful and ancient city with the largest collection of medieval churches in Europe, a Norman Castle and Cathedral, cobbled shopping lanes and alleys. Norwich is also a centre for culture and entertainment.

## Blickling Hall
### Blickling. Tel: (01263) 733084.

Within this Jacobean red brick mansion there are fine tapestries and furniture. Large colourful garden with an orangery. Also parkland and lake. Picnic area, shop and restaurant. Plant centre.

## Bressingham Steam Museum & Gardens
### Bressingham. Tel: (01379) 687382.

A working steam museum with locomotive sheds and engines from all over Europe. Narrow gauge railway rides and Victorian steam roundabout. Gardens, two acre Plant Centre and display area.

## Castle Museum
### Norwich. Tel: (01603) 223624.

Large collection of art, including an important collection by Norwich School artists. Also British ceramic teapots. Archaeology and natural history. Early 12th century keep, tour battlements and dungeons.

## Cockley Cley
### Iceni Village and Museums
### 3 miles SW Swaffham. Tel: (01760) 724588.

The complex comprises a reconstruction of an Iceni Village, a medieval cottage/forge with museum.

## Dragon Hall
### Norwich. Tel: (01603) 663922.

This magnificent medieval merchant's hall has some beautiful features including a crown-post roof, intricately carved and painted dragon and screens passage. The hall was built for the sale and display of cloth which was a staple of the local economy for five centuries.

## Fairhaven Garden Trust
### South Walsham. Tel: (01603) 270449.

Delightful woodland and water gardens filled with cultivated and wild flowers. In Spring there are primroses and bluebells, azaleas and rhododendrons. Bird sanctuary for bird watchers.

## Fritton Lake Countryworld
### Fritton, Gt. Yarmouth. Tel: (01493) 488288.

250 acres of woodland and water which features boating, fishing, 9 hole golf, putting, children's adventure playground, wild fowl collection. The main attraction is the large undercover falconry centre with flying displays twice daily. Cafe and gift shop.

## Holkham Hall
### Weels-next-the-Sea. Tel: (01328) 710733.

The 18th century Palladian style mansion is situated in a 3,000 acre deer park. It was the home of the Earls of Leicester and its attractions include Bygones Museum which has a collection of over 4,000 items from cars, crafts and kitchens. There is also a History of Farming exhibition with audio-visual aids. Garden Centre in a beautiful 18th century walled garden. Pottery, gift shop, art gallery, tea rooms and lake.

## Maritime Museum
### Gt. Yarmouth. Tel: (01493) 842267.

The museum tells the story of maritime history in Norfolk, with displays on herring fishery and Norfolk wherry and a large collection of ship models. World War II and Home Front exhibition.

## Norwich Cathedral
### Norwich. Tel: (01603) 764385.

The roof depicts bible scenes from Adam & Eve

to the Day of Judgment. Saxon Bishop's throne and the largest monastic cloisters in England.

## Norfolk Lavender
**Caley Mill, Heacham. Tel: (01485) 570384.**
Lavender, herb, rose and river gardens. Visitors can find out about the harvest and process of lavender distillation. Gift shop and tea room.

## Norfolk Shire Horse Centre
**West Runton. Tel: (01263) 837339.**
Shire horses demonstrated twice daily. Native ponies, collection of horse drawn machinery. Children's farm.

## Park Farm &
## Norfolk Farmyard Crafts Centre
**Snettisham. Tel: (01485) 542425.**
Safari tours into red deer park, archaeological and discovery trails, sheep centre, indoor animal barn, pets area. Horse riding centre. Craft centre, art gallery and tea room.

## Sandringham
**Sandringham. Tel: (01553) 772675.**
The country retreat of Her Majesty the Queen. The house is set in 60 acres of beautiful grounds and lakes beyond which are 600 acres of country park with Visitor Centre and shop. Also museum of Royal vehicles and memorabilia.

## Sea Life Centre
**Hunstanton. Tel: (01603) 737432.**
Visitors can stroll around over 20 settings and view more than 2,000 fish from 200 different species. Also resident seals and pups in the process of being rehabilitated for their release back into the wild.

## Town House Museum of Lynn Life
**King's Lynn. Tel: (01553) 773450.**
The historic rooms have displays of costumes, toys and a working Victorian kitchen showing the lives of the merchants, tradesman and families of King's Lynn.

## The Tropical Butterfly Gardens
**Great Ellingham. Tel: (01953) 453175.**
The gardens contain hundreds of tropical trees and flowers and several hundred exotic tropical butterflies and birds flying freely around visitors. Garden centre, coffee shop and gift shop.

# NORTHAMPTONSHIRE

## Althorp House
**Althorp, Northampton. Tel: (01604) 770042.**
The house was built in 1508 by Sir John Spencer, remodelled in 1660 by Anthony Ellis and given its present appearance in 1790 by Henry Holland. It is the home of the Earl and Countess Spencer and is filled with a fine art collection.

## Boughton House
**Geddington, Kettering. Tel: (01536) 515731.**
The home of Dukes of Buccleuch and their Montagu ancestors since 1528, the house is a 500 year old Tudor monastic building. It was enlarged around seven courtyards until the French addition was made in 1695. There is armoury and many art treasures inside. Also park with lakes.

## Billing Aquadrome
**Great Billing, Northampton.**
**Tel: (01604) 408181.**
A leisure park set in 270 acres of parkland, woods and lakes. Adventure theme children's play areas and amusement area with giant astroglide, dodgems, crazy golf and other rides. Miniature railway running round the Willow Tree Lake. Rowing boats, paddle boats and canoes available for hire.

## Cottesbrooke Hall
**Northampton. Tel: (01604) 505808.**
A magnificent 1702 Queen Anne house. Furniture, picture collection and porcelain. The house is reputed to be the model for Jane Austen's Mansfield Park.

## Daventry Country Park
**Daventry. Tel: (01327) 77193.**
Country park situated around reservoir. Fishing, nature reserve and trails, Visitor Centre, adventure playground and picnic area.

## Grendon Lakes Water Ski Club
**Grendon. Tel: (01933) 665303.**
Grendon Lakes is a water sports centre providing water skiing, windsurfing and fishing. The Clubhouse looks out onto the beautiful surroundings of the Nene Valley and has a bar, restaurant and shop.

## Hill Farm Herbs
**Brigstock. Tel: (01536) 373694.**
The herb nursery is located behind a traditional

farmhouse and the plants are displayed in the old farmyard. A large stone barn houses the main herb shop and flower room where an excellent selection of dried flowers and baskets are displayed.

## Holdenby House & Gardens
**Northampton. Tel: (01604) 730334.**
This was the prison of King Charles I during the Civil War. Now there is a falconry centre, armoury, 17th century homestead and a collection of rare animals. Beautiful silver and fragrant borders. Tea room and shop.

## John Watson Performance Driving Centre
**Silverstone, nr. Towcester. Tel: (01327) 857177.**
Experience the thrill of driving a racing car around the world famous Silverstone Circuit or try driving a rally car on the special stage.

## Sywell Country Park
**Ecton. Tel: (01604) 810970.**
Waterside walks, picnic meadows, wildlife observation, Visitor Centre, fishing and bird watching.

## Whilton Mill
**Whilton Lock, Daventry. Tel: (01327) 843822.**
The converted water mill provides the backdrop for go-karting on an outdoor track. Also clay pigeon shooting, archery, quad bikes and Landrover driving across rough terrain.

# NORTHUMBERLAND

## Alnwick
In the market town of Alnwick, with its cobbled street, medieval gateways and fine Georgian buildings, is the magnificent castle owned by the Duke of Northumberland, whose family has lived here for over 600 years. There are many varied shops and numerous cafes and restaurants scattered around the town.

## Berwick-upon-Tweed
England's northern most town, situated at the mouth of the River Tweed and near the border with Scotland. Berwick changed nationality 13 times during 300 stormy years of border warfare. It has fine Tudor walled fortifications which form a circuit of the town centre.

## Alnwick Castle
**Alnwick. Tel: (01665) 510777.**
The Ancient Fortress of the Duke of

Northumberland. Home of the Percy family since 1300. In spite of its rugged medieval appearance it has a rich interior housing the most exquisite art treasures.

## Billy Shiel's Farne Islands Boat Trips on M.F.V Glad Tidings
**Seahouses, Northumberland.**
**Tel: (01665) 720308.**
Daily sailings to the Farne Islands' Bird and Seal Sanctuaries. All trips include a visit to the Grey Seal colonies and a commentary en route. Special all day bird watching trips available during the breeding season and cruises to Holy Island by arrangement.

## The Coquet Bird Park
**Weldon Bridge, Longframlington.**
**Tel: (01665) 570387.**
Over 130 rare breeds of birds. Falconry displays. Enclosures with public access to small animals such as rabbits, guinea pigs, goats, lambs, sheep and pot bellied pigs. Adventure playground and picnic areas.

## Energy II Seahouses Angling Trips
**Gavin Shiel. Tel: (01665) 721024.**
Daily fishing trips from Seahouses Harbour for individuals or groups up to 12. 2 hours minimum up to 8 hours in high season.

## Flodden Field
The Battle of Flodden was fought in 1513 between James IV of Scotland and the Earl of Surrey. The Scottish King was slain and his army defeated in the last and most bloody battle fought in Northumberland.

## Iona Art Glass
**Opposite Warkworth Castle.**
**Tel: (01665) 711533.**
Superbly crafted stained glass pictures, lamp shades and nursery lamps.

## St. Aidan's Winery
**Holy Island. Tel: (01289) 89230.**
The winery is situated in the centre of the village, just off the green. Each adult visiting the Winery Showroom has the opportunity to sample the world famous Lindisfarne Mead, manufactured here on the island.

### Marine Life Centre and Fishing Museum
**Seahouses. Tel: (01665) 721257.**
The centre provides the visitor with a unique opportunity to examine local fish in seven spacious tanks, including lobsters, crabs, skate, haddock, whiting, and dog-fish. There is a touch-tank for children and a seabird collection.

### Northumberland Wildlife Trust
**Hauxley Nature Reserve.**
Situated on the Ashington to Alnwick road. Superb bird watching, bird hides and Visitor Centre.

# NOTTINGHAMSHIRE

Nottinghamshire lies right at the heart of the rural leafy East Midlands, where forest and farmland intermingle with charming villages and market towns. This is an area rich in folklore and history including the cosmopolitan city of Nottingham, which reveals its fascinating past in splashes of elegant architecture, traditional industry and its many connections with Robin Hood. The famous outlaw has become synonymous with Sherwood Forest and Nottinghamshire. There are also top sporting facilities, a superb range of shops, restaurants and entertainment in the area.

### Attenborough Nature Reserve
**Attenborough, Beeston. Tel: (0115) 9221221.**
The reserve was reclaimed from 220 acres of disused gravel workings, bounded in the south by the River Trent. Numerous breeds of plants, animals and bird life. Pondlife, waterlife, marshland and woodlands.

### Brewhouse Yard Museum of Social History
**Castle Boulevard, Nottingham.**
**Tel: (0115) 9483504.**
The five 17th century cottages show exhibits of daily life in Nottingham, with period rooms and models.

### British Horological Institute
**Upton Hall, Upton, Newark.**
**Tel: (01636) 813795.**
This Georgian/Victorian manor house has been converted into a museum which features watches, clocks, a horological tool collection and library.

### DH Lawrence's Birthplace
**Eastwood, Nottingham. Tel: (01773) 763312.**
DH Lawrence was born here in 1885. The house

is furnished as at the time. The museum offers an audio-visual presentation and there is a Craft Centre in renovated cottages nearby.

### Holme Pierrepont Hall
**Holme Pierrepont, Nottingham.**
**Tel: (0115) 9332371.**
Early Tudor brick manor house with medieval timber work. Interior has original fireplaces, family furniture and paintings dating from 17th century through to the present.

### The Lace Hall
**Nottingham. Tel: (0115) 9484221.**
The Hall is set in a converted Unitarian chapel containing magnificent stained glass windows. Exhibition showing the story of Nottingham Lace. Lace and coffee shops.

### Newark Castle
**Castlegate, Newark. Tel: (01636) 611908.**
The castle's North Gateway, which dates from 1170 is the largest of any in England. King John died here in 1216. Heritage Centre.

### Newstead Abbey
**Linby, Nottingham. Tel: (01623) 793557.**
The Priory Church, the remains of which date back 800 years, was converted into a country house in the 16th century by the Byron family. Lord Byron lived here and visitors can see some of his possessions and manuscripts. The house also underwent a Neo-Gothic conversion in the 19th century. Parkland stretching over 300 acres, lakes and waterfalls, a Japanese water garden, rock and rose gardens and a sub-tropical garden.

### Nottingham Castle Museum and Art Gallery
**Nottingham. Tel: (0115) 9483504.**
Originally the site of medieval royal castle, the museum was established in 1878 within a 17th century house. It includes an interactive "Story of Nottingham" exhibition, a picture gallery, decorative art and a regimental museum.

### The Pilgrim Father's Story
**Worksop. Tel: (01909) 501148.**
Exhibition telling the story of the Pilgrim Fathers from their origins in Bassetlaw to their settling in the New World.

### Sherwood Forest Visitor Centre and Country Park
**Edwinstone, Mansfield. Tel: (01623) 823202.**
Over 450 acres of Robin Hood's ancient oakland

forest. Woodland paths, picnic areas and a chance to see the famous Major Oak. The Visitor Centre includes a Robin Hood Exhibition, slide shows, films and talks. Also a programme of special events such as the summertime "Robin Hood Festival".

### Tales of Robin Hood
**Nottingham. Tel: (0115) 9482284.**
Visitors can experience the flight from medieval Nottingham to Sherwood Forest in search of Robin Hood. They will meet a minstrel, the Sheriff of Nottingham and hideout in an eerie cave. Educational display on the life and times of Robin Hood.

### Sundown Kiddies Adventureland
**Rampton, Retford. Tel: (01777) 248274.**
Smugglers cove, western street, fantasy castle, miniature farm and pets garden. Ideal for children up to 10 year old.

### Wetlands Waterfowl Reserve and Exotic Bird Park
**Sutton-cum-Lound, Retford.**
**Tel:(01777) 818099.**
Waterfowl reserve with varieties of ducks, geese, swans and parrots. Also wildflowers and fungi.

### Wollaton Hall Natural History Museum
**Wollaton Park, Nottingham.**
**Tel: (0115) 9281333.**
The museum is housed in an Elizabethan house that was built by Sir Francis Willoughby from 1580-88. It offers exhibits on botany, zoology and geology. There are also gardens, a deer park and lake.

# OXFORDSHIRE

### Oxford
There are over 630 listed buildings in the centre square mile of this famous University town. It has some of the finest museums and art galleries in Britain and the Bodlean library is the one of the largest in the world. Two lovely rivers, the Thames and the Cherwell, grace the town and there are many gardens, meadows and parks through which to stroll.

### Blenheim Palace
**Woodstock. Tel: (01993) 811091.**
Birthplace of Sir Winston Churchill, designed by

Vanbrugh. Park designed by Capability Brown. Adventure play area, maze, butterfly house, garden centre and Churchill exhibition.

### Cotswold Wild Life Park
**Burford. Tel: (01993) 823006.**
The park has a tropical house, aquarium, reptile house, butterfly/insect house and there are 200 acres of garden and woodland.

### Didcot Railway Centre
**Didcot. Tel: (01235) 817200.**
The museum recreates the golden age of the Great Western Railway with steam locomotives and trains, an engine shed and small relics museum. Steam days and gala events.

### The Oxford Story
**Oxford. Tel: (01865) 728822.**
Heritage Centre depicting eight centuries of University history in sights, sounds, personalities and even smells.

### Water Fowl Sanctuary
**Wigginton Heath, Banbury.**
**Tel: (01608) 730252.**
Reception barn leading to natural environment for thousands of birds and animals.

### Wellplace Zoo
**Ipsden. Tel: (01491) 680473.**
Small children's zoo.

# SHROPSHIRE

### Whitchurch
This compact and bustling market town in lovely North Shropshire has many fine buildings, dating from medieval, Tudor and Georgian times. The parish church of St. Alkmunds at the top of the High Street is the largest 18th century church in the county outside Shrewsbury. The town is still regarded as the centre of the Cheshire cheese industry. Within the town is the pleasantly wooded Victoria Jubilee Park linked to the town centre by the Harry Richards Memorial Garden.

### Aerospace Museum
**Cosford, Shifnal. Tel: (01902) 374872.**
The museum includes more than seventy aircraft of British, American and German design on an active airfield site. Research and Development aircraft; a collection of historic airliners and

models trace our civil aviation heritage from DH4A to Concorde; German and British experimental and current missiles.

## Attingham Park
**4 miles SE of Shrewsbury.**
Landscaped deer park surrounds an elegant neo-classical house. Ambassadorial silver collection. Napoleonic furniture and extensive picture collection.

## The Dorothy Clive Garden
**Willoughbridge, nr. Market Drayton.**
**Tel: (01630) 647237.**
The Garden accommodates a wide range of unusual plants providing year-round interest. Features include a quarry garden with a spectacular waterfall, flower borders, a scree and water garden.

## Ludlow Castle
**Tel: (01584) 873947.**
The original Norman Castle of the de Lacy's was transformed into a medieval palace by Roger Mortimer and later became a royal palace and headquarters of the Council of Marches. It was the home of the Princes in the Tower and of Prince Arthur, son of Henry VII and his bride Catherine of Aragon. Extensive Norman medieval and Tudor buildings remain.

# SOMERSET/AVON

## Bridgwater
Large country town in the fertile plains of mid-Somerset. Small port. Fine Georgian houses in Castle Street. St. Mary's parish church with 14th century spire. Admiral Blake Museum illustrates the Battle of Sedgemoor and material relating to the Admiral's career. Coleridge's Cottage, Nether Stowey 8m NW. Fyne Court, Broomfield 9m SW. Trout fishing at Durleigh.

## Burnham-on-Sea
Small family resort on North Somerset coast. Good sandy bathing beaches. Championship golf course. Sailing, 'Round Tower' old lighthouse. Bird sanctuary at Bream Down.

## Cheddar
Picturesque village famed for its cheese and Gorge on southern edge of the Mendips. Cliffs of Gorge nearly 500 feet above the winding road. Cox's Cave and Gough's Cave attract thousands

of visitors. Museum contains 12,000 year old skeleton. Nature trails, youth hostel and stock car track nearby.

## Minehead
Largest and most popular of the west Somerset resorts. Situated round wide curving bay on Bristol Channel coast. Close to Exmoor. Nature trail and prehistoric mounds on North Hill. Boat trips from harbour. West Somerset Railway Station.

## Taunton
Historic county town of Somerset in Vale of Taunton Deane. Taunton Castle, scene of Judge Jeffrey's Bloody Assize after the end of the Monmouth Rebellion at Battle of Sedgemoor. Castle now houses museum. Other sights to see include the Tudor house in Fores Street and the 17th century almshouses. Taunton Racecourse is to be found to the SE. Also nearby: Hestercombe House and Gardens, Poundisford Park 4m S, 17th century Gaulden Manor 9m NW and Willows and Wetlands Visitor Centre at Stoke St. Gregory 8m E.

## Wells
Small and beautiful cathedral city, situated at the foot of the Mendip Hills. The cathedral's magnificent West Front dates from the 12th century. There is a mechanical clock with moving figures constructed in 1380 and a 13th century moated Bishop's palace. Also to be seen, Vicars' Close and the 15th century almshouses. Nearby are the Wookey Hole Caves and Papermill 2m NW, Chewton Cheese Dairy 6m NE.

## Admiral Blake Museum
Bridgwater. Tel: (01278) 456127.
Birthplace of the famous seaman. Much of the material displayed here relates to Admiral Blake's career (1598-1657).

## Badger and Wildlife Rescue Centre at Secret World
**East Huntspill, Highbridge.**
**Tel: (01278) 783250.**
Set in 17th century surroundings. Winners of television's Animal Country Awards.

## Barrington Court
**Barrington, nr. Ilminster. Tel: (01460) 241938.**
The beautiful garden was laid out by architects Forbes and Tate and was influenced by Gertrude

Jekyll. It is designed in a series of 'rooms' with basket weave brick paths and fine masonry. Enchanting formal walled garden, fragrant rose garden and lily garden.

### The Cheddar Gorge Cheese Co.
**Rural Village, The Cliffs, Cheddar Gorge. Tel: (01934) 742810.**
In this 1920s style village at the foot of the Cheddar Gorge, visitors can watch the locals at work in the cheese factory and taste the cheddar. Farmhouse Dairy, fudge Kitchen, Candle Works, Cider Tastings. Restaurant and tea room.

### Cheddar Showcaves
**Cheddar. Tel: (01934) 742343.**
Caves inhabited by man in the late Upper Palaeolithic times. New fantasy world "The Crystal Quest". Gorge Walk and Lookout Tower.

### Clapton Court
**Nr. Crewkerne. Tel: (01460) 73220.**
Set over 10 acres there are formal terraces, spacious lawns, a rockery and water garden. Also recently designed rose garden with arbors. Many plants and shrubs of botanical interest, including the biggest ash tree in Great Britain, reputed to be over 230 years old.

### Coleridge Cottage
**Nether Stowey, Bridgwater. Tel: (01278) 732662.**
This was Coleridge's home for three years and was where he wrote The Ancient Mariner and part of Christabel.

### Cricket St. Thomas Wildlife Park
**Cricket St. Thomas, Chard. Tel: (01460) 30755.**
Wildlife park with countryside museum and heavyhorse centre. Location for BBC TV series "To the Manor Born".

### Dunster Castle
**Dunster, nr. Minehead. Tel: (01643) 821314.**
This magnificent stronghold rises dramatically above the village of Dunster. It is set between the wooded hills of Exmoor and the sea. Terraced garden with rare plants and shrubs. Riverside walks.

### East Lambrook Manor Garden
**Nr. South Petherton. Tel: (01460) 240328.**
This listed garden was created by Margery Fish during the 32 years that she lived here. The garden has over 5000 species and cultivars in tiny themed corners with down-to-earth names such as the Ditch and the Green Garden.

### Ferne Animal Sanctuary
**Wambrook, Chard. Tel: (01460) 65214.**
Conservation area, Nature Trail and some animal enclosures.

### Fleet Air Arm Museum
**RNAS, Yeovilton, nr. Ilchester. Tel: (01935) 840565.**
This leading naval aviation museum features World War I and II Wrens, Kamikaze, Korea, Harrier and Concorde 002. Also includes a flight deck with 11 aircraft.

### Forde Abbey and Gardens
**Chard. Tel: (01460) 220231.**
Cistercian monastery founded in 1140. Converted into a private house in mid 17th century and unchanged since. Thirty acres of gardens, trees and herbaceous borders. A magnificent bog garden was created in 1906 with statuesque plants and candelabra primulas in the summer. Plants for sale.

### Glastonbury Abbey
**Galstonbury.**
Ruin of 12/13th century Abbey. Abbot's kitchen, Abbey fishpond. Museum has a model of the 1539 Abbey.

### Hadspen Garden
**Castle Cary. Tel: (01749) 813707.**
The 8 acre garden is set against the backdrop of the magnificent deciduous woodlands of Hadspen House. The classical 18th century hamstone country house and its estate have been the home of the Hobhouse for 200 years.

### Lytes Cary Manor
**Lytes Cary, Somerton. Tel: (01985) 847777.**
The 14th century manor house is surrounded by a garden that is an enchanting mixture of formality and simplicity. The Hall is from 15th century and there is a 16th century Great Chamber. High hedges of yew topiary enclose hidden paths in the garden, evoking an Elizabethan atmosphere. At the foot of the garden is an orchard of medlars, quinces, apple and pear trees.

## Montacute House and Garden
**Montacute. Tel: (01935) 823289.**
Late 16th century with many Renaissance features including heraldic glass. Fine 17th and 18th century furniture. Elizabethan and Jacobean portraits from the National Portrait Gallery. The garden has smooth lawns, yew hedges and a sweeping drive up to the house.

## Perry's Cider Mills
**Dowlish Wake, Illminster. Tel: (01460) 52681.**
Visitors can sample the traditional farmhouse ciders made here. There is a museum of farming bygones and wagons. Also photographic displays of country life. Shop.

## Sheppy's Cider Farm Centre
**Bradford on Tone, Taunton.**
**Tel: (01823) 461233.**
Somerset farm where the tradition of cider making has been handed down over four generations. Cider tastings, country life museum with video of cider making, orchards and shop.

## Tintinhull House Garden
**Tintinhull, nr. Yeovil. Tel: (01935) 822545.**
This is a 20th century formal garden of 1.5 acres surrounding a 17th century house. Only the garden is open. It is divided into separate areas by walls and hedges, with coloured borders and plant themes. A path fringed with catmint leads through a kitchen garden to an orchard gate.

## Tropical Bird Gardens
**Rode, nr. Bath. Tel: (01373) 830326.**
Hundreds of brilliant exotic birds in 17 acres of beautifully laid out gardens.

## Wells Cathedral
**Wells. Tel: (01749) 674483.**
The cathedral dates from the 12th century and was built in the early English Gothic style. The West Front has 296 medieval groups of sculpture.

## Wookey Hole
**Wookey, nr. Wells. Tel: (01749) 672243.**
Show caves that were occupied from Palaeolithic to Roman times. Working Victorian papermill. "Magical Mirror Maze".

# SUFFOLK

## Bury St. Edmonds
An ancient market town full of historic buildings. The Theatre Royal is a Regency theatre designed by William Wilkins and the Market Cross Gallery was designed by Robert Adam. Moyse's Hall Museum in the Market Place is a Norman building that houses local history collections and the Manor House is a new museum of fine arts and time keeping. The coast is within easy reach and there are country parks at Clare and Nowton on the outskirts of the town.

## Lavenham
A magnificent example of a Suffolk wool town with many superb buildings. The church of St. Peter & St. Paul, with its fine 141ft tower stands to the southwest. The 16th century Guildhall is to be found in the Market Place. It now contains an exhibition of local history and of the woollen cloth industry.

## Lowestoft
This coastal town still has an important fishing industry. Visitors can take a guided tour of the fishmarket and witness the great boxes of fish being landed at dawn from the trawlers. The beach here is soft and sandy. Oulton Broad Lake is vast and thickly wooded.

## Cavendish Manor Vineyards
**Nether Hall, Cavendish. Tel: (01787) 280221.**
The first vines were planted in 1972 by owner Basil Ambrose and have been producing wine since 1975. Visitors can tour the house, museum gallery and vines.

## Christchurch Mansion
**Christchurch, Ipswich. Tel: (01473) 253246.**
Manor built between 1548 and 1550. Collection of furniture, panelling and ceramics, clocks and paintings dating from 16-19th century. Suffolk Artists Gallery.

## Clare Castle Country Park
**Station Road, Clare. Tel: (01787) 277491.**
The park consists of 25 acres with the ruins of Clare Castle, a riverside walk, butterfly garden and a nature trail during the summer. The disused Clare Railway Station houses the Information Centre and is of interest to railway enthusiasts.

### Euston Hall
**Thetford. Tel: (01842) 766366.**
Built in the 1660s by the father-in-law of the first
Duke of Grafton, Lord Arlington. Paintings by
Van Dyck, Lely and Stubbs hang inside as well
as a collection of portraits of Charles II, his
family and court. The Pleasure Grounds were
designed by John Evelyn and the Park and
Temple by William Kent.

### Gainsborough's House
**Sudbury. Tel: (01787) 372958.**
The birthplace of Thomas Gainsborough RA
(1727-88). The Georgian fronted town house
contains more of the artist's work than any
gallery. Also 18th century furniture and
memorabilia in chronological sequence following
his career. Contemporary art is displayed in a
varied programme of exhibitions through
the year.

### Ickworth House, Park and Gardens
**Ickworth. Tel: (01284) 735270.**
The house was a Rotunda built in 1795, was the
inspiration of the Earl of Bristol. It houses a
major collection of pictures, including works by
Titian, Gainsborough and Velasquez, fine
furniture and Georgian silver. The surrounding
park was designed by Capability.

### Ipswich Museum and Gallery
**Ipswich. Tel: (01473) 253246.**
Exhibitions include Roman Suffolk Galleries,
Peoples of the World, Suffolk geology and the
Ogilvie Bird Gallery.

### Melford Hall
**Long Melford. Tel: (0187) 880286.**
Turreted brick Tudor Mansion with 18th century
and Regency interiors. It was bought by Sir
Harry Parker of the famous naval family in 1786.
Inside there is Chinese porcelain on display and
ivories captured from a Manilla galleon. Fine
Dutch and naval pictures. There is also Beatrix
Potter memorabilia. She was a member of the
family who often visited the hall.

### Mid Suffolk Light Railway Society
**Brockford.**
The working museum is set in Brockford Station.
There has been restoration of the station and
some of the trackwork on the original route of
the Mid Suffolk Light Railway. Artifacts and

memorabilia relating to the Railway on display.

### Museum of East Anglian Life
**Stowmarket. Tel: (01449) 612229.**
The museum is set in 70 acres of Suffolk
countryside and houses collections of historic
buildings, with exhibition on domestic life,
agriculture, industrial history and crafts. Suffolk
breeds of horses, pigs, sheep and cattle can be
seen around the site. Nature walk along the river.

### Nowton Park
**Nowton Road, Bury St. Edmunds.
Tel: (01284) 757068.**
This park is made up of 112 acres of glorious
English landscape with copses, woods and
magnificent specimen trees as well as meadows
filled with wild flowers. Deer can be seen in
winter and early spring. Recreation areas for
games, picnics etc. Also contains two football
pitches and an all-weather sports pitch.

### The Priory
**Lavenham. Tel: (01787) 247003.**
This timber framed medieval building has been
the home of Benedictine monks, medieval wool
merchants and an Elizabethan rector over its
history. The herb garden has culinary, medical
and dyers herbs. Kitchen garden, orchard
and pond.

### Snape Maltings Riverside Centre
**Nr. Saxmundham, Suffolk.
Tel: (01728) 688303.**
Remarkable collection of 19th century maltings
buildings set on the banks of the River Alde.
Shops and galleries include Snape Craft Shop,
Granary Tea Shop and River Bar.

### Sue Ryder Foundation Museum
**Cavendish. Tel: (01797) 280252.**
The life story of Sue Ryder and the history of the
Sue Ryder Foundation is told in this interesting
museum in the picturesque village of Cavendish.

## SUSSEX

### Arundel
Arundel, dominated by Arundel Castle, has a
history which can be dated back to the
Domesday Book. There is plenty to see including
the castle itself, cathedral, St. Nicholas Church,

the Wildfowl and Wetlands Trust and Trout
Fisheries. There is an open-air swimming
pool, putting, bowls, tennis, horse riding. Boats
can be hired or there are cruises to Littlehampton
or Amberley.

## Brighton
This seaside town is the prefect spot for a
holiday. There are modern shops in Churchill
Square and Western Road, as well as boutiques
and antique shops in the quaint Lanes, once a
17th century fishing village. Visitors can see the
extravagant Pavilion, or take a stroll along the
prom, watch dolphins perform  at the
Aquarium and Dolphinarium, or just take a break
on the beach.

## Chichester
Within Chichester's historic City Walls lie the
ancient Market Cross, the elegant cathedral with
its remarkable tapestry, the quiet Priory Park, the
Bishop's Palace Gardens and Pallant House
Gallery - a restored historic house filled with
antiques, furniture, porcelain, glass and textiles.
The surrounding area contains the picturesque
harbour, including the charming waterside village
of Bosham. Among the many attractions are the
tranquil gardens at West Dean, the modern
racecourse at Goodwood, the Roman
Palace remains at Fishbourne and Uppark
Country House.

## Eastbourne
The elegant resort of Eastbourne has a sweeping
seafront, with a three-tier promenade, featuring
the Carpet Gardens, Victorian Pier and
Bandstand. Princes Park has a boating lake and
mini-golf and Treasure Island is an adventure
theme park. The Redoubt, a Napoleonic fortress,
houses three military museums. Also worth a
visit are the Towner Art Gallery and Local
History Museum. There are four theatres, a
superb marina and many special events during
the year such as International Tennis.

## Arundel Castle
**Arundel. Tel: (01903) 882173.**
Ancestral home of the Dukes of Norfolk for over
500 years. Contains art treasures, paintings and
furniture from the 16th century.

## Arundel Toy and Military Museum
**Arundel. Tel: (01903) 883101.**
Vast collection of old toys, model soldiers,

games, dolls houses, teddy bears, Royal
commemoratives and much more.

## Battle Abbey
**Tel: (01273) 474747.**
The ruins of Battle Abbey stand on the very spot
where the Battle of Hastings was fought.
Four years after his victory, William the
Conqueror founded the Abbey. The high altar
was built on the spot where Harold fell. Little
remains but there are models of Harold's men
and an audio tour.

## Beech Hurst Gardens
**Haywards Heath. Tel: (01444) 441675.**
Ornamental gardens, miniature steam train, pitch
& put, bowls, tennis, children's play area,
beautiful views of the Downs.

## Bodiam Castle
Spectacular moated castle built in 1388 to ward
off a possible French invasion which never came.

## Boxgrove Priory
**Church Lane, Boxgrove.**
Early English architecture. The priory is
renowned for its 16th century painted ceiling,
stained glass and recently restored ruins.

## Brighton's Royal Pavilion and Gardens
**Tel: (01273) 603005.**
These English landscape gardens have been
restored to their original 1820s Nash design.
Flowery shrubberies, typical of the Regency
period, surround the seaside palace of George IV.

## Chichester Cathedral
**Chichester. Tel: (01243) 782595.**
The Cathedral is over 900 years old. Visitors can
see the site of St. Richard's shrine.

## Earnley Gardens
**Earnley, Chichester. Tel: (01243) 782595.**
Tropical butterflies and birds, 17 theme gardens,
small animals farm. Play and picnic areas.

## Fishbourne Roman Palace
**Fishbourne, Chichester. Tel: (01243) 785859.**
The remains of the largest known Roman
residence in Britain. Beautiful mosaics, museum.
Audio-visual programme, gardens and Roman
gardening museum.

## Goodwood House
**Chichester. Tel: (01243) 774107.**
Superb collection of paintings, including

Canaletto and Stubbs, furniture and tapestries. Surrounded by lovely parkland.

### Leonardslee Gardens
**Nr. Horsham. Tel; (01403) 891212.**
Landscape garden in peaceful 240-acre valley with 7 lakes. Famous for rhododendrons and azaleas in spring. Rock garden, Bonsai exhibition and alpine house. Wallabies live in part of the valley and deer in the parks. Restaurant, cafe and gift shop.

### Lewes Castle
**Lewes. Tel: (01273) 486290.**
Imposing Norman castle with octagonal towers. Magnificent views over the town and surrounding countryside. Nearby Barbican House contains exhibits following the progress of Sussex people up to medieval times.

### The Long Man of Wilmington
This mysterious 235 feet figure is to be found on the Sussex Downs near Eastbourne. The earliest record of him was made in 1710 but no one can be sure whether he is prehistoric, Roman, Saxon or perhaps the work of a monk during the Middle Ages.

### Marlipins Museum
**Shoreham-by-Sea. Tel: (01273) 462994.**
The historic Norman building contains Shoreham's local and especially maritime museum. Maritime models and paintings.

### Michelham Priory
**Hailsham. Tel: (01323) 844224.**
The priory was founded in 1229. It is approached through a 14th century gatehouse, spanning the longest medieval moat in the country. Henry VIII demolished most of the original buildings but the remains became a Tudor farm and country house.

### Pashley Manor House
**Ticehurst. Tel: (01580) 200692.**
Peaceful 8 acre gardens, including garden dating from 18th century which surrounds the timber-framed Grade 1 House. Ponds, ancient moats, folly and waterfalls.

### Petworth House and Park
**Petworth. Tel: (01798) 342207.**
Magnificent house set in 700 acres of beautiful parkland. State rooms contain paintings by Turner, Van Dyck and Gainsborough. The old kitchens have been recently restored.

### Royal Botanic Gardens
**Kew at Wakehurst, Ardingly.**
**Tel: (0181) 3325066.**
Formal gardens, natural woodland, wetlands, fields and meadows. Nature trail along a series of lakes and ponds. Restaurant, shop and exhibition rooms in the Elizabethan mansion.

### The Sussex Falconry Centre
**Birdham, nr. Chichester.**
**Tel: (01243) 512472.**
Visitors can fly a hawk, touch and handle owls and see the falcons.

### Weald & Downland Open Air Museum
**Singleton, Chichester. Tel: (01243) 811348.**
A museum of 40 historic buildings rescued from destruction and re-built on a 40 acre site in the South Downs.

### West Sussex History Tours
**Botolphs, nr. Steyning. Tel: (01903) 879317.**
Offers the chance to visit little known areas of West Sussex, calling at private homes of historic and architectural interest for refreshment.

### The Wildfowl & Wetlands Trust
**Arundel. Tel: (01903) 883355.**
Over 100 beautiful ducks, geese and swans from all over the world in wild and attractive surroundings.

# WARWICKSHIRE

### Coventry
Bright modern city with well planned shopping precincts and spacious parks. Splendid modern cathedral designed by Sir Basil Spence. Medieval Guildhall, Herbert Art Gallery, toy Museum and Museum of British Road Transport.

### Kenilworth
A modern town in shakespeare country with impressive ruined castle immortalised by Sir Walter Scott's novel. Stoneleigh Abbey at Stoneleigh 2m E.

### Leamington Spa
Spacious town of Georgian architecture situated on the banks of the River Leam. Visitors should see the Parade, Pump Room, Jephson Gardens, Art Gallery and Museum.

### Rugby
Town famous for its public school which featured

in "Tom Brown's Schooldays". Rugby football originated at the school. Gallery and museum.

### Stratford-upon-Avon
This town at the heart of Shakespeare country and at the edge of the Cotswold, offers the visitor a variety of attractions all year round. There are five, beautifully preserved Tudor homes, administered by the Shakespeare Birthplace Trust. As well as being of architectural interest, the houses contain period furniture and special collections and there is a museum and craft displays. The Royal Shakespeare Theatre is here in Stratford. There are riverside walks along the Avon. Also Holy Trinity Church, a racecourse and the country's largest butterfly safari.

### Warwick
Historic county town with magnificent 14th century castle overlooking the River Avon. Well-preserved Georgian and Tudor buildings. Museum. Racecourse.

# WILTSHIRE

### Salisbury
Old Sarum, originally an Iron Age fort and later the Roman Sorbiodunum, is the site of the original city. Abandoned in 13th century and city of New Sarum -or Salisbury- established on present site. The cathedral offers the best example of pure early English architecture and the highest spire, at 404 feet in England. The extensive Cathedral Close has many fine buildings including Mompesson House, North Canonry, Old Deanery and Malmesbury House. A city of picturesque streets with timbered houses, shops and inns, John A'Port's House, 14th century Cross, Shoemakers' Guildhall, Joiners' Hall. Interesting museums. Racecourse 3m SW. Heale Gardens at Middle Woodford 4m N, Newhouse at Redlynch 9m S.

### Avebury Manor and Garden
**Avebury, nr. Malborough. Tel: (01672) 539388.**
Regularly altered house of monastic origin. Buildings date from early 16th century with Queen Anne alterations and Edwardian renovations by Colonel Jennery. Topiary.

### Lonleat House
**Warminster. Tel: (01985) 844551.**
Renaissance stately home with outstanding collection of books and paintings.

### Mompesson House
**The Close, Salisbury. Tel: (01722) 335659.**
One of the finest 18th century houses in the Cathedral Close. Contains an important Turnbull collection of 18th century English drinking glasses. Attractive walled garden.

### Salisbury Cathedral
**Salisbury. Tel: (01722) 328726.**
Gothic cathedral consecrated in 1258. The superb 404 feet spire, the tallest in Britain, was added to in 14th century. Its treasures include an original Magna Carta and Europe's oldest working clock.

### Stonehenge
**Amesbury. Tel: (01980) 623108.**
Prehistoric monument of worldwide fame, consisting of a series of stone circles.

### Stourhead Garden and House
**Stourton, Warminster. Tel: (01747) 841152.**
This garden, with enchanting lakes and temples, rare trees and plants was designed between 1740-50 by Henry Hoare. The house contains fine works of art.

# WORCESTERSHIRE

### Malvern
Modern Malvern owes its existence to it springs. In 1757, Dr. Wall published evidence of their purity and Malvern rapidly became a fashionable resort. It boasts the Priory, built from a Benedictine Abbey. It is one of the grandest parish churches in England, with a 124 foot tower, unrivalled east window, Norman front, ancient inlaid tiles and enchanting misericord seats. The highest point is Worcestershire Beacon 1394 feet.

### Avoncroft Museum of Historic Buildings
**Stoke Heath, Bromsgrove.**
**Tel: (01527) 831886.**
This open-air museum contains 24 historic buildings spanning 600 years. They were saved from destruction and re-erected on the 15 acre rural site. There are timber-framed buildings, a working windmill, pre-fab, the magnificent 14th century roof form Worcester Cathedral's guest hall and the National Telephone Kiosk collection. Cafe, picnic area and gift shop.

### Bennetts Farm Park
**Lower Wick, Worcester. Tel: (01905) 748345.**
An opportunity to see farm animals, vintage

machinery museum and tour the Milking Parlour at weekends. Children's adventure playground.

### Elgar's Birthplace
**Lower Broadheath, Worcester.**
**Tel: (01905) 33224.**
This lovely cottage houses a unique collection of manuscripts, scores, photographs and memorabilia which portray the life, work and family of Britain's great composer.

### Severn Valley Railway
**Severn Valley Railway, Bewdley.**
**Tel: (01299) 403816.**
The Severn Valley Railway runs 16 miles from Kidderminster to Bridgnorth following the beautiful River Severn.

### Spetchley Park Gardens
**Tel: (01905) 765224/765213.**
30 acre private garden with fine trees, shrubs and plants. Deer park.

### Tudor House Museum
**Friar Street, Worcester.**
Includes a Victorian kitchen, Edwardian bathroom, dolls and toys and "Worcester at War" display.

### White Cottage Garden with Cranesbill Nursery
**Inkberrow. Tel: (01386) 792414.**
Shrubs and herbaceous plants are to found on display in the garden all year round. It contains a stream, bog garden and spring wild flower meadow.

### Witley Court
**10 miles NW of Worcester on the A443.**
**Tel: (01299) 896636.**
The ruins of a country house, designed in the Victorian Italian style of the 1860s. There is a glorious facade with an Ionic portico by Nash. Looking to the gardens, a view enjoyed by Edward VIII, the scene is dominated by the immense Perseus Fountain.

### Worcester Cathedral
King John's tomb, Norman Crypt with pilgrim exhibition, major restoration of 14th century tower and 12th century Chapter House.

### Worcester City Museum and Art Gallery
**Worcester. Tel: (01905) 25371.**
This Victorian building has displays including "On the River", a 19th century chemist's shop. Also museums of the Worcestershire Regiment and Worcestershire Yeomanry Cavalry. The Art Gallery has a programme of exhibitions including contemporary fine art, craft and photography.

### Worcester Woods Country Park & Countryside Centre
**Tel: (01905) 766493.**
Ancient woodlands with walks and orienteering course. Countryside Centre with cafe and events field.

## YORKSHIRE

### Harrogate
Harrogate has an international reputation as one of the most attractive towns in Britain with acres of immaculate gardens, wide open green spaces and elegant architecture. The town evolved as a fashionable spa resort after the first mineral spring was discovered in 1571. Unique to Harrogate, The Stray virtually encircles the town centre.

### Pateley Bridge
The oldest part of the town is built on a hillside rising sharply from the Nidd and is a charming jumble of narrow streets and interesting old buildings. The parish Church of St. Cuthbert was built in 1827. Visitors can reach the ruins of the old Church of St. Mary by climbing a flight of steps at the top of the steep High Street and following the Panorama Walk.

### Scarborough
The centrepiece of this attractive resort are the two majestic sandy bays separated by a dominating headland topped by a Norman castle. Other attractions include beautiful gardens, elegant house and parklands.

### Thornton le Dale
This village lies on the southern edge of the North Yorkshire Moors National Park. There is an excellent choice of cafes, an artist's studio, many interesting buildings and some pleasant walks beside the stream.

## Whitby

Attractive fishing port and seaside resort. The busy harbour with its keel boats and fishing cobles and, more recently, graceful yachts tacking upstream towards the new marina, is ringed by hillside cottages and steep passages in which fishermen mend their nets and little shops sell craftsmen's ware. During July, Viking raids are re-enacted and the century-old three-day regatta in August. Also in August is the annual Folk Festival.

## York

York was built by the Anglo-Saxons and ruled by the Vikings. The city was ravaged by William the Conqueror, nearly crushed by Henry VII and besieged by Cromwell. It was also a great religious centre for centuries. York is one of the best preserved medieval cities in Europe and almost all its historic sites are clustered within the two and a half mile circumference of the ancient city walls. These famous sights include York Minster and the famous medieval street of The Shambles.

## Beningbrough Hall
### Nr. York. Tel: (01904) 470666.

This early Georgian country house has been restored and the rooms hung with portraits on loan from the National gallery. There is a wilderness play area and 7 acres of gardens.

## Brownhill Visitor Centre
## Uppermill. Saddleworth.
### Tel: (01457) 72598.

The centre offers information on the surrounding area and holds regular exhibitions. The Tame Valley Countryside Warden service organises many events including rambles, flora walks, birdwatching, farm visits and horse riding.

## Burnby Hall Gardens
### The Balk, Pocklington. Tel: (01759) 302068.

There are 8 acres of gardens and two lakes. National collection with 60 varieties of water lilies, rose garden picnic area, many varieties of fish. Also museum containing a unique display of sporting trophies.

## The Colour Museum
### Bradford. Tel: (01274) 390955.

The museum has two galleries which explore light, colour, dyeing and textile printing. Interactive displays.

## Dalby Forest Drive
### Eastgate, Pickering. Tel: (01751) 72771.

A nine mile scenic drive through Dalby Forest with parking areas, picnic sites. Forest walks from several locations. Visitor Centre at Dalby Village.

## Emsbay Steam Railway
### Embsay, nr. Skipton. Tel: (01756) 794727.

Talking Timetable: (01756) 795189. Scenic steam railway running 2 miles to Holywell Halt. Station open daily.

## Fountains Abbey & Studley Royal
### Ripon. Tel: (01765) 608888.

The magnificent ruins of Fountains Abbey adjoin the spectacular water garden and beautiful deer garden.

## Harewood House & Bird Garden
### Harewood, Leeds. Tel: (0113) 288 6331.

The home of the Earl and Countess of Harewood is filled with Chippendale furniture, Old Masters and English watercolours as well as a contemporary art gallery. Outside visitors will find beautiful gardens, a bird garden, woodland walks and adventure playgrounds.

## The Henry Moore Institute
### Leeds. Tel: (0113) 2343158.

This building with granite facade houses four gallery spaces for temporary sculpture exhibitions. Bookshop, audio-visual facility, study centre, library.

## Kilnsey Park
### Kilnsey, nr. Skipton. Tel: (01756) 752150.

Visitor centre and nature trail, trout feeding, fly fishing, children's fun fishing, estate shop, children's adventure playground, remote control boats, garden plants. Restaurant and coffee shop.

## Knaresborough Castle
### Castle Yard, Knaresborough.
### Tel: (01423) 503340.

The castle has a 14th century keep, sallyport and old courthouse, now a museum of local history. The original oak courtroom furniture is a rare survival of the period.

## Lightwater Valley Theme Park
### North Stainley, Ripon. Tel: (01765) 635321.

Home of the world's biggest rollercoaster, rides such as "The Ultimate" and "The Rat", a subterranean rollercoaster. Nearby is Lightwater

Village and Factory Shopping centre and Old MacDonald's Farm where children can meet the animals.

## Montpellier Gardens
**Harrogate.**
Montpellier Gardens extend from the town centre in a riot of ever-changing foliage and fragrances. The colour and attention to detail make it a pleasure to stroll around.

## Mother Shipton's Cave and Petrifying Well
**Knaresborough.**
Mother Shipton has become a legend in Knaresborough. Reputedly born in 1488, her predictions have demonstrated a mystical foresight and are revered by many. Visitors can make a wish in the Wishing Well, see the cave of the prophetess' birth and see the petrifying well where absorbent articles are gradually turned to stone. Family attractions include woodland walks, picnic areas and summer barbecues.

## Newby Hall and Gardens
**Ripon. Tel: (01423) 322583.**
Late 17th century house; Robert Adam interior, classical sculptures, Gobelin tapestries, Chippendale furniture. Gardens, children's playground, miniature railway. Restaurant, shop and plant stall.

## The Nidderdale Museum
**Nidderdale.**
Built in an original Victorian workhouse, the museum portrays the life and times of early Dalesfolk through an extensive range of exhibits.

## Nunnington Hall
**Nr. Helmsley. Tel: (01439) 748283.**
A manor house containing the famous Carlisle Collection of miniature rooms, exquisitely furnished to one eighth life size.

## Rievaulx Abbey
**Tel: (01439) 798228.**
Spectacular monastic ruins set in a deeply wooded valley by the River Rye. The church has the earliest large Cistercian nave in Britain. An exhibition shows how the Cistercians ran their businesses.

## Ripon Cathedral
**Kirgate, Ripon.**
The Cathedral's many fine features include the exhibition of ecclesiastical silver in the Cathedral West Front, St. Wilfrid's Saxon Crypt, an Treasury, the Tudor Library, medieval screen, art nouveau pulpit and 15th century choir stalls with canopies, ends and misericords fashioned by local carvers.

## Rochdale Canal
Passing through outstanding scenery and historic communities, this was the first cross-Pennine canal. Now after being closed for some 50 years, boats can be seen on the canal, crossing the border from Yorkshire to Lancashire. The tow provides a superb walk over the Pennines from Sowerby Bridge to Rochdale.

## Selby Abbey
**The Crescent, Selby. Tel: (01757) 703123.**
Founded in 1069 by Monk Benedict of Auxerre. Norman arches, spectacular stained glass windows. The Washington window bears a coat of arms which forms the model for the USA flag.

## Shibden Hall & Folk Museum of West Yorkshire
**Halifax. Tel: (01422) 352246.**
An enchanting half-timbered house dating from the early 15th century. The interior gives an intimate picture of life in a prosperous household of the 17th and 18th centuries. Outside, the folk museum is arranged as an early 19th century village and includes a collection of horsedrawn vehicles. There is also a miniature railway in the park.

## Sion Hill Hall & Bird of Prey Centre
**Kirby Wiske, Thirsk. Tel: (01845) 587206.**
Edwardian mansion and grounds. 20 period room settings with 'members of the household' in costume. Bird of Prey Conservation Centre, with flying demonstrations in the Victorian walled garden.

## Skipton Castle
**Skipton. Tel: (01756) 792442.**
The castle is over 900 years old and one of the best preserved in England. Visitors can discover the Conduit Court with its famous Yew.

## The Stray
**Harrogate.**
These 200 acres of rolling greensward are protected by ancient law to ensure that residents andvisitors alike have access to sports, events, walking or simply watching the world go by.

## Stump Cross Caverns
**Greenhow, nr. Pateley Bridge.**
An underground world of beauty whatever the weather. Displays of stalactites and stalagmites in a natural cave with atmospheric lighting. Visitor Centre.

## Sutton Park
**Sutton on the Forest. Tel: (01347) 810249.**
Charming lived-in house built 1730 by Thomas Atkinson containing beautiful 18th century furniture, paintings mostly from Buckingham House, now Buckingham Palace, an important collection of porcelain and magnificent plaster work by Cortese.

## Yorkshire Sculpture Park
**West Bretton, Wakefield. Tel: (01924) 830302.**
Set Within 100 acres of beautiful 18th century parkland, the collection of sculpture includes Moore, Frink and Hepworth.

## The Arc
**St. Saviourgate. Tel: (01904) 613711.**
Archaeological Resource Centre. Visitors can sort and date authentic archaeological finds, sift through laboratory trays for clues about how our ancestors lived and try out ancient crafts including spinning, weaving.

## The Barbican Centre
**Tel: (01904) 650830.**
Offers a diverse range of sports activities and an exciting series of live presentations.

## Castle Howard
**Tel: (01653) 648333.**
This magnificent 18th century palace was the location for the TV series "Brideshead Revisited". Attractions include richly furnished rooms with collections of important paintings and statuary.
The grounds hold many delights including fountains, lakes, walled rose gardens and woodland trails. Adventure playground, plant centre and cafeteria.

## Jorvik Viking Centre
**Tel: (01904) 643211.**
Reconstruction of the Viking City of Jorvik, complete with sounds and smells evocative of the time.

## National Railway Museum
**Tel: (01904) 621261.**
The Great Railway Show at the National Railway Museum celebrates the Railway age from the 1820s to the present day.

## Treasurer's House
**Minster Yard. Tel: (01904) 624247.**
Treasurer's House, a property of the National Trust, was originally the home of the medieval Treasurers of York Minster. Largely rebuilt in the 17th century, it contains magnificent rooms with fine furniture and pictures. An introductory video describes its history. Attractive garden.

## Yorkshire Air Museum
**Elvington, York. Tel: (01904) 608595.**
The museum is built on the site of a World War II bomber base site. It has aircraft, an authentic control tower, Barnes Wallis Collection, Blackburn Heritage, Air Gunners and general displays.

## York Castle Museum
**Tel: (01904) 653611.**
Authentic Victorian and Edwardian streets, period rooms and settings.

## York City Art Gallery
**Exhibition Square. Tel: (01904) 623839.**
A treasure house of European and British paintings spanning seven centuries. Exciting programme of temporary exhibitions and events.

## York Dungeon
**Tel: (01904) 632599.**
Set in dark, musty atmospheric cellars presenting life-size scenes of medieval punishments, the making saints and the persecutions of heretics. The history of Guy Fawkes, York's most famous citizen, is featured here.

## York Minster
The foundations were created 20 years ago by excavations to secure the Minster from collapse. They are a major archaeological site of the Roman, Saxon and Norman periods, encapsulating 2000 years of York's history.

## Yorkshire Museum
**Museum Gardens. Tel: (01904) 629745.**
The museum is set in 10 acres of botanical gardens and contains displays revealing Yorks fascinating and compelling past.

# Places of Interest *Scotland*

## ABERDEEN

### Art Gallery and Museums
**Tel: (01224) 646333.**
Permanent collection of 18th, 19th and 20th century art with the emphasis on contemporary works. Music, dance, poetry, events film, coffee shop, gallery shop, reference library, print room. Disabled access.

### Bridge of Dee
Built in 1520's by Bishop Gavin Dunbar in James V's reign. Its seven arches span 400 feet and it formerly carried the main road south.

### Gordon Highlanders' Regimental Museum
**Tel: (01224) 311200.**
Displays of regimental uniforms, colours, weapons, silver and pictures.

### King's College
Founded 1494. The chapel, famous for its rich woodwork, is 16th century and the notable 'crown' tower is 17th century.

### St. Machar's Cathedral
**Tel: (01224) 485988.**
This granite cathedral was founded in 1131 on an earlier site, though the main part of the building dates from the mid-15th century. The nave is in use as a parish church.

### St. Mary's Cathedral
Dedicated in 1860 as a church for all the Catholics in Aberdeen, the architecture of St. Mary's is Gothic in style, with a single elegant spire. The High Altar and four Side Altars are embellished with tapestries and paintings by contemporary Scottish artists.

## ANGUS

### Arbroath Abbey
**Arbroath. Tel: 0131-668 8800.**
Founded in 1178 by William the Lion and dedicated to St. Thomas of Canterbury, it was from here that the famous Declaration of Arbroath asserting Robert the Bruce as King was issued in 1320.

### Broughty Castle Museum
**Broughty Ferry. Tel: (01382) 436916.**
Former estuary fort, now a museum. Local history gallery includes sections on fishing, lifeboat, ferries and growth of town.

### Claypotts Castle
**Dundee. Tel: 0131-668 8800.**
Now in suburban surroundings, this is one of the most complete of tower houses, laid out on a Z-plan. It bears the dates 1569 and 1588 and was built for the Strachan family.

### Discovery Point
**Dundee.**
Major attraction entertains visitors with the story of the Royal Research Ship, Discovery, Captain Scott's famous Antarctic exploration vessel, built in Dundee in 1901.

### Glamis Castle
**Nr. Forfar. Tel: (01307) 840393.**
This famous Scottish castle, childhood home of Her Majesty Queen Elizabeth The Queen Mother and birthplace of Princess Margaret, owes it present appearance to the period 1675-87. Portions of the high square tower are much older.

### Kerr's Miniature Railway
**Arbroath. Tel: (01241) 879249.**
Steam and petrol-hauled trains (four locos). Runs for 400 yds alongside BR Edinburgh to Aberdeen main line.

### Mills Observatory
**Dundee. Tel: (01382) 667138.**
A public astronomical observatory with telescopes, displays on astronomy and space exploration, lecture room with projection equipment and small planetarium.

### Restenneth Priory
**Nr. Forar. Tel: 0131-668 8800.**
A house of Augustinian canons, probably founded by David I on the site of an earlier church. A feature of the ruins is the tall square tower, with its shapely broach spire, and an early doorway at its base.

### Tay Bridges
**Dundee.**
The present Railway Bridge carries the main line from Edinburgh to Aberdeen. Built between 1883 and 1887, it replaces the first Tay Railway Bridge which was blown down by a storm in 1879 with the loss of a train and 75 lives after being in use for less than 2 years.

# BORDERS

### Abbotsford House
Nr. Galashiels. Tel: (01896) 752043.
Sir Walter Scott's romantic mansion built 1817-1822. Much as in his day, it contains the many remarkable historical relics he collected, armouries, the library with some 9,000 volumes and his study. He died here in 1832. Free car park, with private entrance for disabled drivers. Teashop and gift shop.

### Loch Carron of Scotland Cashmere Woollen Mill and Museum.
**Galashiels. Tel: (01896) 752091.**
From small beginnings into a weaving shop at the back of a church. Peter Anderson has expanded over a century to the present mill complex where the whole process of tweed manufacture - except for carding and spinning is carried out.

### Ayton Castle
**Ayton. Tel: (01890) 781212.**
Scottish Baronial style castle built in 1846 in red sandstone. Now fully lived in as a family home.

### Biggar Kirk
**Biggar. Tel: (01899) 220227.**
Collegiate Church built in 1545 (on site of earlier building) by Malcolm, Lord Fleming of Biggar, uncle of Mary, Queen of Scots.

### Biggar Puppet Theatre
**Biggar. Tel: (01899) 220521 (Administration). Tel: (01899) 20631 (Box Office).**
Complete Victorian theatre in miniature

seating 100. Attractive grounds with tearoom, shop, games, picnic area and car park. Licensed. Disabled visitors welcome but prior notice required.

### Bowhill
**Nr. Selkirk. Tel: (01750) 22204.**
For many generations Bowhill has been the Border home of the Scotts of Buccleuch. Inside the house, there is an outstanding collection of pictures, including works by Van Dyck, Reynolds, Gainsborough, Canaletto, Guardi, Claude Lorraine, Rayburn etc. Tearoom and gift shop.

### Broughton Gallery
**Broughton Village. Tel: (01899) 830234.**
An imposing building designed by Basil Spence in 1938 in the style of a 16th-century Scottish fortified tower house. Contains continuous exhibitions of paintings and crafts by living British artists for sale.

### John Buchan Centre
**Broughton Village. Tel: (01899) 221050.**
The Centre tells the story of John Buchan, 1st Lord Tweedsmuir, author of " The 39 Steps" and also lawyer, politician, soldier, historian and Governor-General of Canada.

### Jim Clark Memorial Trophy Room
**Duns. Tel: (01361) 883960.**
A memorial to the late Jim Clark, twice world motor racing champion, contains a large number of his trophies.

### The Cornice Museum of Ornamental Plasterwork
**Peebles. Tel: ( 01721) 720212**
Re-creation of a plasterer's casting shop illustrating methods of creating ornamental plasterwork. Car park nearby.

### Coulter Motte
**Nr. Biggar. Tel: 0131-668 8800.**
Early medieval castle mound, originally moated and probably surrounded by a palisade enclosing a timber tower.

### Dawyck Botanic Gardens
**Stobo. Tel: (01721) 760254**
All year round colour from spring bulbs to

autumn tints. Rare trees, including many very fine conifers, shrubs, rhododendron's and narcissi, among woodland walks. In the woods is Dawyck Chapel, designed by William Burn.

## Devil's Beef Tub
**Nr. Moffat.**
A huge, spectacular hollow among the hills, at the head of Annandale.

## Dryburgh Abbey
**Nr. Melrose. Tel: 0131-668 8800.**
Peacefully situated on the banks of the Tweed, Dryburgh Abbey is one of the four famous Border Abbeys founded in the reign of David 1 by Hugh de Morville, Constable of Scotland.

## Dryhope Tower
**Nr. St. Mary's Loch.**
A stout little tower now ruinous, but originally four storeys high, rebuilt c 1613. Birthplace of Mary Scott.

## Dunglass Collegiate Church
**Nr. Cockburnspath. Tel: 0131-668 8800.**
Founded in 1450, the church consists of nave, choir, transepts, sacristy and a central tower; richly embellished interior, in an attractive estate setting.

## Duns Castle
**Nr. Berwick-Upon-Tweed. Tel: (01361) 883211.**
Duns Castle is a 14th century peel tower with Georgian additions, inhabited by the same family for 300 years. Its Gothic stone and plasterwork are of the finest quality, and its furnishings reflect the Scottish, Dutch and French influences of its history.

## Eyemouth Museum
**Eyemouth. Tel: (01890) 750678.**
Opened in 1981 to commemorate the Great East Coast Fishing disaster in which 189 fishermen were lost. 129 of them from Eyemouth. Displays include Eyemouth tapestry.

## Fast Castle
**Nr. Coldingham.**
The scant, but impressive remains of a Home stronghold, perched on a cliff above the sea. Care should be taken on the cliffs.

## Ferniehirst Castle
**Nr. Jedburgh. Tel: (01835) 862201.**
**(Lothian Estates Office, Jedburgh.)**
Scotland's frontier fortress. 16th century Border Castle, ancestral home of the Kerr family, recently restored by the Marquis of Lothian, Chief of the Kerrs. A 17th century stable has been adapted to incorporate an information centre.

## Flodden Monument
**Selkirk. Tel: (01835) 863435.**
The monument was erected in 1913 on the 400th anniversary of the battle and is inscribed ' O Flodden Field'. The memorial is the work of sculptor Thomas Clapperton.

## Floors Castle
**Nr. Kelso. Tel: (01573) 223333.**
A large and impressive mansion, built by William Adam in 1721, with additions in the 1840s by William Playfair. A holly tree in the grounds is said to mark the spot where James II was killed by the bursting of a cannon in 1460. Location of the film ' Greystoke'.

## Gladstone Court Street Museum
**Biggar. Tel: (01899) 221050.**
An indoor street museum of shops and windows . Grocers, photographers, dressmakers, bank, school, library, ironmonger, chemist, china merchant, telephone exchange, etc.

## Grey Mare's Tail
**Nr. Moffat. Tel: 0141-552 8391.**
A spectacular 200-feet waterfall formed by the Tail Burn dropping from Loch Skene. The area is rich in wild flowers and there is a herd of wild goats.

## Halliwell's House Museum and Robson Gallery
**Selkirk. Tel: (01750) 20096.**
This row of 18th- century dwelling houses has recently been extensively renovated and now houses an attractive and lively museum dealing with Selkirk's long and rich history. The building's history and its long link with the ironmongery trade are thoughtfully re-created.

## Harestanes Countryside Visitor Centre
**Nr. Ancrum. Tel: (01835) 830306.**
Harestanes Countryside Visitors Centre is a

group of converted farm buildings which house a variety of facilities designed to introduce the visitor to the borders countryside. As well as interior displays, there are Ranger-led walks and other Ranger activities.

## Hawick Museum & Art Gallery
**Nr. Hawick. Tel: (01450) 73457.**
In the ancestral home of the Langlands there is an unrivalled collection of local and Scottish Border relics, natural history, art gallery, etc. Situated in 107-acre Wilton Lodge Park, open at all times.

## Hermitage Castle
**Liddesdale. Tel: 0131-668 8800.**
This strikingly dramatic 13th-century castle was a stronghold of the de Soulis family and, after 1341, of the Douglases. It has a vivid, sometimes cruel history: to here Mary, Queen of Scots made her exhausting ride from Jedburgh in 1566 to meet Bothwell.

## Jedburgh Abbey and Visitor Centre
**Jedburgh. Tel: 0131-668 8800.**
This Augustinian Abbey is perhaps the most impressive of the four great border abbeys, founded by David 1 in 1138. The noble remains are extensive, the west front has a fine rose window, known as St. Catherine's Wheel, and there is a richly carved Norman doorway.

## Jedburgh Castle Jail & Museum
**Jedburgh. Tel: (01835) 863254 or (01450) 73457.**
On the site of Jedburgh Castle, a 'modern' reform jail was built in 1825. Rooms have been interestingly reconstructed to create the 'reformed' system of the early 19th century. A history of the Royal Burgh is interpreted.

## Jedforest Deer and Farm Park
**Camptown. Tel: (01835) 840364.**
Borders working farm with sheep, suckler cows, corn and red deer. Large displays of rare breeds, including sheep, cattle, pigs, goats, poultry and waterfowl. Old and new breeds are compared.

## Kelso Abbey
**Kelso. Tel: 0131-668 8800.**
This 12th-century Tironensian abbey, was one of the earliest completed by David 1 and was built on a plan unique to Scotland. It was one of the largest of the Border abbeys. The tower is part of the original building.

## Kelso Museum
**Kelso. Tel: (01573) 225470 or (01450) 73457.**
Located in one of Kelso's oldest and most attractive buildings, owned by the National Trust of Scotland, the Museum interprets Kelso's history as a market town. Nearby car parking. Access to ground floor only for wheelchair visitors.

## Kittiwake Gallery
**St. Abbs Village.**
**Tel: (01890) 771504 or 771588.**
Privately - owned gallery, displaying paintings and limited edition prints, greeting cards by Frederick J. Watson, the gallery proprietor. From Easter to September, demonstrations of landscape and wildlife paintings of local subjects.

## Hugh MacDiarmid Memorial Sculpture
**Nr. Langholm.**
Steel and bronze sculpture by Jake Harvey to commemorate the literary achievements of the Langholm-born poet and Scots Revivalist. Nearby is Malcolm Monument.

## Ladykirk
**Nr. Swinton.**
Ladykirk was built in 1500 by James IV, in memory of ' Our Lady ' who had saved him from drowning. As the Border was only 300 yards away and in constant dispute, he ordered it to be built to withstand fire and flood - hence the all-stone construction of the kirk with no wooden rafters and, until this century, stone pews.

## Marjoribanks Monument
**Coldstream.**
Obelisk with a stone figure of Charles Marjoribanks, elected the First Member of Parliament for Berwickshire after the passing of the Reform Act of 1832.

## Mary, Queen of Scots House
**Jedburgh. Tel: (01835) 863331.**
A 16th century bastel house in which Mary, Queen of Scots is reputed to have stayed in 1566 when attending the Court of Justice. Now a museum containing several relics associated with the Queen.

### Melrose Abbey
**Melrose. Tel: (0131) 668 8800.**
This Cistercian abbey is the finest and largest of the Borders abbeys, founded in 1136 by David 1. It is notable for its fine traceried stonework. There is an interesting museum in the Commendator's House, at the entrance.

### Mertoun Gardens
**St. Boswells. Tel: (01835) 823236**
20 acres of beautiful grounds with delightful walks and river views. Fine trees, herbaceous borders and flowering shrubs. Walled garden and well-preserved circular dovecote thought to be the oldest in the country.

### Moat Park Heritage Centre
**Biggar. Tel: (01899) 221050.**
This former church has been adapted to display the history of the Upper Clyde and Tweed Valleys.

### Moffat Museum
Moffat.Tel: (01683) 220868
Situated in an old bakehouse in the oldest part of the town. The Scotch oven is a feature of the ground floor.

### Moffat Pottery
**Moffat.Tel: (01683) 220793.**
Studio pottery known as the home of Moffat's 'Singing Potter', Gerard Lyons. Pots, tapes and paintings of the potter, also metal sculptures by John McPhail and jewellery by Irene McPhail.

## EDINBURGH

### Adam Pottery
**Tel: 0131-557 3978**
'One-Woman' pottery where Janet Adam's wheelthrown stoneware and porcelain is made and sold. Delicate porcelain and bowls, large planters, bread crocks, jugs and decorative platters are all reduction - fired to 1300C, giving a wide palette of subtly colourful glazes.

### Ainslie Park Leisure Centre
**Tel: 0131-551 2400**
Opened in 1989, superbly equipped, brightly designed building on leisure theme with swimming pools, flumes and a leisure complex. Function room for 150. Bar, cafe and audio visual library.

### Brass Rubbing Centre
**Tel: 0131-556 4364.**
Rubbings of the brass commemorating Robert the Bruce and the Burghead Bull. A Pictish incised stone cAD700 are among the selection available. Instruction and materials supplied.

### Calton Gallery
**Tel: 0131-556 1010.**
Family firm of fine art dealers established in 1980 in an elegant Georgian townhouse. Royal Terrace, on the northern face of Calton Hill, was designed by William Playfair around 1820 and is the longest unbroken facade in the New Town.

### Calton Hill
**Tel: 0131-200 2000.**
A city centre hill, 350 ft above sea level, with magnificent views over Edinburgh and the Firth of Forth. The monumental collection on top includes a part reproduction of the Parthenon, intended to commemorate the Scottish dead in the Napoleonic Wars.

### Camera Obscura
**Tel: 0131-226 3709.**
High in the unusual Outlook Tower, an 1850's 'cinema' shows live images of Edinburgh. The scene changes as the guide operates the Camera's system of revolving lenses and mirrors, and tells the story of the city's historic past.

### Cammo Estate
**Tel: 0131-317 8797.**
Forty acres of mature woodland, pond and ruined buildings illustrate the fascinating history of a once private estate.

### Canongate Kirk
The church, built by order of James VII in 1688, is the Parish Church of the Canongate and also the Kirk of Holyroodhouse and Edinburgh Castle. The church silver dates from 1611.

### City Art Centre
**Tel: 0131-200 2000.**
The City of Edinburgh's Art Gallery. A converted warehouse on four floors with a programme of changing exhibitions and displays from the City's collection of paintings.

### Collective Gallery
**Tel: 0131-220 1260.**
'New Art' venue, showing contemporary Scottish

Work in exhibitions that change monthly. Educational programme of workshops, classes, talks and tours.

### Craigmillar Castle
**Tel: 0131-668 8800.**
Imposing ruins of massive 14th century keep enclosed in the early 15th century by an embattled curtain wall. Mary, Queen of Scots frequently stayed here and was in residence in 1566 when the plot to murder Darnley was forged.

### Cramond
This picturesque 18th century village is situated at the mouth of the River Almond. Conducted walks around the village start from The Maltings.

### Dean Village
There was grain milling in this notable village of Edinburgh for over 800 years. A walk along the waterside leads to St. Bernard's Well, an old mineral source.

### Edinburgh Castle
**Tel: 0131-668 8800.**
One of the most famous castles in the world, whose battlements overlook the Esplanade where the floodlit Military Tattoo is staged each year. The castle stands on a rock which has been a fortress from time immemorial. The castle houses the Stone of Destiny.

### Edinburgh Gallery
**Tel: 0131-557 5227.**
The Edinburgh Gallery holds regular exhibitions of contemporary works of art, with a bias towards Scottish figurative, landscape and still life.

### The Fruitmarket Gallery
**Tel: 0131-225 2383.**
An independent gallery hosting varied exhibitions of contemporary painting, sculpture etc from Scotland and the international art world.

### General Register House
**Tel: 0131-535 1314.**
This fine Robert Adam building, founded 1774, is the headquarters of the Scottish Record Office and the home of the national archives of Scotland.

### Greyfriar's Bobby
Statue of Greyfriar's Bobby, the Skye terrier who,

after his master's death in 1858, watched over his grave in the nearby Greyfriar's Churchyard for 14 years.

### Greyfriar's Kirk
**Tel: 0131-225 1900.**
The Kirk, dedicated on Christmas Day, 1620, was the scene of the adoption and signing of the National Covenant on 28th February 1638.

### George Heriot's School
**Tel: 0131-229 7263 (Trust Office).**
Now a school, the splendid building was begun in 1628, endowed by George Heriot, goldsmith and jeweller to James VI and I, the 'jingling Geordie' of Scott's novel Fortunes of Nigel.

### John Knox House
**Tel: 0131-556 9579/2647.**
A picturesque house, said to be the only 15th century house in Scotland, having traditional connections with John Knox, the famous Scottish reformer.

### Lady Stair's House
**Tel: 0131-200 2000.**
Built in 1622, this is now a museum of Burns, Scott and Stevenson.

### Lauriston Castle
**Tel: 0131-200 2000.**
The original tower house built by Sir Archibald Napier, father of the inventor of Logarithms was much extended by William Burn in the 1820's. The last occupant, W.R. Reid, completely refurbished the Castle in 1903 and his Edwardian interior has been carefully preserved.

### Magdalen Chapel
**Tel: 0131-220 1450.**
This 16th Century chapel is notable for its stained-glass windows.

### Museum of Antiquities
**Tel: 0131-225 7534.**
An intriguing and comprehensive collection of the history and everyday life of Scotland from the Stone Age to modern times.

### Museum of Childhood
**Tel: 0131-200 2000.**
This unique museum has a fine collection of toys, dolls, doll's houses, costumes and nursery equipment.

## National Gallery of Scotland
**Tel: 0131-556 8921.**
One of the most distinguished of the smaller galleries of Europe, The National Gallery of Scotland contains a comprehensive collection of old masters, impressionist and Scottish paintings.

## National Library of Scotland
**Tel: 0131-226 4531.**
Founded in 1689, this is one of the four largest libraries in Great Britain. Its unparalleled collection on Scottish history and culture is available to researchers.

## Palace of Holyroodhouse
**Tel: 0131-556 7371/1096
(recorded information).**
The Palace of Holyroodhouse is the official residence of the Queen in Scotland. The oldest part is built against the monastic nave of Holyrood Abbey, little of which remains.

## Parliament House
**Tel: 0131-225 2595.**
Built 1632-39 this was the seat of Scottish government until 1707, when the governments of Scotland and England were united. Royal proclamations are still read from its platform.

## Royal Museum of Scotland
**Tel: 0131-225 7534.**
Part of the National Museums of Scotland in a fine Victorian building. Houses the national collections of decorative arts of the world, natural history, geology, technology and science.

## Royal Observatory
**Tel: 0131-668 8405.**
Situated at the home of the Royal Observatory and University Department of Astronomy, the Visitor Centre demonstrates the work of astronomers.

## Royal Scottish Academy
**Tel: 0131-225 6671.**
The Academy has annual exhibitions and special Festival exhibitions. Ramped wheelchair entrance at side.

## St. Giles Cathedral
Tel: 0131-225 9442.
There has been a church here since the 9th Century. Of the present building, the tower is late 15th Century.

## St. John's Church
**Tel: 0131-229 7565.**
An impressive 19th Century church, the nave of which was built in 1817 by William Burn. There is a fine collection of Victorian stained glass.

## St. Mary's Cathedral
**Tel: 0131-225 6293.**
Built 1879, with the western towers added in 1917. The central spire is 276 feet high and the interior is impressive.

## Scotch Whisky Heritage Centre
**Tel: 0131-220 0441.**
The award winning Scotch Whisky Heritage Centre, located beside Edinburgh Castle, gives the equivalent of a distillery tour in the heart of Edinburgh's Old Town. Visitors learn how and where Scotch whiskies are made.

## Scott Monument
**Tel: 0131-200 2000.**
Completed in 1844, a statue of Sir Walter Scott and his dog Maida, under a canopy and spire 200 feet high, with 64 statuettes of Scott characters.

## Scottish National Gallery of Modern Art
**Tel: 0131-556 8921.**
Scotland's collection of 20th Century painting, sculpture and graphic art.

## Usher Hall
**Tel: 0131-228 1155.**
Edinburgh's premier concert hall which offers a wide and exciting range of concerts and dance performances.

## West Register House
**Tel: 0131-535 1314.**
Formerly St. George's Church, 1811, this now holds the more modern documents of the Scottish Record Office.

## White Horse Close
A restored group of 17th Century buildings off the High Street. The coaches to London left from White Horse Inn and there are Jacobite links.

# LOTHIANS

### Abercorn Church
**South Queensferry. Tel: 0131-331 1869.**
Ancient church dedicated to St. Serf, founded in
5th Century. Abercorn was the first bishopric in
Scotland dating from AD 681.

### Athelstaneford Church
**Haddington. Tel: (01620) 88249/88378.**
The plaque by the church tells the story of the
origins of St. Andrews Cross (the Saltire),
which was first adopted as the Scottish flag at
this place.

### Blackness Castle
**Linlithgow. Tel: 0131-668 8800.**
Interesting 15th century castle built out of the
shore of the Forth, suggesting a fortified ship
in appearance.

### Butterfly and Insect World
**Nr. Lasswade. Tel: 0131-663 4932.**
The farm, housed in a large greenhouse with lush
tropical plants, cascading waterfalls and lily
ponds, provides the setting for butterflies from all
over the world to fly freely around.

### Crichton Castle
**Crichton. Tel: 0131-668 8800.**
The keep dates from the 14th Century,
although today's ruins are mostly 15th/17th
Century. The castle, elaborate in style, has an
arcaded range and impressive Italianate facade,
including piazza.

### Crystal Visitor Centre
**Penicuik. Tel: (01968) 675128.**
Factory tours reveal the secrets of glassmaking
from glassblowing through to cutting to
engraving. Extended Activity tours include the
chance to try glassbowing and cutting
(6-12 persons, booking essential).

### Dalkeith Park
**Dalkeith. Tel: 0131-665 3277.**
Woodland walks beside the river in the extensive
grounds of Dalkeith Palace. 18th Century bridge
and orangery and woodland adventure play area.

### Dalmeny Kirk
**Dalmeny. Tel: 0131-331 1869.**
Dedicated to St. Cuthbert, Dalmeny Kirk has

been described as the most complete example of
a Romanesque (Norman) church in Scotland.

### Deep-Sea World
**North Queensferry. Tel: (01383) 411411.**
Visitors have a 'diver's eye view' of thousands of
fish as they travel along transparent tunnels on an
underwater safari beneath the Firth of Forth.

### Dirleton Castle
**Dirleton. Tel: 0131-668 8800.**
Near the wide village green of Dirleton, these
beautiful ruins date back to 1225 with 15th-17th
Century additions.

### Forth Bridges
**Queensferry.**
For over 800 years travellers were ferried across
the Firth of Forth. Queensferry was named from
Queen Margaret who regularly used this passage
between Dunfermline and Edinburgh in the 11th
Century. The ferry ceased in 1964 when the
Queen opened the Forth Road Bridge. Also here
is the rail bridge of 1883-90, one of the greatest
engineering feats of its time.

### Gleneagles Crystal
**Broxburn. Tel: (01506) 852566.**
Factory where production of Gleneagles of
Edinburgh hand-cut crystal can be seen from the
viewing gallery.

### Gosford House
**Longniddry. Tel: (01875) 870200.**
In fine setting on the Firth of Forth. Central part
of the house by Robert Adam, 1800. North and
South wings by William Young, 1890.

### The Heritage of Golf
**Gullane. Tel: (01875) 870277.**
The exhibition shows how the game of golf
developed after it arrived in Scotland from
Holland in the 15th Century.

### Hopetoun House
**South Queensferry. Tel: 0131-331 2451.**
This great Adam mansion is the home of the
Hope family, Earls of Hopetoun and later
Marquesses of Linlithgow.

### Inchcolm Abbey
**Inchcolm Island. Tel: 0131-668 8800.**
The monastic buildings, which include a fine

13th century octagonal chapter house, are the best preserved in Scotland.

## Inveresk Lodge Garden
**Musselburgh. Tel: 0131-226 5922.**
This garden of a 17th century house (not open to the public) displays a range of plants suitable for the small garden.

## Kinneil Museum and Roman Fortlet
**Bo'ness. Tel: (01324) 24911.**
Converted 17th Century stables, with displays of Bo'ness Pottery and cast iron work.

## Linlithgow Palace
**Linlithgow. Tel: 0131-668 8800.**
This splendid ruin Palace overlooking the loch is the successor to an older building which was burned down in 1424. This now roofless palace still represents on of the most remarkable achievements in Scottish medieval architecture.

## Luffness
**Aberlady. Tel: (01875) 870218.**
A 16th century castle with a 13th century keep built on the site of a Norse camp. There are extensive old fortifications, an old moat and gardens.

## Museum of Flight
**East Fortune. Tel: (01620) 880308.**
Aircraft on display at this World War II former RAF airfield range from a supersonic Lightening fighter to the last Comet 4 which was in airline service.

## Myreton Motor Museum
**Aberlady. Tel: (01875) 870288.**
A varied collection of road transport from 1897, including motor cars, cycles, motorcycles, commercials, World War II military vehicles and automobilia.

## Niddry Castle
**Newbridge. Tel: (01506) 890753.**
Late 15th Century Scottish Castle, a refuge for Mary, Queen of Scots.

## Preston Market Cross
**Prestonpans. Tel: 0131-668 8800.**
An outstanding Scottish market cross, the only one that still stands where and as it was built.

## Rosslyn Chapel
**Roslin. Tel: 0131-440 2159.**
This 15th century chapel is one of Scotland's loveliest and most historic churches, renowned for its magnificent sculpture and Prentice Pillar.

## St. Mary's Collegiate Church
**Haddington. Tel: (01620) 825111.**
14th century medieval church, built on the scale of a cathedral. The home church of Scots Reformer, John Knox.

## Scottish Mining Museum
**Prestongrange. Tel: 0131-663 7519.**
Exhibitions: "The Miner's Skill" and "Cutting the Coal" on mechanical coal extraction.

## Stevenson House
**Nr. Haddington. Tel: (01620) 823217.**
Although the mansion house dates from the 13th century, the present house dates mainly from the 16th century. Well landscaped gardens (both House Garden and Walled Kitchen Garden).

## Tantallon Castle
**Nr. North Berwick. Tel: 0131-668 8800.**
Very impressive fortification in magnificent cliff top setting. Earliest parts date from 14th Century. Associated with the Earls of Douglas.

## Torness Power Station
**Nr. Dunbar. Tel: (01368) 863500..**
Nuclear Power Station. This plant, the most modern power station in Britain, is operated by Scottish Nuclear Ltd and produces a quarter of all the electricity consumed in Scotland.

## Winton House
**Nr. Haddington. Tel: (01875) 341308.**
A gem of Scottish Renaissance architecture dating from 1620. Associations with Charles I and Sir Walter Scott. Terraced gardens.

## Wool Stone
**Stenton.**
The Medieval Wool Stone, used formerly for the weighing of wool at Stenton Fair, stands on the green. See also the 14th century Rood Well, topped by a cardinal's hat and the old doocot.

## Yester Parish Church
**Gifford.**

The Dutch-looking church dates from 1708, and in it is preserved a late medieval bell and also a 17th century pulpit.

# FIFE

### Abbot House Heritage Centre
**Dunfermline. Tel: (01383) 733266.**
A heritage centre in one of Scotland's oldest town houses, part of which date from 1460.

### Aberdour Castle
**Aberdour. Tel: 0131-668 8800.**
Overlooking the harbour at Aberdour, the oldest part is the tower, which dates back to the 14th Century.

### Sir Dougals Badar Garden for the Disabled
**Cupar. Tel: (01334) 653722.**
The garden has raised beds, rock gardens, shrub border, fountains, waterfalls and sheltered seating.

### Balgonie Castle
**Nr. Markinch. Tel: (01592) 750119.**
14th century castle with additions to 1702. 17th century home of Field Marshall Sir Alexander Leslie.

### Balmerio Abbey
**Nr. Newport. Tel: 0131-336 2157.**
Cistercian Abbey founded in 1229 by Queen Ermingade, second wife of William Lyon. Ruined during period of reformation. Peaceful gardens.

### British Golf Museum
**St. Andrews. Tel: (01334) 478880.**
Interesting memorabilia for all golfing enthusiasts dating back to the time when the now world-famous game was originated in this historic town.

### Burleigh Castle
**Nr. Kinross. Tel: 0131-668 8800.**
A fine tower house dating from about 1500. The seat of the Balfours of Burleigh, several times visited by James VI.

### Andrew Carnegie Birthplace Museum
**Dunfermline. Tel: (01383) 724302.**
Weaver's cottage, birthplace of Andrew

Carnegie in 1835, and linked Memorial Hall. The displays tell the story of the weaver's son who emigrated to America, became very rich and then gave away 350 million dollars for the benefit of mankind.

### Crail Museum and Heritage Centre
**Crail. Tel: (01333) 450869.**
Exhibits include relics of golf, HMS Jackdaw, the Royal Burgh, the Collegiate Church, the old harbour, crafts and Crail past and present.

### Crail Tolbooth
**Crail. Tel: (01333) 450310.**
The Tolbooth dates from the early 16th Century, displaying a fish weather vane, and a coat of arms dated 1602. The Tolbooth is a library and Town Hall.

### Culross
**Nr. Dunfermline.**
On the north shore of the River Forth, this is a remarkable example of a small town of the 16th and 17th centuries, which has changed little in 300 years.

### Dunfermline Abbey and Palace
**Dunfermline. Tel: 0131-668 8800.**
This great Benedictine house owes its foundation to Queen Margaret, wife of Malcolm Canmore (1057-93) and the foundations of her modest church remain beneath the present nave.

### Dunfermline District Museum and Small Gallery
**Tel: (01383) 721814.**
The museum, housed in a Victorian villa, has an interesting local history collection, particularly of weaving and linen damask material, the industry that made Dunfermline famous.

### Fife Folk Museum
**Ceres. Tel: (01334) 828380.**
Situated in the 17th Century Weigh House, near an old bridge in an attractive village. Nearby is Ceres Church (1806) with a horse-shoe gallery.

### Kellie Castle and Gardens
**Nr. Pittenweem. Tel: (01333) 720271.**
Fine architecture of the 16th/17th Centuries, though the earliest parts date from 14th Century. Notable plaster work and painted panelling. Four acres of Victorian gardens.

### Kirkcaldy Museum and Art Gallery
**Kirkcaldy. Tel: (01592) 412860.**
Visit this award-winning museum to see the heritage of Kirkcaldy District in a unique collection of fine Scottish paintings and local history exhibitions.

### St. Andrew's Castle
**St. Andrews. Tel: 0131-668 8800.**
This ruined castle, which has been rebuilt over several periods, overlooks the sea and was founded in 1200 as a fortress and principal residence of the Bishop of St. Andrews.

### St. Andrew's Cathedral
**St. Andrews. Tel: 0131-668 8800.**
Founded in 1160 and consecrated in 1318, it was once the largest church in the country. There is a fascinating museum and St. Rule's Tower, dating from 1127.

### St. Andrew's University
**St. Andrews. Tel: (01334) 476161.**
The oldest university in Scotland, founded in 1412. See the 15th century Church of St. Salvator.

### St. Monan's Church
**St. Monan's.**
Possibly a Ninianic foundation, c 400 AD. A place of healing from early times. David I was reputedly cured of an arrow wound here.

### Wemyss Caves
**East Wemyss. Tel: (01592) 414479.**
Several caves, cut into the sandstone cliffs by sea erosion during the last Ice Age, show evidence of prehistoric and recent occupation.

## PERTHSHIRE

### Aberfeldy Water Mill
**Aberfeldy. Tel: (01887) 820803.**
Working oatmeal mill with interpretative gallery and video presentation. Tours stress the importance of mills in the social history of Scotland.

### Abernethy Round Tower
**Abernethy. Tel: 0131-668 8800.**
A round tower, 74 feet high, dating from the 11th century.Tradition has it that Malcolm Canmore did homage to William the Conqueror here.

### Ardblair Castle
**Nr. Blairgowrie. Tel: (01250) 873155.**
Mainly 16th century castle on 2th century foundations, home of the Blair Oliphant family. Jacobite relics and links with Charles Edward Stuart.

### Black Watch Regimental Museum
**Balhousie Castle, Perth. Tel: (01738) 621281.**
Balhousie Castle houses the Regimental Headquarters and Museum of the Black Watch (Royal Highland) Regiment, and displays the history of this famous regiment from 1740 to the present.

### Blair Castle
**Nr. Pitlochry. Tel: (01796) 481207.**
A white turreted baronial castle, seat of the Duke of Atholl, chief of Clan Murray. The oldest part is Cumming's Tower, 1269.

### Caithness Glass
**Perth. Tel: (01738) 637373.**
Visitors are welcome at the factory to see the fascinating process of glass-making. Factory shop. Licensed restaurant.

### Castle Menzies
**Nr. Aberfeldy. Tel: (01887) 820982.**
Outstanding 16th century Z-plan fortified tower house exemplifying the transition between earlier strongholds and later mansions.

### Dunkeld Cathedral
**Dunkeld. Tel: 0131-668 8800.**
Refounded in the early 12th century on an ancient ecclesiastical site, this cathedral has a beautiful setting by the Tay. The nave and the great north-west tower date from the 15th century.

### Huntingtower Castle
**Nr. Perth. Tel: 0131-668 8800.**
A 15th century castellated mansion until 1600 known as Ruthven Castle. This was the scene of the Raid of Ruthven in 1582. There are fine painted ceilings.

### Megginch Castle Gardens
**Nr. Perth. Tel: (01821) 642222.**
The gardens around the 15th century castle have daffodils, rhododendron's and 1,000-year-old yews. There is a double-walled kitchen garden.

## Muthill Church and Tower
**Muthill. Tel: 0131-668 8800.**
Ruins of an important church of the 15th century, incorporating a 12th century tower.

## Rumbling Bridge
The River Devon is spanned here by two bridges, the lower one dating from 1713, the upper one from 1816. A footpath from the north side gives good access to spectacular gorges and falls, one of which is known as the Devil's Mill.

## St. John's Kirk
**Perth. Tel: (01738) 621755.**
Consecrated in 1242, this fine cruciform church largely dates from the 15th century and was restored in 1923-28 as a war memorial.

## Scone Palace
**Nr. Perth. Tel: (01738) 552300.**
The present castellated palace, enlarged and embellished in 1803, incorporates the 16th century and earlier palaces.

## Tourist Island,
## The Highland Motor Heritage Centre
**Nr. Perth. Tel: (01738) 87696.**
A collection of classic and vintage cars, costumes and memorabilia is displayed using authentic period settings.

## Tullibardine Chapel
**Nr. Crieff. Tel: 0131-244 3101.**
Founded in 1446, this is one of the few rural churches in Scotland which was entirely finished and still remains unaltered.

# NORTH EAST

## Alford Heritage Centre
**Alford. Tel: (019755) 62906.**
Extensive exhibition of agricultural and rural life, mounted by Alford and Donside Heritage Association.

## Alford Valley Railway
**Alford. Tel: (019755) 62326.**
Narrow gauge railway running from Alford Station and Museum to Haughton Country Park. Terminus near Alford Transport Museum.

## Ardclach Bell Tower
**Nr. Nairn. Tel: 0131-244 3101.**
A two-storey tower of 1655 whose bell summoned worshippers to the church and warned the neighbourhood in case of alarm.

## Balmoral Castle
**Nr. Ballater. Tel: (013397) 42334.**
The family holiday home of the Royal Family for over a century. The earliest reference to it, as Bouchmorale, was in 1484. Queen Victoria visited the earlier castle in 1848 and Prince Albert bought the estate in 1852.

## Baxter's Visitor Centre
**Nr. Fochabers. Tel: (01343) 820666.**
Slide show with commentary, Old Baxter Shop, replica of the original George Baxter & Sons establishment where Baxters of Speyside were formed. Highland cattle nearby.

## Boath Doocot
**Nr. Nairn. Tel: (01463) 232034.**
A 17th Century doocot (dovecote) on the site of an ancient castle where Montrose flew the standard of Charles I when he defeated the Covenanters in 1645.

## Braemar Castle
**Braemar. Tel: (013397) 41219.**
This turreted stronghold, built in 1628 by the Earl of Mar, was burnt by Farquharson of Inverey in 1689. It was rebuilt about 1748 and garrisoned by Hanoverian troops.

## Brodie Castle and Gardens
**Nr. Forres. Tel: (01309) 641202.**
The castle, associated with the Brodie family for 500 years, was largely rebuilt after the earlier structure was burned in 1645; it is based on a 16th century Z-plan, with additions made in the 17th and 19th centuries.

## Burns Family Tombstones and Cairn
**Nr. Stonehaven.**
The Burnes (Burns) family tombstones in the churchyard were restored in 1968 and a Burns memorial cairn is nearby.

## Castle Fraser
**Inverurie. Tel: (01330) 833463.**
Castle Fraser originated about 1575. Two notable families of master masons, Bel and Leiper, were involved in its construction, completed in 1636.

### Corgarff Castle
**Nr. Ballater. Tel: 0131-668 8800.**
A 16th century tower house, converted into a garrison post and enclosed within a star-shaped loopholed wall in 1748. The castle was burned in 1571 by Edom o'Gordon and the owner, Alexander Forbes, his wife, family and household all perished in the flames.

### Crathie Church
**Crathie.**
This small church, built in 1895, is attended by the Royal Family when in residence at Balmoral.

### Elgin Cathedral
**Elgin. Tel: 0131-668 8800.**
When entire, this was perhaps the most beautiful of Scottish cathedrals, known as the lantern of the North. It was founded in 1224, burned in 1390 by the Wolf of Badenoch. Much 13th century work still remain. There is a 6th Century Pictish slab in the choir.

### Glendronach Distillery
**Between Huntly and Aberchirder.**
**Tel: (01466) 730202.**
Visitor Centre and guided tour around malt whisky distillery dating from 1826.

### Glenfarclas Distillery
**Nr. Keith. Tel: (01807) 500257/500245.**
Tours of a well-known malt whisky distillery, visual exhibition and museum of old illicit distilling equipment in Reception Centre.

### Glenfiddich Distillery
**Nr. Dufftown. Tel: (01340) 820373.**
After an audio-visual programme, visitors are shown around and are offered a complimentary dram.

### The Glenlivet Distillery Visitor Centre
**Nr. Tomintoul. Tel: (01807) 590427 (during season): (01542) 886294 (during winter).**
Guided tours of distillery. Exhibits of ancient whisky tools and artifacts and life-size reproduction of Landseer's painting 'The Highland Whisky Still'. Free whiskey sample.

### Huntly Castle
**Huntly. Tel: 0131-668 8800.**
An imposing ruin which replaced medieval Strathbogie Castle which, until 1544, was the seat of the Gay Gordons, the Marquesses of Huntly, the most powerful family in the north until the mid 16th century.

### Lossiemouth Fisheries and Community Museum
**Lossiemouth. Tel: (01343) 813772.**
Permanent features include Memorial Room for lost/drowned fishermen killed in active service and study of the late J. Ramsay McDonald, Prime Minister.

### Moray Motor Museum
**Elgin. Tel: (01343) 544933.**
Unique collection of over 40 cars and motor cycles housed in an old mill building.

### Nairn Fishertown Museum
**Nairn. Tel: (01667) 453331.**
A collection of photographs and articles connected with the Moray Firth and Herring fishing industries during the steam drifter era.

### Nelson Tower
**Forres. Tel: (01309) 673701.**
The tower has displays on the life of Admiral Nelson, the Forres Trafalgar Club and views of old Forres.

### Rob Roy's Statue
**Peterculter.**
Statue of Rob Roy standing above the Leuchar Burn can be seen from the bridge on the main road.

### Strathisla Distillery
**Keith. Tel: (01542) 783044.**
A typical small old-fashioned distillery, one of the oldest established in Scotland, dating from 1786.

### Tomintoul Museum
**Tomintoul. Tel: (01309) 673701.**
At 1160 ft, Tomintoul is the highest village in the Highlands. Museum has displays on local history, folklife and a reconstructed farm kitchen.

### The Village Store
**Aberlour. Tel: (01340) 871243.**
This old village general store has all the original fittings, records and stock dating back to the 1920's.

# NORTHERN HIGHLANDS

## Ardvreck Castle
**Loch Assynt.**
Built in 1490 by the MacLeods, who in the mid
13th century obtained Assynt by marriage; the
three storeyed ruins stand on the shores of
Loch Assynt.

## Caithness Glass
**Wick. Tel: (01955) 602286.**
See hand-made glass blowing from the raw
materials stage, through all the processes, to the
finished article.

## Castle Stuart
**Nr. Inverness. Tel: (01463) 790745.**
Built in 1625 by James Stuart, 3rd Earl of Moray,
on land bestowed by Mary, Queen of Scots to her
half brother James.

## Choraidh Croft
**Nr. Durness. Tel: (01971) 511235.**
Working croft with rare breeds of domestic farm
animals, aquariums and pond containing sea life.

## Clan Gunn Heritage Centre and Museum
**Latheron. Tel: (01593) 721325.**
Situated in Latheron Old Parish Church. Shows
dramatic story of this ancient Scottish clan from
its Norse origins to the present.

## Croick Parliamentary Church
**Strathcarron.**
Designed by Thomas Telford, Croick Church is
one of the 32 'parliamentary' churches built in the
Highlands and Islands during the 1820s.

## Dornoch Cathedral
**Dornoch.**
Founded in 1224 by Gilbert, Archdeacon of
Moray and Bishop of Caithness, this little
cathedral was partially destroyed by fire in 1570,
restored in the 17th century, in 1835-37 and
again in 1924.

## Dunnet Head
**Nr. Thurso.**
This bold promontory of sandstone rising to 417
feet is the northernmost point of the Scottish
mainland with magnificent views across the
Pentland Firth to Orkney and a great part of the
north coast to Ben Loyal and Ben Hope.

## Falls of Shin
**Bonar Bridge.**
Spectacular falls through rocky gorge, famous for
salmon leap.

## Fortrose Cathedral
**Fortrose. Tel: 0131-244 3101.**
The surviving portions of this 14th century
cathedral include the south aisle with its vaulting
and much fine detail.

## Glen Ord Distillery
**Muir of Ord. Tel: (01463) 870421.**
Licensed in 1838, Glen Ord is in an area with an
ancient tradition of distilling. Guided tours show
the main processes of distilling.

## Highland and Rare Breeds Farm
**Elphin. Tel: (01854) 666204.**
The Scottish Farm Animal Centre has 40 breeds,
ancient and modern in 15 acres of farmland, river
and mountain scenery. There is also an exhibition
of farm tools.

## Mallaig Marine World
**Mallaig. Tel: (01687) 462292.**
Marine aquarium and exhibition featuring local
marine species. Fishing displays on the work of
the Mallaig fishing fleet.

## Hugh Miller's Cottage
**Cromarty. Tel: (01381) 600245.**
The birthplace of Hugh Miller
(1802-56) - stonemason - became eminent
geologist, naturalist, theologian and writer.
Furnished thatched cottage, built c 1711 by his
great grandfather.

## St. Mary's Chapel
**Crosskirk. Tel: 0131-668 8800.**
A rudely-constructed chapel with very low
doors narrowing at the top in Irish style.
Probably 12th century.

## Timespan Heritage Centre
**Helmsdale. Tel: (01431) 821327.**
Award-winning Timespan features the dramatic
story of the Highlands, from Picts and Vikings,
murder at Helmsdale Castle, the last burning of a
witch and much more.

## Wick Heritage Centre
**Wick. Tel: (01955) 603385.**
Prize-winning exhibition of the herring
fishing industry; also displays of domestic and
farming life.

# WESTERN AND
# CENTRAL HIGHLANDS

## Ardchattan Priory
**Loch Etive. Tel: 0131-668 8800.**
One of the Valliscaulian houses founded in
Scotland in 1230, and the meeting place in 1308
of one of Bruce's Parliaments, among the last at
which business was conducted in Gaelic.

## Ben Nevis
**Nr. Fort William.**
Britain's highest mountain and most popular for
both rock-climber and hillwalker. It is best seen
from the north approach to Fort William.

## Ben Nevis Distillery Visitor Centre
**Lochy Bridge. Tel: (01397) 700200.**
Small exhibition, audio-visual display, guided
tours for groups of up to 15, whisky tasting.

## Bonawe Iron Furnace
**Bonawe. Tel: 0131-668 8800.**
The restored remains of a charcoal furnace for
iron-smelting, established in 1753, which worked
until 1876.

## The Cairngorm Reindeer Centre
**Glenmore. Tel: (01479) 861228.**
Visitors may accompany the guide to see
the reindeer herd free-ranging in their
natural surroundings.

## Caledonian Canal
Inverness. Tel: (01463) 233140.
Designed by Thomas Telford and completed in
1822, the Caledonian Canal links the lochs of
the Great Glen (Loch Lochy, Loch Oich and
Loch Ness).

## Carnasserie Castle
**Nr. Lochgilphead. Tel: 0131-668 8800.**
The house of John Carswell, first Protestant
Bishop of the Isles, who translated Knox's
Liturgy into Gaelic.

## Clachan Bridge
**Nr. Oban.**
This picturesque single-arched bridge, built in
1792, links the mainland with the island of Seil.

## Clan Cameron Museum
**Spean Bridge. Tel: (01397) 712052.**
A reconstructed 17th century croft house.
Memorabilia of Bonnie Prince Charlie, the
Commandos, the Camerons and Queen's Own
Cameron Highlanders.

## Clan MacPherson Museum
**Newtonmore. Tel: (01540) 673332.**
Relics and memorials of Clan Chiefs and other
MacPherson families.

## Culloden Moor
**Nr. Inverness. Tel: (01463) 790607.**
Here Prince Charles Edward's cause was finally
crushed at the battle on 16th April 1746. The
battle lasted only 40 minutes and the Prince's
army lost some 1,200 men, and the King's
army 310.

## Fort George
**Nr. Nairn. Tel: 0131-668 8800.**
Begun in 1748 as a result of the Jacobite
rebellion, this is one of the finest late artillery
fortifications in Europe, which is still in use.

## Glencoe and North Lorn Folk Museum
**Glencoe Village.**
Clan and Jacobite relics, also domestic
implements, weapons, costumes, photographs,
dolls' houses, dolls, agricultural tools, dairy and
slate quarrying equipment - all housed in a
number of thatched cottages.

## Highland Wineries
**Kirkhill. Tel: (01463) 831283/831304/831336.**
Tours of the winery show the processes involved
in wine making. Free tasting, tours, shop and
licensed restaurant.

## Inveraray Castle
**Nr. Ineraray. Tel: (01499) 302203.**
Inveraray has been the seat of the chiefs of Clan
Campbell, Dukes of Argyll for centuries. The
present castle originated in 1743 when the third
Duke engaged Roger Morris to build it.

### Inveraray Jail
**Inveraray. Tel: (01499) 302381.**
The living 19th century prison: lifelike figures, sounds, smells and trials in progress, all bring the 1820 courtroom and former county prison back to life.

### Kilravock Castle
**Nr. Nairn. Tel: (01667) 493258.**
The extensive grounds and garden of this 15th century castle are noted for a large variety of beautiful trees, some centuries old and unique in this country.

### Loch Ness
**Nr. Inverness.**
This striking 24-mile long loch in the Great Glen forms part of the Caledonian Canal which links Inverness with Fort William. Famous world wide for its mysterious inhabitant, the Loch Ness Monster.

### James Pringle Weavers of Inverness
**Inverness. Tel: (01463) 223311.**
James Pringle Weavers of Inverness offers tours around a fully-operational weaving mill which dates back to 1790. Mill shop, weaving mill and restaurant.

### Skipness Castle and Chapel
**Skipness. Tel: 0131-668 8800.**
The remains of the ancient chapel and the large 13th century castle overlook the bay.

### Strathspey Steam Railway
**Aviemore. Tel: (01479) 810725.**
The line is part of the former Highland Railway (Aviemore-Forres section) closed in 1965 and re-opened in 1978. Museum of small relics and other static rolling stock on display at Boat of Garten.

# CENTRAL AND SOUTH WEST SCOTLAND

### Alloway Auld Kirk
**Alloway. Tel: (01292) 441252 (a.m.).**
Ancient church, a ruin in Burns' day, where his father William Burns is buried.

### Argyll and Sutherland Highlanders' Museum

### Stirling Castle. Tel: (01786) 475165.
Fine regimental museum, with a notable silver and medal collection.

### Bannockburn Heritage Centre
**Nr. Stirling. Tel: (01786) 812664.**
The audio-visual presentation tells the story of the events leading up to the significant victory in Scottish history (1314).

### Barsalloch Fort
**Nr. Whithorn. Tel: 0131-668 8800.**
Remains of an iron-age fort on the edge of a raised beach bluff, 60-70 feet above the shore, enclosed by a ditch 12 feet deep and 33 feet wide.

### Bothwell Castle
**Uddingston. Tel: 0131-668 8800.**
Once the largest and finest stone castle in Scotland, dating from the 13th century and reconstructed by the Douglases in the 15th C.

### Robert Burns Centre
**Dumfries. Tel: (01387) 264808.**
The Robert Burns Centre is the major feature on the Scottish Tourist Board Burns Heritage Trail which runs through Dumfries and Galloway.

### Burns Cottage and Museum
**Nr. Ayr. Tel: (01292) 441215.**
In this thatched cottage built by his father, Robert Burns was born, 25th January 1759 and this was his home until 1766.

### Burns House
**Dumfries. Tel: (01387) 255297.**
In November 1791 Robert Burns moved to Dumfries as an Exciseman and rented a three-room flat (not open to the public) in the Wee Vennel (now Bank Street). He moved to a better house in Mill Vennel (now Burns Street) and here he died on 21st July 1796.

### Doune Castle
**Doune. Tel: 0131-668 8800.**
Splendid ruins of one of the best preserved medieval castles in Scotland, built late 14th or early 15th century by the Regent Albany.

### Dunblane Cathedral
**Dunblane. Tel: 0131-668 8800.**
The existing building dates mainly from the 13th

century but incorporates a 12th century tower. The nave was unroofed after the Reformation but the whole building was restored in 1829-95.

### Kilwinning Abbey
**Kilwinning. Tel: 0131-668 8800.**
The ruins of a Tironensian-Benedictine Abbey. Most of the surviving buildings date from the 13th century.

### Largs Museum
**Largs. Tel: (01475) 687081.**
The museum holds a small collection of local bygones, with a library of local history books and numerous photographs.

### Loch Lomond
Loch Lomond, largest stretch of inland water in Britain, and framed by mountain scenery, is a popular centre for all watersports. Cruises around the banks and small islands are available.

### Lochmaben Castle
Nr. Lochmaben. Tel: 0131-668 8800.
This castle was captured and recaptured twelve times and also withstood six attacks and sieges. Now a ruin, this early 14th century castle is on the site of a castle of the de Brus family, ancestors of Robert the Bruce.

### Rob Roy's Grave
**Balquhidder Churchyard.**
Three flat gravestones enclosed by railings are the graves of Rob Roy, his wife and two of his sons.

### Roman Bath House
**Bearsden. Tel: 0131-668 8800.**
A Roman bath house built for the use of the soldiers station in the adjacent Antonine Wall fort.

### St Bride's Church
**Douglas. Tel: 0131-668 8800.**
The restored chancel of this ancient church contains the tomb of the 'Bell the Cat' Earl of Angus (died 1514). The nearby tower (1618) has a clock of 1565 said to have been gifted by Mary, Queen of Scots.

### Sanquahr Post Office
**Sanquahr. Tel: (01659) 50201.**
Britain's oldest post office, functioning in 1763,

20 years before the introduction of the mail coach service and still in use today.

# GLASGOW

### Art Gallery and Museum
**Tel: 0141-287 2700.**
This fine municipal art collection has outstanding Flemish, Dutch and Italian canvases, including works by Giorgione and Rembrandt.

### The Barras
**Tel: 0141-552 7258.**
Glasgow's world famous weekend market, with an amazing variety of stalls and shops.

### The Burrell Collection
**Tel: 0141-649 7151.**
Housed in a building opened in 1983, a world famous collection of textiles, furniture, ceramics, stained glass, art objects and pictures gifted to Glasgow by Sir William and Lady Burrell.

### Glasgow Cathedral
**Tel: 0131-668 8800.**
The Cathedral, dedicated to St. Mungo, is the most complete survivor of the Great Gothic churches of south Scotland. A fragment dates from the late 12th century.

### Crookston Castle
**Tel: 0131-668 8800.**
On the site of a castle built by Robert Croc in the mid 12th century, the present tower house dates from the early 15th century.

### George Square
The heart of Glasgow with the City Chambers and statues of Sir Walter Scott, Queen Victoria, Prince Albert, Robert Burns, Sir John Moore, Lord Clyde, Thomas Campbell, Dr. Thomas Graham James Oswald, James Watt, William Gladstone and Sir Robert Peel.

### McLellan Galleries
**Tel: 0141-331 1854.**
The purpose-built exhibition galleries, completely refurbished in time for Glasgow's celebrations as Cultural Capital of Europe, now provide Glasgow Museums with a major exhibition venue for large exhibitions.

### People's Palace
**Tel: 0141-554 0223.**
Opened in 1898, contains important collections relating to the tobacco and other industries, Glasgow stained glass, ceramics and political and social movements.

### Queen's Cross Church
**Tel: 0141-946 6600.**
The only church (1897-1899) designed by Charles Rennie Mackintosh. The church has a small exhibition area, reference library and specialised shop.

### Regimental Headquarters of the Royal Highland Fusiliers
**Tel: 0141-332 0961.**
The exhibits in this regimental museum include medals, badges, uniforms and records.

### Theatre Royal
**Tel: 0141-332 9000 (Box Office).**
A fine Victorian theatre, elegantly restored as the home of Scottish Opera. Performances also by Scottish Ballet, national visiting companies and major concert artists.

### Tron Theatre
**Tel: 0141-552 4267 (Box Office).**
The 200 year old Adam Kirk in the heart of Glasgow's Merchant City, provides the setting for the Tron.

### University of Glasgow Visitor Centre
**Tel: 0141-330 5511.**
Visitor Centre has exhibits of the university at work, interactive slide/computer and video displays plus a 'hands-on' information system.

### Willow Tearoom
**Tel: 0141-332 0521.**
The Willow Tearoom is an original Charles Rennie Mackintosh building, designed for Miss Cranston 1904-1928. Re-opened in 1983, the tearoom still has the original glass and mirror work and doors.

# SCOTLAND'S ISLANDS

## ARRAN
### Arran and Argyll Transport Museum
**Brodick. Tel: (01770) 302150.**
Independent museum run by enthusiasts, with displays of public transport in Arran and Argyll. Photographs, uniforms, advertisements, fittings and equipment from early transport of all kinds.

### Arran Visitor Centre
**Brodick. Tel: (01770) 302140.**
Cheese factory and set of specialist shops stocking locally made foodstuffs, natural body care products, books, clothing and jewellery.

### Brodick Castle Garden and Country Park
**Nr. Brodick Pier. Tel: (01770) 302202.**
This ancient seat of the Dukes of Hamilton dates in part from the 13th century, with extensions of 1652 and 1844. There are two gardens; the woodland garden (1923) and the formal garden which dates from 1710.

## BARRA
### Cille Bharra
**Eolaigearraidh (Eoligary).**
The ruined church of St. Barr, who gave his name to the island and the restored chapel of St. Mary formed part of the medieval monastery.

### Kisimul Castle
**Nr. Castlebay.**
For many generations Kisimul was the home and stronghold of the MacNeils of Barra, widely noted for their lawlessness and piracy.

## IONA
### Iona
**Tel: (01631) 570000.**
In 563 St. Columba with 12 followers came to this tiny island to found a monastery. The oldest surviving building is St. Oran's Chapel, c 1080 (restored). The remains of the 13th century nunnery can be seen and outside the Cathedral is 10th century St. Martin's Cross.

## LEWIS
### Ness Historical Society
**(Comunn Eachdraidh Nis)Ness.**
**Tel: (01851) 810377.**
A permanent display of photographs and

documents relating to local history with artifacts from domestic life, croft work and fishing.

### Shawbost School Museum
**Tel: (01851) 710213/2.**
Created under the Highland Village Competition 1970, the museum illustrates the old way of life in Lewis.

## MULL

### Carsaig Arches
A 3-mile walk from Carsaig leads to these remarkable tunnels formed by the sea in the basaltic rock. Reached only at low tide.

### Duart Castle
**Tel: (01680) 812309.**
The keep, dominating the Sound of Mull, was built in the 13th century. A royal charter of 1390 confirmed the lands, including Duart, to the Macleans.

### Mull Little Theatre
**Dervaig. Tel: (01688) 400377.**
Officially the smallest professional theatre in the country, according to the Guiness Book of Records, providing a variety of performances in summer.

## NORTH UIST

### Balranald Nature Reserve
**Tel: 0131-668 8800.**
Hebridean marsh, machar and shore. Important for plants and nesting birds.

## ORKNEY

### Click Mill
**Dounby. Tel: 0131-668 8800.**
The only working example of the traditional horizontal water mill of Orkney.

### Cubbie Row's Castle
**Island of Wyre. Tel: 0131-668 8800.**
Probably the earliest stone castle authenticated in Scotland. In a graveyard near the castle is St Mary's Chapel, a ruin of the late 12th century.
### Highland Park Distillery

**Kirkwall.**
Famous Orkney distillery which produces malt whisky with a particular 'peaty' taste. Audio-visual display.

## RAASAY

### Brochel Castle
The castle is now very ruinous and is dated somewhere in the 15th century.

### Raasay House
The home of the MacLeods of Raasay until 1834. The house was remodelled early in the 19th century and in 1846 passed into the hands of various owners. It is now occupied by the Scottish Adventure School.

## RHUM

### Kinloch Castle
Isle of Rhum. Tel: (01687) 462037
Magnificent residence built at the turn of the century for Sir George Bullough, still containing many of its sumptuous fittings.

## SHETLAND

### Fort Charlotte
Lerwick. Tel: 0131-668 8800.
A fort roughly pentagonal in shape with high walls containing gun ports pointing seawards. Designed by John Mylne and begun in 1665 to protect the Sound of Bresay, it was burned in 1673 but repaired in 1781.

### Shetland Croft House Museum
**Voe, Dunrossness. Tel: (01595) 695057.**
Typical mid-19th century thatched Shetland croft house, complete with all outbuildings and working water mill. Furnished in period style, c 1860.

### Tingwall Agricultural Museum
**Veensgarth. Tel: (01595) 840344.**
A private collection of tools and equipment used by the Shetland crofter, housed in a mid 18th century granary, stables, bothy and smithy.

## SKYE

### Clan Donald Centre
### and Armadale Gardens
**Armadale. Tel: (01471) 844305/844227.**
Skye's award-winning Visitor Centre, located in a re-built section of Armadale Castle, once home of Lord Macdonald. There are 46 acres of sheltered woodland gardens and several miles of Nature Trails.

# Places of Interest *Wales*

*Please note borders have changed within Wales. Contact WTB: (01222) 499909*

## CLWYD

Colwyn Bay is an attractive seaside resort with a promenade stretching over 3 miles from Penmaen Head to Rhos on Sea. Beaches are safe and sandy. At Rhos on Sea there is the tiny church of St. Trillo, standing by the seashore. Eairas Park, a 50-acre pleasure ground by the sea, includes boating lake, cafeteria, kiosks, children's amusements, trampolines, miniature golf course, crazy golf, tennis, bowls and modern leisure centre.

Visitors can enjoy glorious views of the length of the Clwydian range from Denbigh's hilltop ruined castle. The site of the town was probably an Iron Age fortification and later the seat of the native Welsh princes until 1282. The castle was completed by 1305, built by Henry de Lacy, Earl of Lincoln. The most impressive feature is the Great Gatehouse.

The town of Ruthin is famed for its timber-framed buildings, a mixture of medieval, Tudor and Georgian architecture. In the Town Square, Maen Huail, the stone where King Arthur is said to have had a rival decapitated, survives.

Llangollen, named after the saint Collen, is home of the International Musical Eisteddfod, which for a week in July, attracts musicians and dancers from over 30 nations. Overlooking the town is Castell Dinas Bran, built for a Welsh prince, on a site said by legend to be the location of the Holy Grail.

### Bodelwyddan Castle
**Bodelwyddan. Tel: (01745) 584060.**
An authentically restored Victorian mansion housing a major collection of 19th century portraits and photography from the National Portrait Gallery, as well as furniture from the Victoria and Albert Museum, and sculptures from the Royal Academy. Walled garden, woodland walk, maze, aviary and play areas.

### Chirk Castle
**Chirk. Tel: (01691) 777701.**
A magnificent marcher fortress, over 700 years old, which commands fine views over the surrounding countryside. Beautiful formal gardens with clipped yews, roses and a variety of flowering shrubs.

### St. Asaph's Cathedral
**St. Asaph.**
Probably the smallest cathedral in Britain, St. Asaph's has been destroyed twice since its was founded by St. Kentigern in 537 AD. The cathedral museum has an interesting collection of bronze and stone implements, together with Roman coins.

## DYFED

Encompassing the Pembrokeshire Coast in the South, up round Cardigan Bay to Aberystwyth, Dyfed has much to offer the visitor. Aberystwyth itself is the largest town and principal shopping centre of mid-Wales. It was once a walled town adjacent to one of Edward I's powerful castles. The town is home to the National Library of Wales, where some of the greatest literary treasures of the Celtic lands are stored. It also has its own little train, the narrow-gauge Vale of Rheidol Railway to Devil's Bridge. Visitors can climb to the summit of Constitution Hill on the longest electric cliff railway in Britain. Down the coast at Cardigan, the ruins of the old castle still guard the river passage inland from the sea and the historic rail link with Pembrokeshire. Just south of Cardigan, over the River Teifi, the Pembrokeshire Coast National Park begins, with its noted coastal walks. The ideal base for exploring the National Park is Haverfordwest, also known for its art galleries.

Another popular South Pembrokeshire resort is Tenby, which has two wide beaches ideal for swimming and water skiing. The medieval town that exists today was primarily planned and constructed by William de Valence, Henry III's half-brother, who was made Lord of Pembroke around 1264. Little remains of the castle except the gateway and some of the curtain wall. Since 1878, this has been the home of Tenby Museum. The town's art gallery has an important collection of works with local association, in particular Gwen and Augustus John.

### Dylan Thomas Boathouse
**Laugharne.**
**Tel: (01267) 234567 or (01994) 427420.**
Acclaimed worldwide as one of Wales' leading heritage and visitor attractions, the Boathouse contains original writings and furnishing, audio and visual presentations and an art gallery. Laugharne is the "heron-priested" on which Thomas based his play Under Milk Wood.

### Colby Woodland Garden
**Nr. Stepaside. Tel: (01834) 811885.**
This 8 acre woodland garden is set in a tranquil and secluded valley with one of the best collections of rhododendrons and azaleas in Wales. There is also a walled garden with gothic style gazebo and herbaceous borders.

### Dinefwr Park
**Llandeilo. Tel: (01558) 823902.**
The park as it is today took shape after 1775, when the medieval castle, house, gardens and deer park were fully integrated into a breathtaking landscape.

### Llanerchaeron
**Nr. Aberaeron. Tel: (01545) 570200.**
Set in the beautiful Aeron valley, Llanerchaeron is a rare surviving Welsh gentry estate. The principal house was designed by John Nash and built in 1794-96 along with a model range of domestic and farm buildings.

### Pembrokeshire Islands of Skomer & Grassholm
**For information and bookings contact:**
**Dale Sailing Co., Brunel Quay, Neyland, Milford Haven.**
**Tel: (01646) 601636.**
The pride of Pembrokeshire must surely be its gem-like offshore islands of Skomer and Grassholm. Skomer has cliffs covered with guillemots, kittiwakes and razorbills, while Grassholm is so densely populated with gannets that seen from afar the island is transformed into a snow covered peak.

### Tudor Merchant's House
**Tenby. Tel: (01834) 842279.**
A late 15th century country town house in which

a successful Tudor merchant would have lived. Furnishings recreate the atmosphere of the period and there are remains of early frescoes on three interior walls.

# GLAMORGAN

The capital of Wales, Cardiff, is of course the focus of Glamorgan. It is home to the National Museum of Wales, theatres like the Sherman and the New Theatre, The Welsh National Opera, The Welsh Folk Museum, Cardiff Castle and St. David's Hall. It has some of the best shopping in Britain and miles of parkland.

### National Museum of Wales
**St. Fagans, Cardiff. Tel: (01222) 555105.**
Treasure house of the principality, the National Museum of Wales' headquarters at the heart of Cardiff's civic centre boasts fine displays which include paintings, silver and ceramics, shells, zoological artefacts and dinosaur skeletons.

### Welsh Folk Museum
**St Fagans, Cardiff. Tel: (01222) 555105.**
Situated in 100 acres of parkland, this is one of Europe's leading open-air museums featuring dwellings ranging from an elegant castle to the humble cottage of a slate quarry worker. Galleries focus on the social and cultural life of Wales.

# GWENT

Since the late 18th century Chepstow has been a popular centre for visiting the magnificent scenery of the Wye Valley, a long stretch of which is now a designated Area of Outstanding Natural Beauty. For hundreds of years, Chepstow was the major port of south east Wales. Its castle, situated on the cliffs overlooking the River Wye, defends what was once one of the most vital crossings between England and Wales. Chepstow Museum reveals the rich and varied past of this ancient town. Wine trading, shipbuilding, and salmon fishing are among the town's many industries featured in displays within atmospheric settings.

Further north along the English border, is Monmouth. Geoffrey of Monmouth wrote his "The History of the Kings of Britain" here in the Benedictine Priory in the 12th century. The

Nelson Museum recalls the exploits of Charles Rolls, the co-founder of the Rolls Royce company, who lived in Monmouth. The museum also contains a unique collection celebrating the life and death of Admiral Nelson.

Set in the pastoral heartland of Gwent, on the edge of Wentwood Forest, Caerwent is the only walled Roman civilian town in Wales. There are sites of several temples within the town. Caerleon, meanwhile, was one of three principal military bases in Roman Britain. It possesses the only extant remains of a Roman legionary barracks on view anywhere in Europe. The amphitheatre is also an impressive feature. Newport is Wales's third largest city after Cardiff and Swansea. The museum and art gallery give good insights into the formation of the area.

### Caerphilly Castle
**7m N of Cardiff.**
This vast 13th century fortress is one of Europe's finest medieval strongholds and has a famous leaning tower.

### Monmouth Castle
**Monmouth.**
Henry V was born in this castle in August 1388. A 13th century fortified gateway on the Monnow Bridge was built as an outer defence to the castle, and is the only monument of its kind surviving in Britain.

### Penhow Castle
**By Wentwood Forest.**
Wales's oldest lived-in castle, with a history spanning 860 years. It was here that William de St. Maur founded the famous Seymour family.

### The Taff Trail
A specially constructed cycleway and footpath that runs from Cardiff Bay to the heart of the Brecon Beacons National Park.

### Tintern Abbey
**Tintern.**
The Abbey was founded in 1131 by Walter de Clare, Lord of Striguil, as a Cistercian monastery but was brought into ruins by Henry VIII's Dissolution of the Monasteries in 1536. Stone from the Abbey was taken to construct other buildings and can be seen for example in the fabric of the Anchor Hotel.

### Tredegar House
**Outskirts of Newport.**
The best example of a late 17th century house in South Wales.

# GWYNEDD

On the Northern coast of Wales, Llandudno is an excellent example of an unspoilt Victorian seaside resort. Its pier, opened in 1878, stretches an impressive 2,295 feet into the Irish Sea. The town offers a wide choice of accommodation, fine shops and entertainment from the North Wales Theatre. Visitors can take in the Great Orme Mines, which date from the Bronze Age, for an underground tour and audio-visual presentation. West of the Great Orme Headland, on the wooded banks of a broad estuary, Conwy Castle throws out a ring of medieval town walls. The castle and town walls were built by Edward I between 1283 and 1289. Inside, the ground floor of the Chapel Tower contains a colourful and informative exhibition about castle chapels and a life-size tableau. Visitors can walk along the town walls and admire breathtaking views of the Conwy estuary, the Great Orme and Snowdonia. Betws-y-Coed, situated at the meeting point of three valleys (the Lledr, Llugwy and Conwy), is a popular touring centre for Snowdonia. Caernarfon lies on the traditional route to and from Ireland, via the Menai Strait and Anglesey. The castle and town were built by Edward I as part of his bid to encompass the kingdom of Gwynedd. The Maritime Museum in the town, tells of the later history when boats sailed regularly from Caernarfon to New York with slate. On the Isle of Anglesey, the resort of Beaumaris has a 13th century castle and 15th century early Tudor house in the main street. It is a yachting centre and is excellent for fishing.

### Aberconwy House
**Conwy.**
The only house in Conwy that survives from the 14th century. The stone and timber building is a remarkable example of a merchant's house of the period.

### Anglesey Sea Zoo
**Brynsiencyn, Anglesey. Tel: (01248) 430411.**
Most comprehensive aquarium in Wales, showing

huge collection of marine life in natural seascapes. Visitors can walk through a wreck, watch fierce conger eels and pick up sealife from touch tanks. Children's adventure trail.

## Bangor Cathedral
**Bangor.**
St. Deiniol established a church in Bangor in the 16th century. He later became archbishop and his church therefore became a cathedral.

## Bardsey Island
The island where 20,000 saints are said to be buried and where Merlin is supposedly imprisoned in a building of glass.

## Bodnant Garden
Set on the side of a valley above the River Conwy, the garden has spectacular views of Snowdonia. With terraces, a laburnum walk and splendid collections of rhododendrons, magnolias, camellias and other woodland plants.

## Caernarfon Air World
**Caernarfon Airport, Dinas Dinlle, Caernarfon. Tel: (01286) 830800.**
Snowdonia Pleasure Flights are a holiday highlight. Visitors can fly in Cessna or vintage de Havilland Rapide over mountains, castles and coastline of Snowdonia. The museum has planes, helicopters, a cinema and over 200 model aircraft. Children's adventure playground.

## Dolbadarn Castle
**Llanberis.**
A castle of the Welsh princes, situated on the banks of the Padarn and Peris lakes. It was here that prince Llywelyn imprisoned his brother, Owain Goch, for 23 years.

## Henblas Country Park and Adventure Land
**Bodorgan, Anglesey. Tel: (01407) 840152.**
One of North Wales' oldest properties, Henblas' 200 acres contain all-weather entertainment for the whole family. Undercover play area, guided tours of the manor house and gardens, falconry displays and shirehorse parades, working smithy, cart rides, nature trail and golf driving range.

## Inigo Jones Slateworks
**Tudor Slateworks, Groeslon, Caernarfon. Tel: (01286) 830242.**

Inigo Jones was established in 1861, originally to make school writing slates. Self-guided tour comprises a video, audio commentaries as well as an historical lettercutting and calligraphy exhibition. Tours into the heat of the Victorian slate caverns, locomotives take the visitor through floodlit tunnels on the miners' tramway, while the deep mine 'car' conveys passengers down a 30° underground incline to see the spectacular chambers, tunnels and lake.

## Narrow Gauge Railways of Wales
**Wharf Station, Tywyn. Tel: (01654) 710472.**
Collectively, the eight narrow gauge railways forming the 'Great Little Trains of Wales' are one of the major tourist attractions of Wales.

## Penrhyn Castle
**Bangor. Tel: (01248) 353084.**
A spectacular neo-Norman fantasy castle, designed by Thomas Hopper. It houses an important collection of old masters. The stableblock houses an exciting multi-media exhibition on the estate and the Industrial Railway Museum. The castle is surrounded by extensive pleasure grounds including a Victorian walled garden.

## Plas Mawr
**Conwy.**
The building of Plas Mawr (Great Mansion), commenced in 1576 and finished in 1580 was financed by Robert Wynne of Gwydyr. For 100 years the house was the headquarters of the Royal Cambrian Academy of Art but in 1993 the Academy moved to a gallery next door.

## Plas Newydd
**Anglesey. Tel: (01248) 714795.**
Elegant 18th century house, designed by James Wyatt. It is surrounded by a landscape garden and commands magnificent views of the Menai Straits.

## Portmeirion
The architect, Sir Clough Williams-Ellis, built this fantasy village, incorporating a myriad of styles.

## Power of Wales Museum of the North
**Llanberis. Tel: (01286) 870636.**
The museum takes the visitor on a journey through time with the aid of the most modern

technology. It tells the story of the Celts, the Druids, the Romans, Norman Knights and some of the other famous figures who used their power to shape the face of Wales such as Llywelyn ap Gruffyd and Owain Glyndwr.

### Snowdonia National Park

640 miles of divergent landscape including mountains, lakes, three beautiful estuaries and 28 miles of coastline, make this National Park a stunning place to explore. And of course Snowdon is the highest mountain in England and Wales.

## POWYS

The main touring centre for the 519 square miles of the Brecon Beacons National Park is Brecon. It has its own castle, priory, museum and shopping centre. There are a wide range of inns, guest houses and hotels. Brecon is also a centre for riding and pony trekking and hosts a popular summer jazz festival.

### Centre of Alternative Technology
**Machynlleth. Tel: (01654) 702400.**
A superb attraction for all the family, the centre's five acre display circuit shows working windmills, water power, solar energy exhibits, organic gardens, self-build and low-energy homes. Adventure playground and maze.

### Equilibre
**Abercegir, Machynlleth. Tel: (01650) 511222.**
This Horse Theatre, situated in magical mid-Wales, brings together classical horsemanship, drama, dance, music and poetry in a unique event that appeals to all.

### King Arthur's Labyrinth
**Corris Craft Centre, Machynlleth. Tel: (01654) 761584.**
Involves a boat ride along a beautiful underground river into the huge caverns where the Welsh tales of King Arthur are told with tableaux and stunning sound and light effects.

Photograph: **Bryn Bras Castle, Nr. Caernarfon,** was built at the entrance to Llanberis Valley in 1830 in the Romanesque style around an older structure. See page 170.

# Places of Interest *Northern Ireland*

## COUNTY ANTRIM

The major resort on the coast is Ballycastle, ideally positioned as a base for touring the northern part of the Antrim coast. It has beautiful sandy beaches and some of the best grass tennis courts in Ireland. Since the 16th century it has been the focus of the whole area. It was from the White Lodge at Ballycastle that George Kemp, assistant to Guglielmo Marconi, sent his first radio transmission to Rathlin Island in 1898. Marconi himself later joined Kemp in Ballycastle, and the Marconi Memorial in the town now bears tribute to this great inventor.

For long-distance walkers, the Ulster Way, the age-old footpath which meanders around the Province, covers some of the  most enjoyable scenery both wild and tamed, in Northern Ireland. It is joined by the newer Moyle Way to make a truly wondrous circuit of North Antrim, passing through a number of Forest Parks which are a feature of the area.

There are nine Glens of Antrim: Glenarm, Glencoy, Glenariff, Glenallyeamon, Glencorp, Glendun, Glenshesk, Glentaise and Glenann. Glenariff Forest Park is situated at the top of the valley, with miles of walks and waterfalls. In the park there is a restaurant, small museum and Visitors Centre.

Another popular attraction is the Giant's Causeway. The Causeway is a World Heritage Site. An award-winning Visitor Centre explains the significance of this landscape of basalt columns and also tells the story of the Armada treasure ships which foundered nearby.

Carrickfergus is dominated by its 800-year old castle but it is also the home of Knight Ride, a themed mono-rail designed so that visitors can relive the town's exciting history from 531 AD onwards.

A visit to the county town of Ballymena will lead to Slemish, the volcanic mountain on which St Patrick, it is said, was a boy shepherd.

Deep sea angling boats can be hired from Ballycastle, Balintoy and Cushendall. Rathlin Island has a scuba diving centre which runs frequent trips to explore the 30 or so wrecks around the coast.

Visitors can also try rock-climbing on some of the most difficult cliffs in the British Isles.

### Andrew Jackson Centre
**Boneybefore, Carrickfergus. Tel: (01960) 366455.**
Site of the ancestral home of the 7th US President (1829-37) and hero of the Battle of New Orleans, Andrew Jackson. His parents emigrated in 1765 from Carrickfergus. US Rangers' Centre has an exhibition on the 1st Battalion US Rangers, raised in Carrickfergus in 1942.

### Arthur Ancestral Home
**Dreen, Cullybackey. Tel: (01266) 44111.**
Restored 18th century farmhouse with open flax-straw thatched roof. Ancestral home of Chester Alan Arthur, 21st US President 1881-85. Arthur's father left Dreen in 1815 for America.

### Ballycastle Museum
**Tel: (012657) 62024.**
Folk social history of the Glens in the town's 18th century courthouse.

### The Ballance House
**2m SE of Glenavy. Tel: (01846) 648492.**
Birthplace in 1839 of John Ballance, New Zealand's Prime Minister 1891-93, a pioneer of the welfare state. Tea shop.

### Dunluce Castle
**On A2 E of Portrush.**
Dramatic ruins on a rocky headland. Most of the fortifications date from the 16th and 17th centuries. Visitor Centre.

### Leslie Hill Heritage Farm Park
**1m W of Ballymoney. Tel: (012656) 66803.**
Horse trap and pony rides through an 18th century estate. Deer, ornamental fowl. Garden, lakes, trails. Museum, shop and cafe.

### Rathlin Island Bird Sanctuary
**Boats from Ballycastle. Tel: (012657) 63935.**
Kebble National Nature Reserve, near the West

Lighthouse, is home to the island's main breeding colonies of kittiwakes, razorbills and puffins.

# BELFAST

This robust northern metropolis of nearly half a million people - a third of Northern Ireland's population - is buzzing with vitality as never before. The city and the river front are being transformed. Lagan Weir Lookout Visitor Centre is the place to start exploring the river, docks and shipyards.

Much of the city centre is now pedestrianised and there are plenty of shops, from big-name stores to local craft shops. The downtown area is dominated by City Hall, built in 1903. It has a pristine Portland stone facade and visitors can tour its opulent interior. It is surrounded by many examples of Victorian and Edwardian architecture. There is the Grand Opera House, which can be viewed from the comfort of a 'snug' in the ornate Crown Liquor Saloon across the road.

Other sights include St. Anne's Cathedral, the leaning tower of the Albert Clock, St. Malachy's Church, the Customs House and Clifton House, a former poorhouse in Irish Georgian style. The southern part of the city is good for moderately priced restaurants, pubs and accommodation, as well as shopping and theatre. The Botanic Gardens and Ulster Museum are here too.

Visitors also have easy access to unspoiled countryside. Cavehill Country Park is to the north and there are panoramic views from the Belfast Castle Heritage Centre and the nearby plateau of the Zoological Gardens.

### Arts Council Sculpture Park
**Sranmillis Rd. Tel: (01232)) 381591.**
Works in bronze, steel, wood, iron and ceramics by local sculptors.

### Belfast Castle
**Antrim Road. Tel: (01232) 776925.**
Beautiful Scottish Baronial Castle set on the side of Belfast's Cave Hill. Gardens and Heritage Centre.

### Belfast Zoo
**Antrim Road. Tel: (01232) 776277.**
Also set on the slopes of Cave Hill, the zoo houses over fifty endangered species.

### Colin Glen Woodland Park
**Stewartstown Rd. Tel: (01232) 776925.**
A 200-acre park set at the foot of Black Mountain. There are nature trails and wildlife ponds as well as a Visitor Centre.

### Giant's Ring
**Off B23 1m S of Shaw's Bridge.**
Prehistoric enclosure, over 600 ft in diameter, with a dolmen in the centre.

### Malone House
**Barnett Demesne. Tel: (01232) 681246.**
Elegant Georgian Mansion, set in the parkland of Barnett Demesne in South Belfast. Home of the Higgin Art Gallery.

### Royal Ulster Rifles Museum
**War Memorial Building. Tel: (01232) 232086.**
Contains relics of the Royal Ulster Rifles and its predecessor foot regiments.

### Ulster Museum
**Botanic Gardens. Tel: (01232) 381251.**
Noted for its Irish antiquities, art collections and natural sciences. Treasures from the Armada shipwreck Girona. Shop and cafe.

# COUNTY ARMAGH

Visitors to this county are constantly reminded of its associations with St. Patrick, who founded his first church here in the 5th century. In this land Celtic mythology mingles with Christian history. Emain Macha (Nevan) is an ancient and mysterious fort of Ulster Kings and home of legendary heroes. The Nevan interpretive centre helps unravel history through a series of dramatic visual and interactive experiences. The St. Patrick Trian complex, meanwhile, has exhibits recounting the history of Armagh and the Land of Lilliput exhibition marks Jonathan Swift's links with the area.

Also worth exploring are the County Museum and Planetarium with Astro Park.

The Craigavon waters are excellent for watersports and trout-fishing. Lough Neagh Discovery Centre is also well equipped for water-related activity, centering around Oxford Island. Birdwatchers, ramblers and youngsters are also catered for.

### Ardress
**7 miles W of Portadown. Tel: (01762) 851236.**
17th century house with an 18th century front

and neo-classical plasterwork in the drawing room. Farmyard with livestock. Woodland walk and garden.

### Armagh Friary

Ruins of the longest friary church in Ireland (163ft). Founded by Archbishop Patrick O'Scanail in 1263.

### Cardinal O'Fiaich Heritage Centre
**Cullyhanna, Newry. Tel: (01693) 868757.**

Exhibition on Cardinal Thomas O'Fiaich (1923-90) who was born near here. Photographs, telephone handsets allowing visitors to listen to songs and poems of South Armagh and memorabilia. Research library and coffee shop.

### Gosford Forest Park
**Markethill off B28. Tel: (01861) 551277.**

Gosford Castle is an example of the mock-Norman style. The estate itself has associations with Dean Swift. There are traditional breeds of poultry in open paddocks, a deerpark, ornamental pigeons in a dovecote and 200-year old broadleaved trees.

### Peatlands Park
**7m E of Dungannon. Tel: (01762) 851102.**

Peat faces and small lakes in south west corner of Lough Neagh basin. Outdoor exhibits on peat ecology. One mile trip on narrow-gauge railway. Visitor Centre and shop.

### Royal Irish Fusiliers Museum
**Sovereign's House, The Mall, Armagh. Tel: (0186) 522911.**

Story of the regiment 1793-1968. Exhibits include a soldier's uniform from the Peninsular War and a 1943 Christmas card from Hitler.

### Tannaghmore Gardens & Farms
**Silverwood, Craigavon. Tel: 901762) 343244.**

Victorian and rose gardens. Rare breeds include Irish Moiled, Kerry and Dexter cattle, Soay sheep, Saddleback pigs. Picnic area.

## COUNTY DOWN

When St. Patrick came to Ireland in 432, he meant to sail up the coast to County Antrim where as a young slave, he had tended flocks for six years on Slemish mountain. But strong currents swept his boat through Strangford's tidal narrows and he landed where the Slaney river flows into the lough. Undaunted by this change of plan, Patrick went about his missionary business, starting with Dichu, the local chieftain. Over the next 30 years, Patrick converted the Irish to Christianity. He died at Saul in 461 and was buried in Downpatrick.

### Ark Open Farm
**Newtownards. Tel: (01247) 820445.**

Rare breeds include Vietnamese pot-bellied and Berkshire pigs, Nigerian pygmy goats, Chinese and Pilgrim geese, llama and guanaco. Pets'corner, pony rides. Picnic sites and cafe.

### Butterfly House
**Seaforde. Tel: (01396) 811225.**

Hundreds of free-flying exotic butterflies. Reptiles and insects behind glass. Also maze, viewing tower, nursery garden and play area.

### Castlewellan Forest Park
**Castlewellan. Tel: (013967) 78664.**

Includes the national arboretum, begun in 1740, a three-mile trail around the lake with natural sculptures and Queen Anne-style courtyards. Visitor Centre and cafe.

### Clough Castle
**Clough village.**

Anglo-Norman motte-and-bailey earthwork castle with added stone tower. Offers fine views from the top of the mound.

### Down County Museum
**The Mall, Downpatrick. Tel: (01396) 615218.**

Local Stone Age artefacts and Bronze Age gold on display within a former jail building. Also tells the story of St. Patrick and has a restored 18th century cell block with life size figures of prisoners. Shop, tea room. Nearby is the Mound of Down, where John de Courcy built his first Norman castle.

### Dundrum Castle
**Dundrum village.**

This fine Norman castle was built by John de Courcy in about 1177 and later occupied by the Magennises. Views to the sea and the Mourne mountains.

### Grey Abbey
**East side of Greyabbey village.**

Ruined Cistercian Abbey founded in 1193 by

Affreca, wife of John de Courcy. Parkland setting, medieval 'physick' garden. Visitor Centre.

### Mount Stewart House and Gardens
**SE of Newtownards. Tel: (012477) 88387.**
Boyhood home of Robert Stewart, Lord Castlereagh. Its gardens have an amazing collection of plants, colourful parterres and vistas. Temple of Winds overlooks Strangford Lough.

### Murlough National Nature Reserve
**2m S of Dundrum. Tel: (01396) 751467.**
Sand dune system with heath and woodland surrounded by estuary and sea, rich in botanical and wildlife interest. Guided walks.

### Scarva Visitor Centre
**Main St., Scarva. Tel: (01762) 832163.**
History of the canals in Ireland, including the building of the Newry canal and the history of Scarva.

### Scrabo Country Park
**Nr. Newtownards. Tel: (01247) 811491.**
Scrabo Tower was built in 1857 as a memorial to the 3rd Marquess of Londonderry. Woodland walks, old quarries.

### Tollymore Forest Park
**Newcastle. Tel: (013967) 22428.**
Numerous stone follies and bridges, wildlife and forestry exhibits in barn. Pony trekking, fishing, walks in the Mournes. Lecture theatre and cafe.

### Ulster Wildlife Centre
**Crossgar. Tel: (01396) 830282.**
Learn about wildlife on the wetland, raised bog and meadowland of Tobar Muire monastery. Plants and flowers in Victorian conservatory attract butterflies.

# COUNTY FERMANAGH

Fermanagh is a paradise for fishing, canoeing and other water-based activities. Anglers and walkers often share the waterside paths along the Ulster Way. There are five Lakeland Trails forming a continuous part of the 500-mile Way encircling Northern Ireland.

Enniskillen, one of Ireland's most charming county towns, is a natural hub for excursions. Visitors can see its Watergate and towering Castle, with its museum complex. It also has good restaurants, convivial pubs and high-quality shops.

There are dozens of islands dotted around the Lower Lough region, including Devenish with its round tower and sheep and Boa with its Celtic idols.

### Castle Coole
**1m SE of Enniskillen. Tel: (01365) 322690.**
A perfect example of late 18th century Hellenism with a fine Palladian front, the castle was designed by James Wyatt for the Earls of Belmore and completed in 1798. Inside there are fine furnishings and plasterwork. Mature oak woodland and lake.

### Crom Estate
**3m W of Newtownbutler. Tel: (013657) 38174.**
Over 100 acres of woodland, farmland and loughs, supporting rare plants and abundant wildlife. Walks around the old estate take in the ruins of Crom Old Castle. Visitor Centre, shop and tea room.

### Enniskillen Castle
**Tel: (01365) 325000.**
The castle was once the stronghold of Gaelic chieftains. There are exhibitions on the Maguires, and the landscape and people of Fermanagh. Regimental museum of the Royal Inniskilling Fusiliers and the Fifth Dragoon guards in the castle keep. Shop and cafe.

### Devenish Island, Lough Erne
Famous for its perfect 12th century round tower and ruined Augustinian Abbey. Intricately carved 15th century high cross in graveyard. Small museum.

### Marble Arch Caves
**12m SW of Enniskillen. Tel: (01365) 348855.**
Underground boat trip past stalactites and stalagmites, lasting one and a half hours. Geology exhibitions, shop and cafe.

# NOLTON HAVEN

**Mr. Jim Canton, Haverfordwest,
Pembrokeshire SA62 9NH.
Tel: (01437) 710263.**

St. David's, Nolton Haven Farm Cottages, in the Pembrokeshire National Park is situated beside Nolton Havens' sandy beach which they overlook.
These six stone slate and pine cottages offer discerning guests the ideal situation to enjoy the superb Pembrokeshire coastline. The cottages are fully equipped with colour TV, microwave, fridge/freezer. 30 yards to the beach and 75 yards to the local Inn restaurant. Pony trekking, surfing, fishing, excellent cliff walks, boating and canoeing are all available.

Colour brochure on request.

**Prices range from £130 - £400 per week**

# *Bed and Breakfast*

## Accommodation

# Our World by the Sea

Map Ref. H8

## FOR INEXPENSIVE QUALITY

FEATURED BY **BBC**

Q EXCELLENT

## BEACH MODERN LUXURY HOLIDAY HOME *or Caravan*

With the beach moments from your door. Top Grade 5 Award Park, in an area of outstanding natural beauty. This is a quiet secluded cove and Park with sub-tropical plants confirming Gulf Stream mild climate. Safe bathing, water sports, sea & river fishing. Ramble along the flat coastal strip. The local post office & shop is only 3 min. walk. Nearby restaurants, Bar Snacks, Take Aways, golf, pony trekking, three modern leisure centres, Nature Trails in the Historic Glynllifon Country Park. Tour **beautiful Snowdonia** and the famous Llŷn peninsula, beaches & Portmeirion. Featured by the BBC, Wales Tourist Board & British Holiday Home Parks. Families return to us year after year with the new Dual expressway making the journey so easy. Come & view anytime. All our Accommodation comprises Shower, W/basin & Toilet, 2 or 3 Bedrooms, Remote Control Colour TV, Well Heated, **Free Electric & Gas,** Fridge/Freezer, Cooker, Electric Blanket, Kettle, Hoover, Blankets, Pillows, Crockery, Cutlery, Cooking Utensils. Bring your own sheets, pillow cases & towels or own duvet. Most have **Heated Bedroom,** Microwave & Toaster. **Full Central Heating to 65°** on Request. Some are double glazed. Try a **"Super 12"** Home which is 20% more spacious. Park next to your Accommodation. Try a £12 Minibreak Special. Holiday Home Caravans for sale on Park. Phone for our detailed Brochure.

| SUPER 12 20% more spacious | 1998 | Model Type | Sleeps | Bed rooms | MARCH 21/28 | APRIL GF 4 | 11 | BH 18 | 25 | MAY 2 | 9 | BH 16 | BH 23 | 30 | JUNE 6 | 13 | 20 | 27 | JULY 4 | 11 | 18 | 25 | AUGUST 1/8 | 15/22 | BH 29 | SEPTEMBER 5 | 12 | 19 | 26 | OCTOBER 3 | 10/17 | 24 | Model Type |
|---|---|---|---|---|---|---|---|---|---|---|---|---|---|---|---|---|---|---|---|---|---|---|---|---|---|---|---|---|---|---|---|---|---|
| | Week Commencing | | | | | | | | | | | | | | | | | | | | | | | | | | | | | | | | | |
| | Economy older Caravan | A | 4-6 | 2 | 35 | 45 | 65 | 39 | 45 | 49 | 45 | 45 | 99 | 69 | 79 | 89 | 95 | 105 | 119 | 129 | 179 | 189 | 189 | 189 | 139 | 89 | 79 | 65 | 55 | 49 | 39 | 49 | A |
| | Economy Standard older Caravan | B | 4-8 | 2 | 45 | 59 | 85 | 55 | 49 | 59 | 55 | 55 | 149 | 89 | 95 | 105 | 115 | 125 | 149 | 155 | 219 | 229 | 229 | 229 | 199 | 119 | 89 | 75 | 65 | 59 | 49 | 69 | B |
| | Economy Standard older Caravan | C | 6-10 | 3 | 49 | 69 | 99 | 59 | 49 | 69 | 59 | 59 | 159 | 99 | 105 | 109 | 125 | 139 | 159 | 159 | 229 | 239 | 249 | 239 | 209 | 139 | 95 | 79 | 69 | 65 | 55 | 79 | C |
| | Superior Holiday Home | D | 4-8 | 2 | 65 | 89 | 119 | 69 | 69 | 89 | 89 | 95 | 189 | 125 | 139 | 145 | 155 | 165 | 179 | 179 | 259 | 275 | 279 | 279 | 239 | 149 | 119 | 99 | 85 | 75 | 69 | 99 | D |
| | Superior Holiday Home | E | 6-10 | 3 | 69 | 115 | 129 | 79 | 75 | 99 | 95 | 99 | 199 | 139 | 149 | 159 | 169 | 179 | 199 | 199 | 279 | 299 | 309 | 279 | 169 | 139 | 115 | 99 | 89 | 75 | 119 | E |
| | Superior Plus Holiday Home | F | 4-8 | 2 | 69 | 99 | 129 | 79 | 75 | 99 | 95 | 99 | 199 | 139 | 149 | 149 | 169 | 179 | 199 | 199 | 279 | 289 | 299 | 299 | 169 | 139 | 109 | 99 | 85 | 75 | 109 | F |
| | Superior Plus Holiday Home | G | 6-10 | 3 | 75 | 119 | 159 | 85 | 79 | 129 | 99 | 119 | 239 | 159 | 169 | 169 | 189 | 199 | 219 | 239 | 299 | 319 | 329 | 299 | 179 | 159 | 129 | 109 | 95 | 85 | 129 | G |
| | UP MARKET PLUS Holiday Home | H | 4-6 | 2 | 75 | 119 | 159 | 85 | 89 | 119 | 109 | 129 | 229 | 159 | 169 | 179 | 199 | 219 | 239 | 289 | 319 | 329 | 319 | 319 | 189 | 149 | 129 | 119 | 99 | 89 | 119 | H |
| SUPER 12 | Superior Holiday Home | I | 4-8 | 2 | 69 | 115 | 169 | 89 | 89 | 129 | 109 | 119 | 249 | 159 | 169 | 179 | 199 | 219 | 239 | 239 | 289 | 319 | 329 | 329 | 289 | 189 | 159 | 129 | 119 | 95 | 89 | 129 | I |
| SUPER 12 | Superior Holiday Home | L | 6-10 | 3 | 85 | 159 | 219 | 119 | 89 | 159 | 129 | 159 | 279 | 205 | 219 | 229 | 249 | 259 | 279 | 289 | 349 | 369 | 375 | 369 | 339 | 229 | 179 | 159 | 139 | 119 | 109 | 169 | L |

**SUPER SHORT BREAKS – ANYTIME**
3 nights weekend. 4/3 nights midweek, **HALF** weekly price to next £ and add →
Other dates/nights by arrangement. Phone for quotation.
**ANY DATES TO SUIT YOU**

**NO HIDDEN EXTRAS. COME AND INSPECT ANYTIME & CHOOSE**

| 10 | 20 | 45 | 20 | 15 | 25 | 20 | 20 | 45 | 25 | 25 | 25 | 25 | 25 | 25 | 30 | 40 | 45 | 45 | 40 | 25 | 15 | 15 | 30 |

Deposit £33 P.W. and Insurance £1 Nightly for caravan. Cots & High Chairs £2 Nightly each. Dogs £2 Nightly.
Full Central Heating to 65° Request. Over 6 persons £5 per night each. All prices inc. VAT @ 17½%.

### INSTANT HOLIDAYS – ANYTIME
Should you be able to take a last minute break, please ring **01286 660400,** and we will do our best to accommodate you – the same day if you wish.

**MINIBREAK – A few days, week-end or mid-week**
4-6 Berth FROM £10 per night per Holiday Home, Caravan **A Type**
4-8 Berth FROM £12 per night per Holiday Home, Caravan **B Type**
6-10 Berth FROM £14 per night per Holiday Home, Caravan **C Type**

**ANY 4 DAYS** - BEACH MODERN LUXURY HOLIDAY HOME, ANY 3 NIGHTS. Extra nights available. **Model A, B or C. FROM**

| | MARCH BERTH | APRIL BERTH | MAY BERTH | JUNE BERTH | JULY BERTH | AUGUST BERTH | SEPTEMBER BERTH | OCTOBER BERTH |
|---|---|---|---|---|---|---|---|---|
| | 4-6 4-8 6-10 | 4-6 4-8 6-10 | 4-6 4-8 6-10 | 4-6 4-8 6-10 | 4-6 4-8 6-10 | 4-6 4-8 6-10 | 4-6 4-8 6-10 | 4-6 4-8 6-10 |
| | 21 28 35 | 4th 43 49 55 | 2nd 49 55 59 | 6 65 73 78 | 4 89 104 109 | 1 139 159 169 | 5 79 99 109 | 3 39 45 48 |
| | 28 33 33 | 11th 69 79 95 | 9 48 55 79 | 11 95 108 109 | 8 139 159 169 | 12 69 79 95 | | |
| | | 18 38 48 49 | 16 43 48 49 | 23 78 83 88 | 15 129 145 149 | 19 53 63 65 | 17 34 39 43 | |
| | | 25 29 39 39 | 23rd 59 119 125 | 27 78 88 95 | 25 139 159 165 | 26 48 53 55 | 24 55 69 73 | |
| | | | 30 55 65 69 | | 29th 125 155 159 | | | |

### EASTER WEEK-END
8th April to 15th April

| | 4-6 Berth | 4-8 Berth | 6-10 Berth |
|---|---|---|---|
| 2 nights | £39 | £75 | £79 |
| 3 nights | £69 | £79 | £95 |
| 4 nights | £75 | £89 | £99 |

Also "Super 12" 20% more spacious. Villa chalets & Executive Bungalows.

### MAY DAY BANK HOLIDAY WEEK-END
1-8 MAY 4-6 Berth 4-8 Berth 6-10 Berth
Any 3 nights f £49 £75 £79

### WHIT BANK HOLIDAY WEEK-END
21-29 MAY 4-6 Berth 4-8 Berth 6-10 Berth
Any 3 nights f £89 £119 £125

### AUGUST BANK HOLIDAY WEEK-END
28 AUG 2 SEPT 4-6 Berth 4-8 Berth 6-10 Berth
Any 3 nights f £99 £149 £155
Also "Super 12" 20% more spacious. Villa chalets & Executive Bungalows.

**ALSO VILLA CHALET**

## Also FOR SALE
New & one owner Villa Chalets, Holiday Homes & Caravans for sale on the Park.
*Come and inspect anytime*

### HOW TO FIND US

So easy to get to on new A55 Expressway

BEACH HOLIDAY, WEST POINT, THE BEACH, PONTLLYFNI, CAERNARFON, NORTH WALES, LL54 5ET
## PERSONAL ATTENTION, BROCHURE & RESERVATIONS – TEL. 01286 660400

**Bedfordshire**

# POND FARM

**Mrs. Tookey, Pulloxhill, Bedfordshire MK45 5HA.**
**Tel: (01525) 712316.**

Pond Farm is situated opposite the village green in Pulloxhill. Three miles from the A6 and five miles from the M1 Junction 12. we are within easy reach of Woburn Abbey and Safari Park, Whipsnade Zoo, The Shuttleworth Collection of Historic Aircraft at old Warden and 11 miles from Luton Airport. Flitwick mainline station is only three miles away and 45 minutes by train to London.

Pond Farm was built in the 17th Century, mainly arable although we have horses grazing on the meadow land. We also have a resident great Dane.

Accommodation comprises double, twin and family rooms all with washbasins, tea/coffee making facilities, colour TV's, separate toilets and shower rooms. Children welcome at reduced rates. Parking space available. Evening Meals at local Inn.

**Prices from £16.00**

# NETHERTON HOTEL

**Mr. Robert Sousa, 96/98 St. Leonards Road, Windsor, Berkshire SL4 3DA.**
**Tel: (01753) 855508  Fax: (01753) 621627.**
**E.mail: http://www.leisurehunt.com/ad-html/nethert.htm**

This recently refurbished hotel offers a comfortable friendly atmosphere. All rooms are en-suite and have colour TV and tea/coffee making facilities, also available hair dryer and ironing facilities. There is a TV lounge for guests' use. Full English breakfast is served, packed lunches by arrangement. Private car park. Facilities for the disabled. Children welcome. Shop nearby. Only 5 minutes walk from the town centre, train station, Castle, gardens etc.

**Bed and Breakfast from £55 - £110.**

**RAC Highly Commended**                    **AA QQQ Recommended**

# ROCKLANDS GUEST HOUSE

**Mrs. D. J. Hill, The Lizard, Helston, Cornwall TR12 7NX.**
**Tel: (01326) 290339.**

Mixed farm with pigs and beef cattle, Rocklands is situated away from the farm overlooking uninterrupted sea views. There are 4 double rooms, 2 family rooms; 2 toilets, bathroom; dining room with separate tables; lounge with colour TV and sun lounge. Visitors are made to feel at home. The Lizard is well known for its lovely scenery and walks along the cliff tops. Good fishing, safe beaches. Golf at Mullion 5 miles; horse riding. Shop nearby. Children welcome, baby minding. Dogs welcome if well trained. Shingle and sandy beaches 1/2 mile distance. Parking available.
Open Easter to October.

**Bed & Breakfast from £20 per person per night.**

# CORNERWAYS

**John & Andrea Leggatt, 5 Leskinnick Street, Penzance, Cornwall TR18 2HA.**
**Tel: (01736) 364645.**

John and Andrea Leggatt extend a warm welcome to their small, friendly, centrally situated guest house, close to rail/coach stations, car park, Heliport and docks for day trips to Isles of Scilly. Beaches within easy reach. Excellent touring and walking base for exploring West Cornwall. All rooms have a colour TV and tea making facilities. Packed lunch available. Vegetarian menu available. Children welcome. Shop and beach nearby. Dogs welcome. Open all year. **10% discount weeks stay.**

**Bed & Breakfast: Single £15.00, Double £30.00, En-suite £35.00.**
**Optional Evening meal £6.50.**

## "SEAWAYS"

**Mrs. P. White, Polzeath, Cornwall PL27 6SU.**
**Tel: (01208) 862382.**

"Seaways" is a small family guest house, 250 yards from safe sandy beach. Surfing, riding, sailing, tennis, squash, golf all nearby. Two family, one double, one twin and one single room, all with private or en-suite facilities. Sitting room; dining room; children welcome (half price for under 10's). Cot, high chair and babysitting available. Comfortable family holiday assured with plenty of good home cooking. Lovely cliff walks nearby. Padstow a short distance by ferry. Other places of interest: Tintagel, Boscastle and Port Isaac. Open all year round.
**Bed & Breakfast from £17.50 per person or Bed, Breakfast and Evening Meal from £25.50 per person.**
S.A.E. for information

## PENKERRIS

**Mrs. D. Gill-Carey, Penwinnick Road, St. Agnes, Cornwall TR5 0PA.**
**Tel: (01872) 552262.**

Enchanting Edwardian residence with own grounds in unspoilt Cornish village. Beautiful rooms, log fires in winter, good home cooking. Dramatic cliff walks and beaches nearby. Bedrooms: 1 single. 3 double, 1 twin and 2 triple.

Bathrooms: 2 private and 3 public.
Parking for 8.

**Lunch and Evening Meal available.**
**Bed and Breakfast from £13.50 p. p. p. for a double room.**

**ETB 2 Crowns.**

## "BELLA VISTA GUEST HOUSE"

**Mrs. B. Delbridge, St. Ives Road, Carbis Bay, St. Ives, Cornwall TR26 2SF.**
**Tel: (01736) 796063.**

Small, friendly guest house. Highly recommended, satisfaction guaranteed. Colour TV, washbasins, radio intercom and baby listening in all rooms. Personal supervision. Use of lounge. Excellent food. Fresh farm produce. Packed lunches available. Shop nearby. Extensive views of sea and coastline. Beach Nearby. Free parking on premises. No smoking. Fire certificate held.

S.A.E. for brochure.

**Bed and breakfast from £16.00 per person.**

**CCC Registered**

## KINGSWOOD

**Mrs. Culbert, Old Lake Road, Ambleside, Cumbria LA22 0AE.**
**Tel: (015394) 34081.**

Kingswood is ideally situated near the town centre yet off the main road. Good restaurants and shops. Ample parking, well equipped and comfortable rooms with H. & C., tea/coffee making facilities, colour TV, central heating. Single/double/twin and family rooms.

No smoking. Pets welcome. Please telephone for details.

Open most of the year.

 **Commended**

## SUNDIAL HOUSE

**Mrs. Maggie Bowker, 51 Milnthorpe Road, Kendal, Cumbria LA9 5QG.**
**Tel: (01539) 724468.**

Sundial Guest House is located on the A6, 1/4 mile from Kendal town centre. Kendal is a charming and historic town and is a perfect centre for visiting the Lakes. Whether on holiday or business, we offer you a warm welcome. Some en-suite bedrooms, all have TV and tea making facilities. There is a residents' lounge and ample parking. Children welcome. Baby minding facilities. Packed lunches available. Shop nearby.

**Bed and Breakfast prices from £15.50 - £19.50.**

 **Approved**

**Mrs. Cath Blundell, 5 Portland Place, Penrith, Cumbria CA11 7QN.**
**Tel: (01768) 863072.**

A warm welcome awaits you in my large Victorian bed and breakfast offering a high standard of comfort, cleanliness and friendly personal attention at all times. Attractively decorated spacious bedrooms, 1 large en-suite family room sleeps five. All have tea/coffee facilities, colour satellite TV. In-house movies and central heating. Within 4 minutes walking distance of town centre yet only 1 mile from M6 (Junction 40) and A66. Ideal base for touring Lake District, Eden Valley, Scottish Borders or stop over on your journey north or south. On C2C cycle route with secure storage for bikes and free drying for your clothes. Children welcome Packed lunches available.

**Please write or telephone for further information.**
**Bed and Breakfast from £16 - £25 per person. ETB Commended   AA QQQ**

# PALLET HILL FARM

**Mrs. Brenda Preston, Penrith, Cumbria.**
**Tel: (017684) 83247.**

Pallet Hill Farm is pleasantly situated 2 miles from Penrith (B5288) gateway to the Lakes, easy access to the Scottish Borders and Yorkshire Dales. Good farmhouse food and personal attention. Family, double and single rooms. Sitting room, dining room with separate tables. Children welcome. No pets. Car essential, parking. Excellent local bar meals.

**Bed and Breakfast from £10.00**

# ROCKSIDE GUEST HOUSE

**Mr. & Mrs. J.N. Fowles, Ambleside Road, Windermere, Cumbria LA23 1AQ**
**Tel: (015394) 45343**

A Lakeland Guest House full of character, Rockside is RAC Acclaimed and BTA 2 Crowns. Centrally situated two minutes from railway station and the shops and restaurants of Windermere. Car parking for 12 cars. All bedrooms have hot and cold, central heating, colour TV and telephone. Most rooms with private bathroom, tea/coffee making facilities. Breakfast is served from 8.30 - 9.15. Open all year for singles twins, doubles and families to enjoy "the most beautiful corner of England". Help is given to plan a day out in the car or on foot. Maps and routes available.

**Bed and Breakfast from £16.50 - £24.50**

**RAC Acclaimed**                                              **BTA 2 Crowns**

# WINBROOK HOUSE

**Mrs. J.R. Phelps, 30 Ellerthwaite Road, Windermere, Cumbria LA23 2AH.**
**Tel: (015394) 44932.**

Beautifully appointed guest house situated 450 yards from the centre of Windermere, and only 2 minutes drive away from Bowness-on-Windermere, with all the lake facilities, hire boats, steamer trips, tennis, putting, miniature golf and pony trekking.

| | |
|---|---|
| Tea/coffee facilities | Full Central Heating |
| Most rooms with private facilities | Private car park |
| Residents' lounge | Colour TV in all bedrooms |
| Access to rooms at all times | Open all year |

**Bed and Breakfast from £16.50 per person**

**ETB 2 Crowns Commended    RAC Acclaimed**

# Villa Lodge

**John & Liz Christopherson, 123 Cross Street, Windermere, Cumbria LA23 1AE.**
**Tel: (015394) 43318  Fax: (015394) 43318.**

Friendliness and cleanliness guaranteed. Extremely comfortable accommodation situated in peaceful area overlooking village yet 2 mins. from BR/bus stations and local restaurants. All bedrooms mostly en-suite (some 4 posters) have colour TV, tea/coffee making facilities with full central heating. Use of lounge. Wonderful views of Lake and mountains. Packed lunches available. Shop nearby. Safe, private parking. An excellent base for exploring all the Lake District.

**Bed and Breakfast from £18 - £25**

AA  QQQ  👑👑  **Commended**

---

# WEST TITCHBERRY FARM

**Mrs. Yvonne Heard, (F.C.H), Hartland, Bideford, Devon EX39 6AU.**
**Tel: (01237) 441287.**

Completely renovated 18th Century farmhouse, comfortably furnished and well appointed. One family room with washhand basin, one double with washhand basin and one twin bedded room. Shared bathroom and separate shower room. Lounge with log fire and colour television. Hot drink making facilities, dining room with separate tables where excellent home cooking is served using farm produced meat and fresh vegetables, wherever possible. A games room and walled garden are available for guests use. The coastal footpath winds its way around this 150 acre mixed farm situated between Hartland Lighthouse and The National Trust beauty spot of Shipload Bay. Hartland Village 3 miles, Clovelly 6 miles, Bideford, Westward Ho! and Bude approximately 17 miles. Children welcome at reduced rates; cot, high chair and babysitting.

**S.A.E for terms. Bed and Breakfast or Evening meal.** Sorry, no pets.
**Also self catering cottage available from £90 - £320.**

---

# BROCK HOUSE BED & BREAKFAST

**Mrs. E.M. Cracknell, "Brock House" 3 Barton Terrace, Dawlish, Devon EX7 9QH.**
**Tel: (01626) 863311.**

*For your holiday or Mini Break. A welcome awaits you!*
*Bed and choice of English Breakfast.*
*All rooms with CTV, H & C, Shaver point and hot drink facilities.*
*Children welcome, TV Lounge, Parking (Pay and Display Council parking 50 yards nearby).*
*Beach is 700 yards as the crow flys or 5 minutes walk.*

Terms per person from: Weekly £83.00. Nightly £14.50.
Over one night but under one week from £13.50 nightly.

Strictly No Smoking.

**ETB 1 Crown Approved**

## STILE FARM

**Mrs. K. Williams, Starcross, Exeter, Devon EX6 8PD.
Tel: (01626) 890268.**

A 30 acre grass farm, off Dawlish coast road, surrounded by beautiful countryside/farmland. Close to Powderham Castle, Exe Estuary, sandy beach 2 miles. Ideal touring, shopping (Exeter, Newton, Abbot and Torquay) and exploring. Golf, fishing, racing etc. all nearby. Full English breakfast is served in pleasant dining room. Tea making facilities, H & C and shaver points in all rooms. En-suite available. Linen provided. Nice garden with picnic table. Ample safe parking. Children welcome.

**We Are A Non Smoking Establishment**.

Please phone for a brochure.

**Bed and Breakfast from £15.00.**

## BURTON FARM

**Anne Rossiter, Galmpton, Kingsbridge, Devon TQ7 3EY.
Tel: (01548) 561210.**

A working dairy farm also specialising in breeding pedigree sheep. Situated in the South Huish Valley, 1 mile from fishing village of Hope Cove, 3 miles famous sailing haunt of Salcombe. Walking, beaches, sailing, windsurfing, bathing, diving, fishing, and horse riding. We offer traditional farmhouse cooking and home produce. Four course Dinner, Bed and Breakfast. Access to rooms at all reasonable times. Tea/coffee making facilities, many en-suite. Family games room. Guests lounge with colour TV, video and stereo. No Smoking. Open all year, except Christmas. Warm welcome assured. Dogs by arrangement. Small functions catered for (up to 25 people). **Self Catering also available.** Tourist Board inspected.

Details and terms on request. **2 Crowns Highly Commended**

## TREGONWELL RIVERSIDE GUESTHOUSE

**Mrs. J. Parker, 1 Tors Road, Lynmouth, Devon EX35 6ET.
Tel: (01598) 753369.**

Elegant award winning Victorian, former Sea Captains Riverside House, snuggled amidst Oak Wooded Valleys, waterfalls, cascades, romantic beaches in the heart of Exmoor's famous "Olde Worlde" smugglers village. Pretty bedrooms, log fires, garage parking. Spectacular scenery.

**Standard rooms £19.50. En-suite £25.00**

Open all year. Group discounts.

**2 Crowns Commended    AA**

# THE OLD COACH HOUSE HOTEL

**Ed & Merl Stevens, Ottery, nr. Tavistock, Devon PL19 8NS.
Tel: (01822) 617515.**

A lovely 19 century country hotel of character, amid peaceful farming countryside on the edge of Dartmoor, 2 miles from the ancient Stannary town of Tavistock. Superbly converted in 1988 to provide 6 bedrooms all with en-suite bathrooms. **Three bedroom cottage annex and adj. s/c cottage added in 1997.** CTV, telephones, radio, hospitality tray and central heating. A small restaurant and bar provide a warm, friendly atmosphere. Many National Trust Properties, Beauty spots, sporting venues and tourist attractions, in Devon and Cornwall nearby. Ed and Merl would be delighted to arrange a relaxing break at any time of the year. **3 night bargain breaks £64 - £92 per person inc. Bed and Breakfast & Evening meal. Self Catering cottage from £200 - £360 per week.**

---

**Ruth Hill King, Little Holwell, Collipriest, Tiverton, Devon EX16 4PT.
Tel/Fax: (01884) 257590.**

Little Holwell is a traditional Devon Longhouse. The house is centrally heated, with log fires in the winter, and is open all year round except Christmas. An optional evening meal is available, cooked on our  traditional Aga using the best local produce. All bedrooms have hand basins, clock/radio, hairdryer, tea/coffee making facilities. Two rooms are en-suite and one room has a private bathroom. Little Holwell is in a very quite area, only 15 minutes from the M5, situated 1.5 miles from the centre of Tiverton, an historic market town. Local attractions include: Bickleigh Castle, Coldharbour Mill Working Wool Museum and the National Trust properties: Knightshayes Court and Killerton House. This is a non smoking house.

**Bed & Breakfast £16.20 per person. Bed & Breakfast and Evening Meal £25.29 per person.**

---

# GROSVENOR HOUSE HOTEL

**Nigel & Angela Pearce, Falkland Road, Torquay, Devon TQ2 5JP.
Tel: (01803) 294110.**

Licensed Hotel run by friendly Christian family in quiet central position 400m from seafront. Good sized rooms all with en-suite, teamaking and CTV. Use of lounge. Excellent home cooked food with choice of menu at Breakfast and Dinner. Packed lunches available. Shop nearby. Car parking at front of Hotel, 600m from rail station. Open all year including full Christmas programme. Write or Phone for brochure.

**Bed and Breakfast from only £113 per week with reductions for children sharing. Daily prices from £18**

## THE OLD FORGE AT TOTNES

**Jeannie Allnutt, Seymour Place, Totnes, Devon TQ9 5AY.**
**Tel: (01803) 862174  Fax: (01803) 865385.**

A charming 600 year old stone building, converted from Blacksmith and Wheelwright workshops and coach houses. Very close to the River Dart steamer quay, shops and station. Ideally situated for touring most of Devon, including Dartmoor and Torbay coasts. Luxury suites for family/disabled. All suites have colour TV, beverage tray, radio alarm clocks and central heating. Walled gardens, parking. Excellent choice of breakfast menu. Conservatory style leisure lounge complete with whirlpool spa.

**Bed and Breakfast from £26.00 per person en-suite.**

*AS FEATURED ON THE BBC TV'S HOLIDAY PROGRAMME.*

**AA selected QQQQ    ETB Highly Commended**

## LAGUNA HOTEL

**Mr. & Mrs. B.T. Gwynne, Suffolk Road South, Bournemouth, Dorset BH2 6AZ.**
**Tel: (01202) 767022.**

A family run hotel set in two acres of land a few minutes' walk to Bournemouth town centre. Large free car park. All bedrooms are en-suite and have TV and tea making facilities. Lift. Licensed cocktail bar. Come and enjoy our heated indoor swimming pool, spa bath, sauna, solarium; games rooms; children's play area; sun patios. Entertainment every evening (seasonal).

**Terms from £16 per night.**

Discounts for weekly stays. Send for full colour brochure.

**Self-catering holiday apartments also available in same complex.**

## MAYFIELD PRIVATE HOTEL

**Mrs. S. Barling, 46 Frances Road, Knyveton Garden, Bournemouth, Dorset BH1 3SA.**
**Tel: (01202) 551839.**

* Overlooking gardens, bowls, crazy golf, tennis  * Short walk to sea, shops, shows, rail, and coach stations.
* High standard of catering and comfort  * Linen Provided  * Colour TV and tea making in all rooms
* Residential licence  * Some rooms toilet and shower en-suite  * Evening refreshments  * Own keys
* Parking  * Central heating  * Diets on request, vegetarian etc  * Packed lunches available
* Children over 6 years  * Bed & Breakfast £14 - £17 daily  * Room, full English breakfast and four course dinner from £110 - £130 weekly.

**ETB 2 Crowns Commended**                                                    **AA QQQ**

## RAVENSTONE HOTEL

**RAC Acclaimed**

**Mrs. S. Cowan, 36 Burnaby Road, Alum Chine, Bournemouth, Dorset BH4 8JG.
Tel: (01202) 761047.**

**"A beautifully appointed Licensed Hotel"**

* A few minutes walk to beach through delightful pine woods
* Easy reach of town centre * B & B from £16 per person
* Super 4 course evening meal with choice of menu * packed lunches available * Basement games room * Cosy bar
* Full central heating * All bedrooms en-suite with colour TV, Tea making * Linen provided * Radio/Intercom/Child listening
* Free parking

**Mini Breaks & Reductions for Senior Citizens.
AVAILABLE OUT OF SEASON.**

## BEECHMOUNT

**Mrs. P. M. Carter, Birdlip, Gloucestershire GL4 8JH.
Tel/Fax: (01452) 862262.**

A warm wecome awaits you in our family run Guest House. Ideal central base for exploring the beautiful Cotswolds by car or foot. Cheltenham, Cirencester, Stroud and Gloucester all within equal distance. M5 Junction 11a, is only 10 minutes away making us an ideal stop over. All rooms tastefully decorated, some en-suite. With tea and coffee making facilities as well as colour TV's.

Choice of menu for breakfast. Evening meal is by prior arrangement.

**Prices from £15.00 per person.**

**Members and registered with the Heart of England Tourist Board. 2 Crowns Commended**

## BURROWS COURT

**Mr. P. Rackley, Nibley Green, North Nibley, Dursley, Gloucestershire GL11 6AZ.
Tel: (01453) 546230.**

This 18th century mill is idyllically set in an acre of garden surrounded by open country with beautiful views of the Cotswolds. Decorated and furnished in the country style, there are 6 bedrooms all with private bathroom, colour TV, beverage facilities and radio. There is a residents' lounge/bar and a separate lounge on the ground floor. Children and dogs are welcome. Packed lunches available. Parking facilities. Convenient for the M5 junction 13/14. There are severasl good restaurants and pubs in the area

**Bed and Breakfast price per person per night range from £20 - £25 depending on length of stay.**

**AA QQQ**          **RAC Highly Acclaimed**          **ETB 2 Crowns Commended**

# SEVERN BANK

**Mrs. S. Carter, Minsterworth, Nr. Gloucester GL2 8JH.
Tel: (01452) 750357.**

A fine country house set in 6 acres of riverside grounds 4 miles west of Gloucester. Large en-suite bedrooms with superb views, colour TV, tea making facilities and central heating. Non smoking throughout. Ideal for touring Cotswolds, Forest of Dean, Wye Valley and Severn Vale and for viewing Severn Bore tidal wave. Restaurants and shops nearby. Packed lunches available. Parking facilities.

**Bed and continental Breakfast £18.00 - £22.00**

**ETB 2 Crowns Commended**

# FIFIELD COTTAGE

**Mrs. Valerie Keyte, Fosse Lane, Stow-on-the-Wold, Gloucestershire GL54 1EH.
Tel: (01451) 831056.**

Guest house in the centre of the Cotswolds, has attractive garden, situated in private road. Only 4 minutes walk to town centre. Central for places to visit like Stratford-upon-Avon, Burford, Cheltenham, Oxford, Broadway, Evesham, Chipping Camden etc., all within 20 miles radius. Good size bedrooms, family, twin and double. Two rooms en-suite. One with private bathroom. All rooms have satellite TV and tea/coffee facilities. TV lounge, dining room. Cot, with reduced rates for children under 11 years. Established for 22 years, many guests return each year, even from abroad booking one or two nights, then staying for a week. Vegetarians catered for. C.H. Car park. Pets welcome. Closed Christmas.

**Bed and Breakfast from £17.00. En-suite £20 per person.**

# OAKLEA GUEST HOUSE

**Mrs. C. Field, London Road, Hook, Basingstoke, Hampshire RG27 9LA.
Tel: (01256) 762673 Fax: (01256) 762150.**

Oaklea, is a fine Victorian House 1 mile M3 Junction 5, is ideally placed for Heathrow and West Country. Accommodation in single, double and family rooms (some en-suite with TV, some non-smoking). Packed lunches available. Baby minding facilities. Use of lounge. Linen provided. Licensed. Ample parking. Large garden. Dogs welcome.

Write or telephone for further information.

Prices from £25 single to £36 double or twin. Double/twin en-suite £44.

**AA QQQ     RAC Highly Acclaimed.     ETB 2 Crowns Commended**

# EFFORD COTTAGE BED & BREAKFAST

**Mrs. Patricia J Ellis, Everton, Lymington, Hampshire SO41 0JD.**
**Tel: (01590) 642315  Fax: (01590) 641030 or 642315**

Our friendly, award winning Guest House is a spacious Georgian cottage, standing in an acre of garden. All rooms have en-suite facilities together with central heating, full beverage facilities, CTV, telephone, mini fridge, trouser press,heated towel rail, hair dryer and electric blanket. We offer a four course, multi-choice breakfast, with homemade bread and preserves. Patricia is a qualified chef and uses our homegrown produce. An excellent centre for exploring both the New Forest and the South Coast with sports facilities, fishing, bird watching and horse riding in the near vicinity. Shop nearby. Use of lounge. Linen provided. Private parking. Dogs welcome. Sorry no children under 12 years.

**Bed and Breakfast from £21.00 per person, Evening Meal from £15.**

**AA Selected QQQQ      RAC Highly Acclaimed      ETB 3 Crowns Commended**
**Welcome Host                                                                 STB Member**

# THE TANNER OF WINGHAM

**Mrs. D.J. Martin, 44 High Street, Wingham, Canterbury, Kent CT3 1AB.**
**Tel: (01227) 720532.**

Family run restaurant with Bed & Breakfast accommodation, situated in a building dating from 1440, in historic and picturesque village, midway between Canterbury and Sandwick. Ideal for touring East Kent and convenient for docks and Chunnel. Relax in a friendly atmosphere and enjoy optional evening meal from our monthly-changing menu - which includes the largest vegetarian and vegan options in East Kent. Rooms are individually decorated with antique beds and furniture - some rooms heavily beamed. Families welcome, cot available. The many local attractions include historic houses and gardens, wildlife and bird parks.

Don't forget your day trip to the Continent!

**Double room Bed & Breakfast £39-£49. Family room £44-£49. Evening meal £12.50.**

# ELMO GUEST HOUSE

**Mr. Christo, 120 Folkestone Road, Dover, Kent CT17 9SP.**
**Tel: (01304) 206236.**

A warm welcome  awaits you from Patricia, Steve and family. Ideal for overnight stops and short breaks. Catered for late arrivals and early departures. Single, double and family rooms all with CTV, wash basin and tea/coffee facilities. Private parking and Lockup garage available. Situated 2 mins. Dover's Priory station. Town centre, 5mins. from Ferry, Hoverport and Liner Terminal. 10 mins. Channel Tunnel.

**Bed and Breakfast £12.00-£18.00.**

# MALVERN HOTEL

**29 Eastern Esplanade, Cliftonville, Margate, Kent CT9 2HL.**
**TEL/FAX: (01843) 290192.**

Small Private Hotel overlooking the "Oval Bandstand", Lawns and Promenade with panoramic views over the sea. Ideally situated as a base for visiting and touring the area. Take a stroll through Historic **Canterbury** (Cathedral), **Deal** and **Herne Bay** for shopping, together with the **Ports** of **Ramsgate**, **Dover** (Castle) & **Folkestone (Channel Tunnel)**. All within easy reach.

* **En-suite Rooms** (most).
* Colour Television.
* Tea and Coffee making facilities

* **French & Belgium** (and local) Day trips Arranged.
* Close Margate Winter gardens, Indoor/Outdoor Bowls. and amenities. * The beach is 100m.

**ACCESS & VISA Telephone Booking Accepted**
Bed & Breakfast per night; Double/Twin £36 - £42: Family Room £48 - £65; Single £22 - £30.
Reductions for longer stays. (Overnight stays accepted - as available)
Send 'Stamp' only for details. Mention **"PASTIME 1998 GUIDE"** when booking.

---

# THE OLD COACH HOUSE

**Mark & Claire Smith, 50 Dean Street, Blackpool, Lancashire FK4 18P.**
**Tel: (01253) 349195.**

This Historic Tudor style detached House built in 1851 is surrounded by its own award winning gardens in the heart of Blackpool's South Shore, minutes from the promenade, pleasure beach and south pier. All bedrooms are en-suite with TVs, tea/coffee makers, telephone, trouser press, hairdryers etc. Private car park, licensed restaurant, conservatory, deluxe four poster rooms and non smoking rooms available. Open all year round. For further details please contact Mark or Claire.

**Bed and Breakfast from £20.50 and VAT with reduction for children sharing parents' room.**

**ETB 3 Crowns Highly Commended      AA QQQQ Selected      RAC Highly Acclaimed**

---

# DALMACIA HOTEL

**71 Shepherds Bush Road, Hammersmith, London W6 7LS.**
**Tel: 0171-603 2887  Fax: 0171-602 9226.**

We offer comfortable and value for money accommodation.

* All rooms en-suite
* Satellite TV & Remote
* Listed by Les Routiers & LTB

* All major Credit Cards Accepted
* Direct Dial Telephones
* Send for Brochure

**Single £35.00. Double £55.00. Family Room £65.00.**

# Lincoln House Hotel
## London W1

**33 Gloucester Place, London W1H 3PD**

A Georgian hotel of distinctive character
in the heart of London. Close to
Oxford Street shopping,
theatreland and nightlife.
En-suite rooms with all modern comforts
including Satellite TV. Moderately priced,
excellent value and quality service.
Commended by world distinguished
guide books including LTB and the
' "Which ?" publication.'

**Tel: 0171 - 486 7630 (3 lines)  Fax: 0171 - 486 0166**
**For reservations call Free: 0500 007208**

---

 # CENTRAL LONDON - HAVE A NICE STAY

### Close to Hyde Park, Lancaster Gate,
### Main Tube/Bus Routes/A2 Air Bus.

| **OXFORD HOTEL** | **ROYAL COURT APARTMENTS** | **LONDON GUARDS HOTEL** *(formally Gards)* |
|---|---|---|
| 14 Craven Terrace, London W2 3QD. | 51 Gloucester Terrace, London W2 3DQ. | 36/37 Lancaster Gate, London W2 3NA. |
| **Budget rates** Including Continental breakfast. Recently refurbished. All rooms with en-suite toilet/shower, fridge, microwave, crockery/cutlery | Self Catering Apartments. Let on hotel type daily basis. Serviced daily. 24 hr reception/security. Breakfast room and leisure centre. | Fully air conditioned. 40 rooms with bath/WC. hairdryer and fridge. Licensed coffee shop. |
| **Nightly rates** Twins from £65, Triples from £75, Family (sleeps 4) £80. | **Nightly Rates (April/Oct)** from - Studio-standard £90, Superior £105. Apartments 1 bedroom (sleeps 3) £120, 2 bedrooms (sleeps 4/5) £195, 2 bedrooms (5/6) £225. | **Daily rates per room.** Twin rooms from £95 - £135, Triple rooms from £105 - £140, Family rooms (4) rooms from £120 - £150. |
| **Tel: 0171-402-6860** | | **Tel: 0171-402 1101** |

**CENTRAL RESERVATIONS**
**Freephone: 0800-318 798  Tel: 0171-402 5077  Fax: 0171-724 0286**

# *Gower Hotel*

## 129 Sussex Gardens, Hyde Park, London W2 2RX.
## Tel: 0171-262 2262  Fax: 0171-262 2006.

The Gower Hotel is a small family run Hotel, centrally located, within 2 minutes' walk from Paddington and Lancaster Gate stations, also the A2 airbus to and from Heathrow. Excellent for sightseeing London's famous sights and shops, Hyde park, Madame Tussaurd's, Oxford Street, Marble Arch, Buckingham Palace and many more close by.

All rooms have private shower, WC radio, TV (includes satellite and video channels), direct dial telephone and tea and coffee facilities.
All recently refurbished and fully centrally heated.

Single Rooms from £30 - £44
Double/Twin Rooms from £22 - £32
Triple & Family Rooms from £19 - £27
**Prices are per person.**

*Discount available on 3 nights or more if you mention this advert.*

**All prices are inclusive of a large traditional English Breakfast & VAT
Credit cards welcome**

*WE LOOK FORWARD TO SEEING YOU.*

# QUEENS HOTEL

## 33 Anson Road, Tufnell Park, London N7 0RB.
## Tel: 0171-607 4725  Fax: 0171-262 2006.

The Queens Hotel is a large double-fronted Victorian building standing in its own grounds five minutes' walk from Tufnell Park Station. Quietly situated with ample car parking spaces; 15 minutes to West End and close to London Zoo, Hampstead and Highgate. Two miles from Kings Cross and St. Pancras Stations.

**Many rooms with shower and WC, TV
and tea and coffee making facilities.
Singles from £20 - £36
Double/Twins from £28 - £48
Triples and family rooms from £17 per person**

**All prices include full English Breakfast plus VAT.
Children half price.
Discounts on longer stays.
Credit Cards Accepted.**

*WE LOOK FORWARD TO SEEING YOU.*

# DOLPHIN HOTEL

### 34 Norfolk Square, Paddington, London W2 1RT.
### Tel: 0171-402 4943  Fax: 0171-723 8184.

**An ideal hotel for your stay in central London**

Hyde Park, Madame Tussaurds, London Zoo, Oxford Street and many other London attractions are all easily accessible.

**SINGLE ROOM:** £32 - £46
**DOUBLE ROOM:** £42 - £60
**FAMILY ROOMS AVAILABLE.**

All rooms with TV, telephone, refrigerator and kettle. Children welcome. Shop nearby. Baby minding available. Use of lounge. Nice breakfast and friendly service. Parking space. Nearest underground station: Paddington Station.

---

*AN INEXPENSIVE HOTEL IN LONDON SW1*

### 37 Eccleston Square, Victoria, London SW1V 1PB.
### Tel: 0171-828 6812.

Friendly, private hotel, with English character and charm, in ideal, central, quiet location overlooking magnificent gardens of stately residential square (c. 1835) on fringe of Belgrave and not far from Buckingham Palace, Westminster etc.
Comfortable Single, Double, Twin and Family Rooms. Lift.

GOOD ENGLISH BREAKFAST. MODERATE PRICES.
SPECIAL CAR PARKING ARRANGEMENTS. FREE COLOUR BROCHURE.

**HIGHLY COMMENDED in the Considerate Hoteliers of Westminster 1997 Awards.**
**Recommended by Egon Ronay/RAC**

---

# EDGAR HOUSE

### Mr. G. Anstey, 1 Wyndham Park, East Runton, Cromer, Norfolk NR27 9NJ.
### Tel/Fax: (01263) 513045.

Fine peaceful non-smoking accommodation Guest House, out of town, centre of this picturesque village ideal for exploring, walking, touring, local sports, angling and famous cromer crab seafood cafe's, and a magnificent coastline, seaview, car parking, friendly and children welcome, baby minding available, lounge with open fire (in chilly weather), full central heating, dining room. English breakfast menu and superb home cooking with evening meals and vegetarians (optional). Packed lunches available. We have four comfortable bedrooms, one single, one twin, two double or family room some with wash basin plus own luxury bathroom.

**Bed & Breakfast from £10 - £15 and offer special rates for out-of-season breaks.**

# STRENNETH

**Mr. K. Webb, Airfield Road, Fersfield, Diss, Norfolk IP22 2BP.**
**Tel: (01379) 688182  Fax: (01379) 688260  E-mail: ken@mainline.co.uk**

Strenneth is a well established, family run business, situated in unspoiled countryside just a short drive from Bressingham Gardens and the picturesque market town of Diss. Offering first class accommodation. The original 17th Century building has been carefully renovated to a high standard with a wealth of exposed oak beams and a newer single storey courtyard wing. There is ample off road parking and many nice walks near by. All the seven bedrooms, including a Four Poster and an Executive, are tastefully arranged with period furniture and distinctive beds. Each having remote colour television, hospitality trays, central heating and full en-suite facilities. The main house is smoke free and the guest lounge has a log fire on cold winter evenings. There is an extensive breakfast menu using local produce. Ideal touring base. Pets most welcome at no extra charge. Hair and Beauty salons now open. **Bed and Breakfast from £22.00**

# ROSE FARM

**Mrs. J. Durrant, School Lane, Suton, Wymondham, Norfolk NR18 9JN.**
**Tel: (01953) 603512.**

Rose Farm is situated near Attleborough and Wymondham, which are steeped in local history and architectural interest and 5 miles from Snelterton Race Course. Easy access to Norwich, Norfolk Broads, Breckland Forest and coastal resorts. All bedrooms are equipped with TV and tea/coffee making facilities. Packed lunches available. Children and dogs welcome. Baby minding facilities. Use of lounge. Parking space. Open all year, except Christmas.

**Bed and Breakfast from £19.00; reductions for children.**

**ETB Listed Approved**

# THE HAYES

**Mr. F. J. Matthews, Newcastle Road, Corbridge, Northumberland NE45 5LP.**
**Tel: (01434) 632010.**

Spacious, attractive stone-built guest house set in seven acres of grounds.
Single, double, twin and family bedrooms. Lounge and dining rooms.
Open 11 months of the year. Stair lift for disabled guests. Car parking.

**Also self catering properties - three cottages, flat and caravan.**

For brochure or booking, telephone or send S.A.E.

**Bed and Breakfast £16.50 per person per night. Children's reductions.**

**ETB 1 Crown Approved**

*Norfolk*

*Northumberland*

# WILLOW HOUSE

**Mrs. V. Baker, 12 Willow Wong, Burton Joyce, Nottingham NG14 5FD.
Tel: (0115) 9312070.**

Attractive and interesting period house in quiet village location within walking distance of beautiful stretch of River Trent, yet only 4 miles from Nottingham City. Convenient for Trent Bridge, Holme Pierrepont International Watersports Centre, golf course, Sherwood Forest and Historic Southwell Minster. Good local eating. Clean, spacious, comfortable rooms with drinks facilities, TV. French/Italian spoken. Children welcome. Packed lunches available. Shop nearby. Baby minding facilities. Use of lounge. Parking space.

Please phone first for directions.

**Bed and Breakfast from £16.00 per person per night.**

# WRESTLER'S MEAD

**Mrs. B.B. Taphouse, 35 Wroslyn Road, Freeland, Oxford OX8 8HJ.
Tel: (01993) 882003.**

A warm welcome awaits you at the home of the Taphouses. We are conveniently located for Blenheim Palace (10 minutes), Oxford (20 minutes) and the Cotswold (25 minutes). Accommodation comprises one double and one single room, both with washbasins and at ground level. Our first floor family room has its own en-suite shower room with washbasin and toilet. The double and family room each have a colour television. Cot, high chair and babysitting service available. Pets by arrangement. No hidden extras.

**Bed and Breakfast £17.00 - £20.00 per person per night.**

# GORSELANDS FARMHOUSE AUBERGE

**Mrs. B. Jones, Boddington Lane, nr. Long Hanborough,
nr. Woodstock, Oxfordshire OX8 6PU.
Tel: (01993) 881895  Fax: (01993) 882799.**

Gorselands is a beautiful old Cotswold stone farmhouse situated in idyllic countryside with its own grounds of 1 acre. Convenient for Woodstock, Blenheim Palace, North Leigh Roman Villa and Oxford. The house has flagstone floors, exposed beams and a guest lounge. Evening meals are served in the candlelit galleried dining room. Large family/double/twin en-suite rooms available. There is a full size billiards table and tennis court for guests' use (rackets available). Cot and babysitting service.

**Bed and Breakfast from £19.75. Evening Meal from £10.95. Drinks licence.**

**RAC Listed          ETB 2 Crowns Commended          Elizabeth Gundrey Recommended**

## ABBEY RISE

**Jill Heath, 97 Wells Road, Bath, B.A.N.E.S. BA2 3AN.**
**Tel: (01225) 316177.**

Highly recommended Bed and Breakfast accommodation in a Victorian Town House. Attractively furnished rooms offering panoramic views of the city. All with colour TV's, tea/coffee facilities. En-suite rooms available. A short walk to the city centre, rail and coach stations.

**Bed and full English Breakfast from £18.00 per person.**

**B.I.G.H.A.**                                                   **AA QQQ**

## "ELLSWORTH HOUSE"

**Mrs. Margaret Gentle, Fosseway, Midsomer Norton, Bath, N. E. Somerset BA3 4AU.**
**Tel: (01761) 412305.**

Ellsworth is eight miles from Bath and within easy reach of Bristol, Wells, Glastonbury, Cheddar and the heart of the West Country. The guest house is surrounded by an attractive garden with plenty of garden furniture for relaxing. Ample parking space. There are three double/family rooms and two single rooms, all with colour TV's, en-suite, shaver points, electric kettle for early morning tea or coffee. One bathroom, TV lounge. Central heating throughout. Facilities for the disabled. Shop nearby. Dogs welcome. Open all year.

**Bed and full English breakfast from £18 - £22.50 per person. Reductions for children in family room.**

## BRINSEA GREEN FARM

**Mrs. Delia Edwards, Brinsea Lane, Congresbury, nr. Bristol, North Somerset BS49 5JN.**
**Tel: (01934) 852278.**

**Quality Self Catering Apartment. Bed and Breakfast with en-suite.**

Brinsea Green is a 500 acre dairy beef and sheep farm, situated at the end of a quiet country lane surrounded by open fields. Easy access from M5 Exit 21, A38 and Bristol Airport. Built in 18 century the farmhouse still has many of its original features including inglenook fireplaces and bread-oven. The accommodation comprises two en-suite rooms and two with basins sharing a bathroom. All with hot drinks facilities. The historic towns of Bath, Bristol and Wells, the natural wonders of Cheddar and Hookey Hole are close by.

**Bed and Breakfast from £20.00 per person.**

## PANBOROUGH BATCH FARM

**Mrs. Pamela Borthwick, Panborough, Nr. Wells, Somerset BA5 1PN.**
**Tel: (01934) 712882.**

Panborough, near Wells. Bed and Breakfast in superb accommodation in lovely old 17th century farmhouse, surrounded by beautiful scenery. Every comfort and choice of breakfast. Central for Glastonbury, Cheddar, Bristol, Bath, Minehead, Burnham and Wookey. Close to old Inn. Packed lunches if requested. Use of lounge. Parking space. Beach 8 miles away.

**Bed and Breakfast from £15.00 - £16.00 per person.**

Open all year.

## HUNGERFORD FARM

**Mrs. Sarah Richmond, Washford, Watchet, Somerset TA23 0JZ.**
**Tel: (01984) 640285.**

Hungerford Farm is a comfortable 13th century farmhouse on a 350 acre mixed farm. Situated in beautiful countryside on the edge of the Brendon Hills and Exmoor National park. Within easy reach of the North Devon Coast, 2.5 miles from the Bristol Channel and Quantock Hill. 3/4 mile from Somerset Railway. Open all year. Marvellous country for walking, riding and fishing on the reservoirs. Stabling available for own horses. Family room and twin-bedded room; with TV, bathroom, shower, toilet; own lounge with TV and open fire. Children welcome at reduced rates, cot and high chair. Sorry, no pets.

**Bed and Breakfast from £16.00 evening drink included. Reductions for longer stays.**

## MILL LANE HOUSE

**Peter & Sarah Fuente, Slindon, Arundel, W. Sussex BN18 0RP.**
**Tel: (01243) 814440.**

Magnificent views to the coast. Situated in beautiful National Trust village on South Downs. Direct access to many miles of footpaths; superb bird watching locally, also Pagham Harbour and Amberley Brooks. Easy reach of Arundel Castle, Goodwood, Chichester with Roman Palace, Cathedral and Festival Theatre. Beaches 6 miles. Excellent pubs within easy walking distance. Central heating, log fires. All rooms en-suite and with television. Facilities for the disabled. Children welcome. Packed lunches available. Baby minding. Parking space. Dogs welcome.

Weekly terms available.

**Bed and Breakfast from £20.00 per person per night**

## AMBLECLIFF HOTEL

**Mr. C. Kelman, 35 Upper Rock Gardens, Brighton, Sussex BN2 1QF.**
**Tel: (01273) 681161  Fax: (01273) 676945.**

This stylish hotel, highly recommended as the place to stay when in Brighton by a national newspaper and two television programmes, has been awarded the AA's coveted Select QQQQ, only given to 2 or 3 hotels in Brighton and RAC's Highly Acclaimed, for quality and customer satisfaction. Excellent location, close to the seafront, with historic Brighton, the Conference Centre, Royal Pavilion and the Marina only a stroll away. All double, twin and family rooms are en-suite. Individually designed rooms with four poster and king size bed.

Best in its price range for excellent service. Children over 5 years.

**Bed and Breakfast from £20.00.**

**A Non-Smoking Hotel**          **RAC Highly Acclaimed**          **AA selected QQQQ**

## CAPRICE GUEST HOUSE

**Jane French, Bonnetts Lane, Ilfield, Crawley, Sussex RH11 0NY.**
**Tel: (01293) 528620.**

Caprice is a small family run guest house offering quality accommodation at affordable prices in a warm and friendly atmosphere. Ideally situated five minutes from Gatwick in a rural country lane. Tea/coffee and TV in all rooms, en-suite facilities and guest lounge. Children of all ages welcome. Easy access to M23/M25.

**ETB Commended**

## CLEAVERS LYNG COUNTRY HOTEL

**Church Road, Herstmonceux, East Sussex BN27 1QJ.**
**Tel: (01323) 833131  Fax: (01323) 833617.**

This family run hotel in the heart of East Sussex is set in 1.5 acres of landscaped gardens with views to the South Downs. All bedrooms fully en-suite with central heating and tea/coffee facilities. Home cooked food served in the Oak beamed restaurant featuring inglenook fireplace. Residents' lounge. Lounge bar. Fully licensed. Within easy reach of Eastbourne and Bexhill and numerous historical houses and castles.

**Bed and Breakfast £55.00 per room per night**
**(based on two people sharing)**

# DENE HOTEL

**Mr. V. P. Venayak, 38-42 Grosvenor Road, Newcastle-upon-Tyne, Tyneside NE2 2RP.
Tel: 0191-281 1502  Fax: 0191-281 8110.**

Fully licensed, centrally heated. Hot and cold, TV, Radio clocks, hair dryers and tea/coffee making facilities. Guests' lift. Lounge, packed lunches available, facilities for the disabled. Children welcome. Dogs allowed. Parking space.

Bed and Breakfast (single) from £25.50
Bed and Breakfast (double) from £47.50
Dinner £7.50

**3 Crowns Commended**

# THE COACH HOUSE

**Mrs. R. Hancock, Snowford Hall Farm, Hunningham, nr. Leamington Spa,
Warwickshire CV33 9ES.
Tel: (01926) 632297  Fax: (01926) 633599.**

The Coach House is set in a 200 acre mainly arable working farm. The House stands on elevated ground overlooking the peaceful surrounding countryside. Rooms (1 double, 2 twins) are centrally heated, have tea/coffee making facilities. Baby minding and packed lunches available. Children welcome. Parking space. A comfortable lounge with colour TV awaits the visitor. A full English breakfast is served. There are excellent pubs and restaurants nearby. Warwick, Stonleigh Park, Exhibition centre, Sky Blue Centre, Stratford-upon-Avon and the Motor Museum are all nearby.

Restricted smoking. Open all year except Christmas and New Year.

**Bed and Breakfast from £19.00**

# HAYBURN WYKE GUEST HOUSE

**Alan & Dawn Curnow, 72 Castle Road, Salisbury, Wiltshire SP1 3RL.
Tel/Fax: (01722) 412627.**

Situated by Victoria Park $\frac{1}{2}$ mile from City Centre, Cathedral (a walk by the River Avon) and Old Sarum, 3 miles Wilton House and 10 miles from Stonehenge. Full English breakfasts. Some rooms with en-suite facilities. All rooms with hot and cold water, television and tea/coffee making facilities. Children welcome. Shop nearby. Baby minding. Use of lounge. Car parking. Guide dogs only.

**Bed and Breakfast from £18.00.
CREDIT CARDS ACCEPTED.**

**AA QQQ  RAC Accredited**

## WHITFIELD HOUSE HOTEL

**Adrian & Sue Caulder, Darnholm, Goathland, North Yorkshire YO22 5LA.**
**Tel: (01947) 896215.**

On the fringe of Goathland in the beautiful North York Moors, we are ideally situated for walking or touring the National Park. The North York Moors Railway is close by and Whitby and the coast just nine miles away. A former 17th century farmhouse - Whitfield House Hotel offers a warm and friendly atmosphere with personal attention and superb country cuisine. We have nine attractive cottage-style bedrooms (all with en-suite bathrooms), with hairdryer, teamaker, radio, telephone and colour TV. Central heating throughout. Bar lounge and TV lounge. Children welcome. Packed lunches available. Shop nearby. Use of lounge. Parking space. Dogs allowed. Open all year. For brochure write to proprietors.

**Prices from £26.00 - £28.00**          **ETB 3 Crowns Commended**

## BRIMHAM GUEST HOUSE

**Mrs. Judy Barker, Silverdale Close, Darley, Harrogate, Yorkshire HG3 2PQ.**
**Tel: (01423) 780948.**

With beautiful views across The Dales and a warm friendly atmosphere, the Brimham Guest House is situated in the heart of Nidderdale, convenient for Dales, Harrogate, York and Skipton. All our rooms are en-suite with tea/coffee making facilities and full central heating. TV and sun lounge. Full English breakfast served in the private dining room.

**Bed and Breakfast £17.50 - £20.00 per person per night.**

## WHEELGATE GUEST HOUSE

**Mrs. Jean A. Tomlinson, 7 Kirkgate, Sherburn-in-Elmet, Leeds, Yorkshire LS25 6BH.**
**Tel: (01977) 682231.**

Wheelgate Guest House is easily accessible in the pleasant village of Sherburn-in-Elmet on the B1222 road only 3 miles off the A1, 20 minutes drive from York, Selby or Leeds. Easy access to M62 and M1 motorways. The house is Olde Worlde with central heating throughout. Colour TV, wash basins and tea/coffee making facilities in all rooms. Guest lounge and dining room. Excellent home cooking. Packed lunches available. Shop nearby. Private car parking. Children and pets welcome. Open all year. Licensed.

Terms on request.

**Bed and Breakfast prices from £18.00 - £25.00 per person per night.**

# Howgill Lodge

**Ann & Bernard Foster, Howgill Lodge, Barden, Skipton, Yorkshire BD23 6DJ.
Tel: (01756) 720655.**

Howgill Lodge Barn is a 17c Barn tastefully converted to 4 characterful en-suite rooms. Overlooking Dales scenery in the heart of Wharfdale on the Duke of Devonshire's Bolton Abbey Estate. A perfect centre from which to explore the Dales or just relax in comfort. Excellent home cooking with friendly service.

**ONCE EXPERIENCED YOU WILL RETURN.**

---

## THE NEW INN MOTEL

**Mrs. Birkinshaw, Main Street, Huby, York, Yorkshire YO6 1HQ.
Tel: (01347) 810219.**

The New Inn Motel is in the Idyllic village of Huby (twixt York and Easingwold). York is 15 minutes by car, 40 minutes by bus and 10 minutes to park and ride. The Motel is in an ideal centre for York, the east coast, Scarborough, Harrogate, Ripon, Heriot and Heartbeat country, the North York Moors and the Yorkshire Dales. The bungalows are purpose built. All en-suite, central heating, colour TV and hospitality tray. Partial facilities for the disabled. Children welcome. Parking space. Dogs allowed.

**Special 2 and 3 day breaks throughout the year.
Bed and Breakfast from £22.50 per person per night.**

**AA Listed**

---

## YORK LODGE GUEST HOUSE

**Mr. W. Moore, 64 Bootham Crescent, Bootham, York, Yorkshire YO3 7AH.
Tel: (01904) 654289.**

Your hosts extend a warm welcome to their family-run Guest House, situated just ten minutes walk from the city centre attractions.

* Full central heating
* En-suite bedrooms available
* Colour TV and tea/coffee making facilities
* Freshly cooked full English breakfast
* All major credit cards accepted
* Children welcome

**Bed and Breakfast from £16.00 per person. Off season Breaks on request (minimum two nights).**

Please write or telephone Joe or Margaret, anytime.

# DALESCROFT

**Iris & Dennis Blower, 10 Southlands Road, York, Yorkshire YO2 1NP.
Tel: (01904) 626801.**

∗ 10 minutes walk to City and Race Course
∗ En-suite available
∗ All rooms with tea/coffee facilities and colour TV
∗ Children welcome
∗ Packed lunches available
∗ Dogs allowed
∗ Low Season Breaks from £18.00 per person per night (min 2 nights)
∗ Bed and Breakfast from £13.00 - £20.00
∗ Evening Meal available - £8.00

**ETB Listed Commended**

# CLIFTON VIEW GUEST HOUSE

**Mrs. Carol Oxtoby, 118/120 Clifton, York, Yorkshire YO3 6BQ.
Tel/Fax: (01904) 625047.**

Victorian style family-run guest house overlooking attractive village green. 12 minutes walk to city walls and tourist attractions. All rooms have wash basin, colour TV and tea/coffee making facilities. Most rooms have a shower cubicle. En-suite available. Full central heating. Private car park. Children and pets welcome. Use of lounge. Baby minding available. Parking space. Evening meals by arrangement.

S.A.E. for brochure.

**Bed and Breakfast from £13.00 - £18.00 per person.**

# WELLGARTH HOUSE

**Mrs. Helen Butterworth, Wetherby Road, Rufforth, York, Yorkshire YO2 3QB.
Tel: (01904) 738592/738595.**

A warm welcome awaits you at Wellgarth House, ideally situated in Rufforth (B1224) 3 miles from York and 1 mile from the ringroad, A1237. Also convenient for 'park and ride' into York city. This country guest house offers a high standard of accommodation with en-suite **Bed and Breakfast from £18**, all rooms have complimentary tea/coffee making, colour TV. Excellent local pub, 2 minutes walk away provides lunches and dinner. Large private car park. Dogs allowed. Telephone or write for brochure. Access/Visa accepted.

**AA Listed    ETB 2 Crowns**

# ROWANTREE FARM

**Mrs. B. Tindall, Danby, Whitby, Yorkshire YO21 2LE.
Tel: (01287) 660396.**

Rowantree Farm is situated in the heart of the North Yorks Moors. It is a large stone built old farmhouse with panoramic moorland views. It is a working farm comprising 120 acres. It is set in ideal walking country and is also close to the coast. The Moors Information Centre is close at hand where trained staff are always willing to hand out information on the whole of the North Yorks Moors. There are 3 bedrooms: 1 twin, 1 double and 1 family. There is a spacious residents lounge and separate dining room with colour television. Children are welcome and babysitting can be arranged.

Ample car parking space.

**Bed and Breakfast from £15.00. Evening Meals provided on request, £7.50.
Discounts for weekly bookings.**

**St. John's Road, St. Helier, Jersey, Channel Islands.
Tel: (01534) 887666  Fax: (01534) 880746  Freephone:
0500-242393.**

*51 YEARS OF HAPPY HOLIDAYS*

Comfortable hotel and self-catering apertments in an ideal location overlooking the town of St. Helier. Well situated for exploring the beautiful Island of Jersey. All rooms are furnished in a modern style and include full en-suite facilities, colour TV, radio, direct dial telephone, hairdryer and tea making facilities. The hotel is well known for its good food and service.

**Room rates from £27.00 per night. Bed and Breakfast half board available. Short breaks welcome.
Packages inclusive of airfare are available from £199.00 (min. 3 nights).**

JERSEY TOURISM GRADED    **AA 2 Star**

**Jersey Tourism top graded
"Three Diamond"**

**Mrs. Angela Jeffrey, Greve D'Azette, St. Clement,
Jersey C.I. JE2 6SA.
Tel: (01534) 22861  Fax: (01534) 69668.
E-mail: jjeff10693@aol.com**

Angela & John offer a warm welcome to the Playa D'or Guest House. All 15 Bedrooms are comfortably furnished and have en-suite showers or bath, TV, clock/radio's, hairdryers & Tea/Coffee facilities, some rooms have sea views. There is a south facing terrace, a comfortable breakfast room & guest lounge overlooking the sea. The Playa D'or has a private residential bar license, and its own car parking for guest use only. Golf, tennis and squash is all close by, as are two nice restaurants. The main town of St. Helier is 1 mile or 10 mins walk away. We are also on a main bus route.

**Open from Feb/Nov inclusive, Tariff from £17.00 - £28.00 on a Bed & Breakfast basis.
ALL MAJOR CREDIT CARDS ACCECPTED**

# Bed and Breakfast
## *Accommodation*

## CHAPELBANK HOUSE HOTEL AND RESTAURANT

**Mrs. Douglas, 69 East High Street, Forfar, Angus DD8 2EP.
Tel: (01307) 463151.**

Elegant town house with four luxurious bedrooms.
This family run hotel offers first class cuisine. Ideally situated for golf,
fishing, shooting, hillwalking and visiting the Glens and castles
of Angus. Facilities for the disabled. Children over 12 welcome.
Packed lunches available. Shop nearby. Baby minding. Use of lounge.
Linen provided. Parking space.

**Bed and Breakfast from £36.00 - £55.00 per person per night.**

**STB 4 Crowns Highly Commended**

# CAIRNDOW STAGECOACH INN
## & Stables Restaurant

COMMENDED

Douglas and Catherine Fraser extend a warm welcome in the best traditions of Scottish hospitality, at one of the oldest coaching inns in the Highlands. The inn is delightfully situated just off the A83 on the upper reaches of Loch Fyne in Argyll. It presents to the visitor a haven of sparkling views, high mountains and magnificent woodlands and rivers. We offer excellent accommodation in 14 bedrooms in a relaxed country atmosphere. All rooms are en-suite with central heating, radio & TV., direct dial telephones and tea/coffee making facilities. There is a residents lounge, sauna, sunbed and a multi-gym. In our friendly bar and lounge you can sample many malt whisky's and enjoy a chat with the locals. Two deluxe bedrooms with 2 person spa baths and king size beds.

Bed and Breakfast from £28 - £30, Deluxe £50 per person. ALL MAJOR CREDIT CARDS ACCEPTED. Bed, Breakfast and Evening Meal £285 weekly.

**Douglas & Catherine Fraser, Cairndow, Argyll PA26 8BN**
**Tel: (01499) 600286  Fax: (01499) 600220**

# DUNIRE GUEST HOUSE

### Anne Cameron, Glencoe, Argyll.
### Tel: (01855) 811305.

Family run Guest House in historic village of Glencoe. Ideal base for touring West Coast, climbing and walking. All rooms have colour TV, en-suite and tea/coffee facilities. Drying room. Private car park.

For further details contact Anne Cameron.

**Bed and Breakfast from £15.00 - £19.00.**

## STB 2 Crowns Commended

# Southfield Hotel

An elegant Georgian house quietly located in its own grounds convenient to town centre, beach, bowling greens, tennis courts, golf courses (5 miles from Turnberry). 40 cover restaurant. Lounge bar. Open all day. Food all day. Open to non-residents. Children welcome. All bedrooms ensuite. Group and weekly discounts available. Douglas, Jean, Craig and all the staff guarantee a homely welcome and comfortable stay.

**Southfield Hotel, The Avenue, Girvan KA26 9DS.**
**Tel: (01465) 714222.  Fax: (01465) 712405.**

# THE LAURELS

### Mrs. Angus, 29 West Road, Irvine, Ayrshire KA12 8RE.
### Tel: (01294) 278405

Privately run Bed and Breakfast centrally situated in small town of Irvine. Close to Shopping Mall, Harbour area and Beach, Maritime Museum and eating places. Royal Troon Golf Course, Irvine Golf Course and many others. 30 mins train services to Glasgow. 15 mins from Ayr. TV, tea/coffee facilities. 1 Twin, 1 Double, 1 Single.

**Bed and Breakfast from £12.50 - £16.00 per person per night.**

## BUSBIEHILL GUEST HOUSE

**Mr. & Mrs. P. Gibson, Knockentiber, Kilmarnock KA2 0DJ.
Tel: (01563) 532985.**

Busbiehill is the oldest guest house in the area with many recommendations from home and abroad. This homely county guest house with panoramic views, overlooks Irvine to the Arran hills. Very central for overnight stays to Erskine Bridge A52 or ferry to Arran. Kilmarnock is one of the best planned towns with every facility for tourists and homely friendly people, also suitable for a relaxed holiday for golfers with 22 courses within easy reach. We are 1 mile from A71, Glasgow 22, Largs 22, Edinburgh 63. Nearest station Kilmaurs. 5 double with 2 en-suite, 3 twin bedded, 5 bathrooms with toilet upstairs. Ladies, gents toilet downstairs. No pets. Children welcome over 5 years. Tea making facilities.

**Bed and Breakfast from £15.00**

## WOODBURN COTTAGE

**Mrs. Catherine Harris, Woodwynd, Kilwinning, Ayrshire KA13 9DP.
Tel: (01294) 551657  Fax: (01294) 558297.**

A warm welcome awaits you at 'Woodburn Cottage', a former 19th century farmhouse, now in the centre of Kilwinning. Easily accessible from Glasgow and the south and well placed to visit Burns' country, golf courses, country parks and west coast beaches. Also ideal for the ferry to Arran (15 mins). Accommodation consists of 2 twin and 1 single bedroom all with colour TV, tea/coffee facilities. There is also a lounge for guests to relax in during the day. Large mature garden (a little piece of countryside in the centre of town). Private parking.

**Scottish Tourist Board Commended Listed**

## SOROBA GUEST HOUSE

**Mrs. Irene Archibald, Blairingone Village, By Dollar, Clackmannanshire FK14 7NU.
Tel/Fax: (01259) 742785.**

Peter and Irene welcome guests old and new to their Guest House. Set in beautiful open countryside with magnificent views of the Ochil Hills. Ideally located in central Scotland on the A977 Kincardine Bridge - Perth Road with over 100 golf courses within easy reach. We offer high standard accommodation. Most bedrooms with en-suite facilities. Delicious home cooking. Ideal for golfing, walking or simply relaxing.

Please contact the above address for further information.

# WOODLEA HOTEL

**Mr. & Mrs. McIver, Moniaive, Dumfriesshire DG3 4EN.**
**Tel: (01848) 200209  Fax: (01848) 200412.**

Robin and Sandi McIver invite you to stay at their friendly country Hotel set amid beautiful scenery. Comfortable rooms: en-suite facilities, tea/coffee, hairdryer, bedroom bar. Varied menus: tasty, hot and plenty! Heated indoor pool, sauna, golf and more FREE! Ideal centre to explore this undiscovered part of Scotland on quiet roads.

Weekly, mini-break, daily, O.A.P. and longer stay rates quoted.

---

## THE FOREST HILLS HOTEL
### The Square, Auchtermuchty, Fife  Tel/Fax: 01337 828318

STB
COMMENDED

Traditional Inn in the square of this Royal Burgh (once a busy weaving centre surrounded by forests and hills which were a favourite venue for deer and boar hunting by noblemen visiting nearby Falkland Palace). Ten bright bedrooms with central heating, teamakers, TV. radio and all facilities. Cocktail bar, comfortable lounge, bistro, intimate restaurant. 2 day break from £80.

**Leisure facilities available in sister Hotel, The Lomond Hills Hotel, Freuchie, nr Glenrothes**
**Tel: 01337 857329/857498**

---

# SCOTSTARVIT FARM

**Mrs. Morna Chrisp, by Cupar, Fife KY15 5PA.**
**Tel: (01334) 653591.**

Make this unusually quiet and scenic spot a must to enjoy the stunning unspoilt views over and beyond the bonnie home of Fife to the Lomond Hills, the Lidlaws and the Grampian Mountains. Nestled beside National Trust places of interest our traditional working farm is a few minutes from the country town of Cupar and the historic village of Leeres with St. Andrews 10 minutes drive away. Comfortable characteristic farmhouse where you can gaze on panoramic views whilst enjoying a hearty breakfast or preparing for bed. The wonderful scenery is endless. Perfectly situated for golfing or touring. Open all year. Realistic rates.

**STB 2 Crowns Commended**

## CLAN MACDUFF HOTEL

**Mr. Angus Fyfe, Achintore, Fort William, Inverness-shire PH33 6RW.
Tel: (01397) 702341  Fax: (01397) 706174.**

This family run hotel overlooks Loch Linnhe, two miles south of Fort William. Situated in its own grounds in a quiet peaceful location ideal for touring and experiencing the rugged mountains and enchanting coastline of the West Highlands. All bedrooms have colour TV, hairdryer and hospitality tray, most with private facilities. The hotel offers great value hospitality.

Colour brochure on request.

**Bed and Breakfast with Evening Meal from £32.00 per person.**

## BEINN ARD

**Mrs. Patricia Jordan, Argyll Road, Fort William, Inverness-shire PH33 6LF.
Tel: (01397) 704760.**

Situated in a quiet street in an elevated position just above the town with panoramic view of Loch Linnhe and surrounding hills. Only five minutes' walk from town centre, pier and station. This is a most attractive wooden house which has recently been extended and renovated to a high standard. We offer our guests a pleasant informal and comfortable base from which to view the magnificent local scenery and experience the many attractions Fort William has to offer. One family room en-suite, one double room en-suite, one twin room and two single rooms; all have colour TV and tea/coffee making facilities. Children welcome. Dogs allowed. Packed lunches available. Open 28th December to mid October. Skiers welcome.

**STB 2 Stars Commended**  **Bed and Breakfast from £15.00 - £18.50**

*Letterfinlay Lodge Hotel*

**Mr. & Mrs. Forsyth, Spean Bridge, Inverness-shire PH34 4DZ.
Tel: (01397) 712622.**

Set in a magnificent situation on the shores of Loch Lochy. Family run former shooting lodge offering traditional Scottish fayre. Pleasant motoring in the glorious highland scenery, 20 minutes from Fort William, the hotel is an excellent centre for visits to places of interest in the Western Highlands. Surrounded by hills and mountains, many of which are Munroes, there are numerous chances for climbing, pony-trekking, shooting, boating, fishing and hill walking.

*Enjoy Our Highland Hospitality.*

**RAC    AA**        ALL MAJOR CREDIT CARDS        **STB 3 Crowns**

# HIGH PARK FARM

**Mrs. J.E. Shaw, Balmaclellan, Castle Douglas, Kirkcudbrightshire DG7 3PT.
Tel: (01644) 420298.**

A warm welcome awaits guests at High Park. This 171 acre family run farm is situated by Loch Ken, popular for fishing and boating. 12 miles from Castle Douglas and 2 miles from New Galloway. All bedrooms have washbasins, shaver points, tea/coffee making facilities plus central heating. Our comfortable sitting/dining room has colour TV and on colder nights an inviting log fire.
**Contact the above address for further information.**

 **Commended**

# THE ROSSAN

**Mr. & Mrs. Bardsley, Auchencairn, Castle Douglas, Kirkcudbrightshire DG7 1QR.
Tel: (01556) 640269.**

3 bedrooms. C.H. tea/coffee hair dryer in room.
Clothes dried overnight. Meat/Vegetarian/Vegan/Gluten free always available.
Home grown/organic fruit and veg whenever possible.
We have our own hens. Ample parking, large garden.
Dogs welcome free.
Two nearby beaches, wonderful walks, Bird Watches paradise.

**Please phone for brochure.**

# KIRKLAND HOUSE
# 42 ST. VINCENT Crescent,
# GLASGOW G3 8NG

### S.T.B. Listed Commended

*City Centre guest house located in Glasgow's little Chelsea, a beautiful Victorian Crescent in the area known as Finnieston offers excellent rooms most with en-suite facilities, full central heating, colour TV, tea/coffee makers. The house is located within walking distance of Scottish Exhibition Centre, Museum-Art Gallery and Kelvingrove Park. We are very convenient to all City centre and West End facilities also only ten minutes from Glasgow's International Airport. Our house is featured in the Frommers Tour Guide and we are also Scottish Tourist Board Listed Commended. St. Vincent Crescent runs parallel with Argyle Street and Sauchiehall Street in the central Kelvingrove area near to Kelvingrove Park and Art Gallery Museum.*

### ROOM RATES
*Singles £25-£35 Twins/Doubles £50-£70*
TEL: 0141-248 3458 FAX: 0141 - 221 5174
MOBILE NUMBER 0385 924282
*Members of the "Harry James Appreciation Society".*
*Ask for details.*

# HOLLY HOUSE

### S.T.B. Listed Commended

Holly House is a mid terrace Early Victorian building standing in a tree lined terrace with ample car parking in the city centre South area. Local places of interest being Burrell Gallery, Rennie Mackintosh Art Lovers House, Ibrox Football Stadium. The SECC, airport and city centre are all within 5-10 minutes whilst the Ibrox Underground is just around the corner. The accommodation is set out as singles, twins, doubles and a few large family rooms  all well appointed with central heating, colour TV's etc. Being privately owned, you are assured a warm welcome awaits you.

**Holly House recommends**
**Dorsey's Restaurant at 195 Brand Street. 0141-419-0589.**

Room rates to include breakfast:
Singles £20-£30
Twins/Doubles £36-£60
Family £60-£70

**Contact: Peter N. Divers,**

**Holly House, 54 Ibrox Terrace,**

**Glasgow G51 2TB.**

**Tel: 0141-427 5609. Fax: 0141-427 5608. Mobile 0850 223500.**

**E-mail: PND.HOLLYdor@Gisp-net**

"Member of The Harry James Appreciation Society"

# NUMBER THIRTY SIX

36 St. Vincent Crescent, Glasgow G3 8NG.
Tel/Fax: 0141-248 2086
Mobile: 0585 562382

S.T.B. Listed Commended

*Number Thirty Six is a Victorian House situated on the edge of Glasgow City Centre close to the West End. We are just a stones throw away from the S.E.C.C., the Art Galleries and Museum and some of the best restaurants, pubs and shops in Glasgow. Our bedrooms are tastefully and individually decorated with all rooms having private facilities. Room rates include a continental breakfast served in the comfort and privacy of your own room.*

TARIFF
SINGLES £25-£35
TWINS/DOUBLES £46-£60

# BLAIR MAINS FARM

**Mrs. Moira Ireland, Harthill, Lanarkshire.**
**Tel/Fax: (01501) 751278.**

Attractive farmhouse on small farm - 72 acres,
immediately adjacent to M8, Junction 5 motorway.
Ideal centre for touring.
Edinburgh, Glasgow, Stirling 30 minutes' drive.
Fishing (trout and coarse) and golf nearby.
Clay pigeon shooting.
1 family, 1 double, 2 twin and 4 single rooms. Bathroom, sitting room, dining room
and sun porch. Central heating. Children welcome - babysitting offered. Pets accepted.
Car essential - parking. Reduced rates for children.
Open all year.
**Phone for further information.**

WE'LL KEEP A WELCOME
IN..............
THE HILLSIDE HOTEL
& RESTAURANT

3 Queen's Road,
Dunbar,
East Lothian EH42 1LA.

Overlooking the East Lothian coast at the fishing port of Dunbar, close to the Lammermuir Hills and 30 minutes from Edinburghs 2 golf courses (1 championship course). Sea fishing, walking and climbing, scuba diving a short walk from hotel. 18 golf courses within 20 minutes drive from hotel.
Excellent restaurant and bar. Parties of 10 or more-Dinner (table d'hote), Bed and Breakfast from £37.50pp.
Some rooms en-suite.

**Brochure & Reservations from Joan & Barrie Bussey**
**Tel/Fax: (01368) 862071**

# THE HAYMARKET HOTEL

**Mrs. Pauline Brock, 1 Coates Gardens, Edinburgh, Lothians EH12 5LG.**
**Tel: 0131-337 1775.**

A small family run hotel in the west end of Edinburgh and only 10 minutes walk from Princes Street. All rooms en-suite with tea/coffee making facilities and colour television.

Evening Meals on request. Packed lunches available. Children welcome. Baby minding facilities. Use of lounge. Dogs allowed. Open all year and fully licensed. A warm welcome awaits you. Horse riding on request.

*Lanarkshire*

*Lothians*

# CRAIGHALL FARMHOUSE

**Mrs. Mary Fotheringham, Forgandenny, Bridge of Earn, Perthshire PH2 9DF.
Tel: (01738) 812415.**

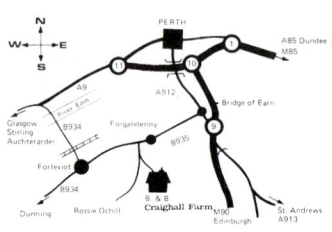

Situated in the lovely Earn Valley we offer true Highland hospitality in our farmhouse only 6 miles south of Perth and half a mile west from Forgandenny on the B935. The farm is within easy reach of Edinburgh, St Andrews, Glasgow and Pitlochry. Golf, tennis and swimming nearby, hill walking and lovely scenery. Accommodation includes rooms with private facilities and en-suite; tea/coffee making facilities; guest lounge with colour TV. Children welcome. Sorry no pets.

**Bed and Breakfast from £16.50**

**STB 3 Crowns    AA & RAC Highly Acclaimed**

## John & Barbara Riley, Tyndrum, by Crianlarich,
## Perthshire FK20 8RY.
## Tel: (01838) 400219  Fax: (01838) 400280.

A family-run hotel set in beautiful mountain scenery on the West Highland Way near the Junction of the A82 and A85. Accommodation in 5 single, 5 double, 7 twin and 4 family bedrooms. 18 private and 1 public bath/shower rooms.

**Term per person:** Bed and Breakfast £20 single standard. £28.00 all en-suite rooms, with Evening Meal £40.00. Open all year.

## STB 2 Crowns Approved

# DUISARY

**Miss I.M. MacKenzie, Strath, Gairloch, Ross-shire IV21 2DA.**
**Tel: (01445) 712252.**

Enjoy true Highland hospitality at Duisary, a modernised traditional croft house with all mod cons. All bedrooms have wash hand basins (one en-suite) and tea making facilities. There is central heating throughout. The house, on the outskirts of the village, has magnificent views of the sea, the beach and the Skye and Torridon hills. Here one can relax and enjoy some of the finest scenery in Scotland. The picturesque golf course (9 hole) is 1 mile away. The world famous Inverewe Gardens are close by. There are ample opportunities for sea and loch fishing and walking. Children welcome. Use of lounge.
Open April - October
**Bed and Breakfast from £16.00. Evening meals are not provided but there are several good eating places nearby.**

**STB 2 Crowns Commended**

# DRISEACH

**Mrs. J. MacLennan, Plockton, Ross-shire IV52 8TU.**
**Tel: (01599) 544362.**

Magnificent views of the Cuillin mountain range over the sea to Skye also of Applecross mountains. Many beautiful walks. Arts and crafts from traditional knitwear to jewellery and paintings nearby. There is also 40 acres of 19th century exotic gardens and woodland trails. 1 double, 1 family and 1 twin rooms. Packed lunches available. Shop nearby. Baby minding facilities. Parking space. Dogs allowed.

**Bed and Breakfast £16 - £25**

# Trade Description Act

The accommodation mentioned in this
guide has not been inspected, and the publishers rely
on information provided.

The publishers have every confidence in their advertisers but cannot be
held responsible for the accuracy of the descriptions published.

# INCHYRA GRANGE HOTEL

**Grange Road, Polmont, Falkirk, Stirlingshire FK2 0YB.
Tel: (01324) 711911  Fax: (01324) 716134.**

Set in 44 acres of private grounds, the original country house that was Inchyra Grange has been delightfully extended and now offers every modern amenity including the superb Pelican Leisure Club with its swimming pool, resident beautician and gym. A choice of dining is always available from traditional fayre in the Pelican Grill or a la carte dining in the hotel restaurant. Inchyra is ideally situated for touring Central Scotland. Many beautiful and interesting places can be reached easily from the hotel, including Stirling Castle, Loch Lomond and the Trossachs, Linlithgow Palace and of course the exciting and historic cities of Edinburgh and Glasgow.

**Dinner, Bed and Breakfast from £52 per person.**
**STB 4 Crowns Commended**

## GARYBUIE GUEST HOUSE

**Mrs. G.J. Wilson, 4 Balmeanach, Glenhinnisdale, Snizort,
Portree, Isle of Skye IV51 9UX.Tel: (01470) 542310.**

Situated in the glen by the side of the River Hinnisdal. Turn off A856 at Hinnisdal Bridge, over cattle grid to telephone box next to house. Accommodation can be provided in two family rooms, one double, one twin, one single. Warm family house, home cooking. Dinner on request. Tea/coffee trays and TV all rooms. Lounge. 10 minutes Uig ferry to Outer Hebrides. River fishing, walking Trotternish Ridge, scenic area. Children from the age of 2 years welcome. Parking and Packed Lunches available.

**Bed and Breakfast from £15.00. Bed, Breakfast and Evening Meal from £25.00. Brochure available.**

**STB Approved Listed**

# Bed and Breakfast
## *Accommodation*
### Wales

## MIN Y GAER HOTEL

**Mrs. Rita Murray, Porthmadog Road, Criccieth, Conwy LL52 0HP.**
**Tel: (01766) 522151  Fax: (01766) 523540  E-mail: minygaer.hotel@virgin.net**

A pleasant licensed hotel, conveniently situated near the beach with delightful views of Criccieth Castle and the Cardigan Bay coastline. Ten comfortable centrally heated rooms (9 en-suite), all with colour TV and tea/coffee facilities. Use of lounge. An ideal base for touring Snowdonia. Reduced rates for children. Private parking.

**Bed and Breakfast from £19.50 - £22.50**

**AA Recommended    RAC Acclaimed**
**WTB 3 Crowns Highly Commended**

## CUCKOO MILL FARM

**Mr. & Mrs. D.D. Davies, Pelcomb Bridge, St. David's Road,**
**Haverfordwest, Pembrokeshire.**
**Tel: (01437) 762139.**

Cuckoo Mill Farm is a 320 acre mixed farm in central Pembrokeshire, two miles out of Haverfordwest on St. David's Road. The sea is six miles away. The accommodation is warm and comfortable . The bedrooms are well appointed with H. & C., tea making facilities and hair dryer. Linen provided. Children welcome - cot, high chair and baby sitting provided. Pets allowed. Parking space. Meal times arranged to suit guests. All poultry and meats are home-produced. There are peaceful country walks on the farm and a small trout stream. Six miles from nearest beach coastline. Open all year for Bed & Breakfast or Bed, Breakfast and Evening Dinner.

**Reductions for children and senior citizens.**

## CHURCH FARM GUEST HOUSE

**Rosemary & Derek Ringer, Mitchel Troy, Monmouth, Gwent NP5 4HZ.
Tel: (01600) 712176.**

A spacious and homely 16th century former farmhouse with oak beams and inglenook fireplaces, set in large attractive garden with stream. An excellent base for visiting the Wye Valley, Forest of Dean and Black Mountains. All bedrooms have washbasins, tea/coffee making facilities and central heating; most are en-suite. Own car park. Terrace, barbecue. Colour TV. Non smoking. We also offer a programme of guided and self-guided walking holidays and short breaks. Separate "Wysk Walks" brochure on request.

**Bed and Breakfast from £18.00 - £21.00 per person. Evening meals by arrangement.**

**WTB 2 Crowns Commended    AA QQQ**

## HEATHER DEAN

**Mrs. V. Boycott, Maryland, nr. Trellech, Monmouth, Monmouthshire NP5 4QJ.
Tel: (01600) 860566  Fax: (01600) 860566.**

Heather Dean is situated in the heart of the Wye Valley. Set in its own grounds, a warm welcome and cosy atmosphere welcome our guests. All rooms Tourist Board highly commended. Bedrooms all en-suite, colour TV, tea/coffee etc. centrally heated. Cosy sitting room, sunny breakfast room. Noted for its breakfasts. Evening meal by arrangement. Children welcome, packed lunches available. Linen provided. Parking space. Wonderful scenery and walks on the doorstep. Easy access to Monmouth, Chepstow, Symonds Yac and the Forest of Dean. Plenty of local pubs serving good food.

**Prices from £25.00 - £35.00**

## MAES-Y-GWERNEN HOTEL

**Mrs Elsie Moore, School Road, Abercraf, Swansea Valley, Powys SA9 1XD.
Tel: (01639) 730218  Fax: (01639) 730765.**

Country hotel in private grounds, all rooms have en-suite bathroom, colour TV, tea/coffee facilities, telephone etc. Bar, lounges, dining room, conservatory and gardens exclusively for use of guests. Children welcome. Dogs allowed. Packed lunches are available and there are available and there are facilities for the disabled. Winners of AA and Tourist Board National Awards and of the Les Routiers UK Guest House of the Year 1995. Situated in Abercraf village on southern edge of Brecon Beacons National Park. "Everything about Maes-Y-Gwernen is delightful, and I give superb ten out of ten marks for all" - A Satisfied Guest.

**Bed and Breakfast from £26 - £33. Major Credit Cards Accepted.**

**AA QQQQ  Les Routiers Selected  RAC Highly Acclaimed  WTB 4 Crowns Highly Commended**

# *Self Catering*

## Accommodation

**Photograph: Gara Mill, Kingsbridge, Devon.**

# Self Catering
## *Accommodation*

### England

### and the Channel Islands

*Cornwall*

# LOWER KITLEIGH COTTAGE
**Week St. Mary, Bude, Cornwall.**

Pretty listed farmhouse in unspolit country near magnificent coast. Newly renovated but retaining all its charm. Peaceful garden with picnic table and parking. Large sitting room, period furniture, inglenook with free logs, colour TV, fully equipped kitchen: Fridge/freezer, electric oven, washer/dryer, constant hot water. Three bedrooms with duvets and panoramic views. Facilities for the disabled. Electric cooker. Children welcome. Shop 1 mile. Baby minding on request. Dogs permitted. Riding, golf, fishing, safe sandy beaches. National Trust cliffs. Cornish moors. Central heating ensures a cosy stay throughout the year.

**For further details contact:** Tim Bruce-Dick, 114 Albert Street, London  NW1 7NE.  Tel: 0171-485 8976  Fax: 0171-267 7529

**Prices from £175 - £350.**

# TREAGO MILL
**Mrs. Angela Harty, Crantock, Newquay, Cornwall TR8 5QS.**
**Tel: (01637) 830213.**

Treago is situated in a peaceful valley a few minutes walk from lovely sandy Porth Joke Cove, 1 mile from Crantock village and surrounded by magnificent National Trust scenery. Good coastal walks. Near golf, riding, fishing, leisure park, safe bathing and surfing. Good food pub, cafe and shop. Private spacious grounds with well equipped cottage and 3 bungalows. Sleeps 5-6. Ample parking. Personal attention.

**Terms from £116.00 to £378.00 weekly.** July 4th - Aug 29th already full. Colour brochure available on request.

# PENLEE CARAVAN PARK
**Christine & David White, Mousehole, Penzance, Cornwall TR19 6QT.**
**Tel: (01736) 741173.**

Small quiet caravan park and holiday bungalow located along the sea front in the picturesque fishing village of Mousehole which has shops, restaurants, pubs, post office and beaches. Penlee is ideal for a peaceful holiday yet is within easy reach of all activities and amenities. The caravans are fully equipped (except linen) and the bungalow has three bedrooms. Gas central heating and parking.

**Short breaks available on request.**

# PENMARLAM QUAY COTTAGE

## A.M. Oliver, Yeate Farm, Bodinnick-by-Fowey, Cornwall PL23 1LZ.
## Tel: (01726) 870256.

Penmarlam Quay Cottage, overlooking the Fowey estuary, has been carefully
converted from a 14th century barn. With its own quay, slipway and moorings it is
ideal for boating and fishing. Good walks abound over mainly National Trust land.
The Old Ferry Inn is nearby with Fowey just across the river. Dogs are
welcome if well behaved as sheep are kept on the farm.
All modern amenities. Baby minding. Beach 2 miles.

**Prices from £130 - £380 per week.**

# TREGEATH COTTAGE

**Tregeath Lane, Tintagel, Cornwall PL34 0DZ.**
**Tel/Fax: (01840) 770217.**

**2 Keys Approved**

Tregeath is an old modernised detached cottage, built of stone and slate (sleeps 5 + cot), with grass and clothes line. Situated beside a quiet parish road, connected to 50 acres of farmland. Two double bedrooms upstairs, one single room downstairs, all with small eleric fires. Cot and high chair. Bathroom/toilet downstairs; immersion heater; airing cupboard; shaving point. Dining/sitting room with coal grate, electric fire, two night storage heaters, colour TV, kitchen; stainless steel sink, electric cooker, microwave, fridge/freezer, kettle, spin dryer; well equipped. Mains water and electricity on £1 meter. One dog only, no cats. Parking space, car essential. No linen. Near shops 1 mile.

Write to: **Mrs. E. M. Broad, "Davina", Trevillett, Tintagel, Cornwall PL34 0HL.**

# RAMSTEADS

**Mr. G.B. Evans, Outgate, Ambleside, Cumbria LA22 0NH.**
**Tel: (015394) 36583.**

Seven timber lodges on a country estate of 26 acres of natural woodland and open grassland, situated between Ambleside and Hawkshead in central Lakeland and within easy reach of its many attractions. The chalets are furnished and fully equipped for four or six people, providing a base for quiet relaxation or exploring the surrounding villages and countryside. Lettings are normally Saturday to Saturday, but other arrangements may be made if required.

# GREAVES FARM CARAVAN PARK
### Field Broughton, Grange-Over-Sands, Cumbria LA11 6HR.

A small, quiet park, family owned and supervised, beautifully situated in an old farm orchard. It offers peaceful holidays in a pleasant rural setting.The luxury caravans are 4/6 berths, self-contained and fully equipped to high standards. Each caravan has colour TV, refrigerator, calor gas cooker.
**Prices range from £180 - £220 per week**
**British Graded Holiday Parks 4 Ticks**          **ETB Graded**          **Welcome Host**

# CORNERWAYS
### Field Broughton, Grange-Over-Sands, Cumbria LA11 6HR.

A delightful detached bungalow with good all-round lakeland views. Linen, colour TV, fridge/freezer, microwave, cooker. **Prices from £250 -£350 per week**
**Tourist Board Member Graded 3 Keys (Commended)**

**Enquiries/Bookings to:** Mrs. E. Rigg, Prospect House, Barber Green, Grange-O-Sands, Cumbria LA11 6HU. Tel: (01539) 536329/536587

# HIGH DALE PARK BARN.

**Grizedale Forest, Cumbria.**

Newly converted 17th century barn. Two centrally heated units sleeping 8 + 2. Glorious position, secluded valley, superb wildlife, walking.

**Write to:**
**Mr. Peter J.G. Brown, High Dale Park Farm, Satterthwaite, Ulverston, Cumbria LA12 8LJ.**
**Tel: (01229) 860226.**

**Prices from £165.00 - £657.00**

**ETB 3-4 Keys up to Highly Commended**

# THE ULLSWATER CARAVAN, CAMPING & MARINE PARK

**Mr. & Mrs. R.F. Dobinson, Watermillock, Penrith, Cumbria CA11 0LR.**
**Tel: (01768) 486666.**

**SITUATED WITHIN THE LAKE DISTRICT NATIONAL PARK.**

For hire: 6 berth caravans, mains services, W.C. showers. Also Self Catering holiday houses, sleeps 6, all mains services and TV - (available all year round). Tents and tourers welcome, mains electric points available for tourers. Children's playground, shop, licensed bar.

Own lake access one mile.

Caravan Sales.

# DOVE COTTAGE

**Mr. A. Tatlow, Ashview Calwich, Ashbourne, Derbyshire DE6 2EB.**
**Tel: (01335) 324443/324279.**

Modernised 200 year old cottage in Mayfield Village. Comfortably furnished with colour TV, fridge/freezer, automatic washing machine, tumble dryer, microwave and gas central heating.
Convenient for busy market towns, sporting facilities, the Peak District, Alton Towers and much more.

Available for long or short lets, also mid week bookings.

**ETB 4 Keys**

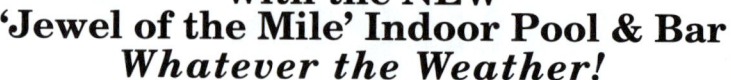

# PARKERS FARM HOLIDAY PARK

**Mr. & Mrs. Parker and family, Ashburton, Devon TQ13 7LJ.**
**Tel: (01364) 652598  Fax: (01364) 654004.**

A friendly, family run farm site, set in 400 acres and surrounded by beautiful countryside. 12 miles to Torbay, overlooking Dartmoor National Park.
Ideal for touring Devon/Cornwall. Perfect for children and pets, with all farm animals, play area and plenty of space to roam. Also large area for dogs. Holidays cottages and caravans fully equipped except for linen. Level touring site with some hard standings. Free showers in very clean, fully tiled block. Laundry room and games room. Small family bar, restaurant, shop and phone.

**GOOD DISCOUNTS FOR COUPLES.**

# WEST TITCHBERRY FARM

**Mrs. Yvonne Heard, (F.C.H), Hartland, Bideford, Devon EX39 6AU.**
**Tel: (01237) 441287.**

Completely renovated 18th Century farmhouse, comfortably furnished and well appointed. One family room with washhand basin, one double with washhand basin and one twin bedded room. Shared bathroom and separate shower room. Lounge with log fire and colour television. Hot drink making facilities, dining room with separate tables where excellent home cooking is served using farm produced meat and fresh vegetables, wherever possible. A games room and walled garden are available for guests use. The coastal footpath winds its way around this 150 acre mixed farm situated between Hartland Lighthouse and The National Trust beauty spot of Shipload Bay. Hartland Village 3 miles, Clovelly 6 miles, Bideford, Westward Ho! and Bude approximately 17 miles. Children welcome at reduced rates; cot, high chair and babysitting.
**S.A.E for terms. Bed and Breakfast or Evening meal.** Sorry, no pets.
**Also self catering cottage available from £90 - £320.**

# SOUTH MOLTON

### Court Green, Bishop's Nympton, Devon.

A most attractive well-equipped, south -facing cottage with large garden, on edge of Bishop's Nympton village, 3 miles from South Molton. Ideal holiday centre - east reach of Exmoor, the coast, sporting activities and places of interest. Children welcome. Sleeps five. 3 bedrooms, 1 double, 1 twin-bedded, 1 single, bathrooms and toilets. Sitting room and dining rooms, large kitchen, C.H., wood burning stove, TV. One mile sea trout/trout fishing on River Mole. Well behaved pets welcome. Parking space. Terms April to October.

**Prices range from £150 - £200**

Please write for further details to:
**Mrs. J. Greenwell, Tregeiriog, nr. Llangollen, Denbighshire LL20 7HU.**
**Tel: (01691) 600672.**

*Devon*

Devon

# GARA MILL

**Mrs. Marcia Green, Slapton, Kingsbridge, Devon TQ7 2RE.**
**Tel: (01803) 7702295.**

Gara Mill offers peace and tranquillity in a riverside setting between Dartmouth and Kingsbridge. There are eight comfortable, two-bedroomed cedar lodges which sleep 5, a large flat in the 16th century millhouse and a cosy cottage. All are well-equipped for self-catering, inc. colour TVs and microwaves. Games room, childrens' play area, laundry, outdoor badminton court. Dogs welcome. Secluded, yet convenient to Slapton Ley Nature Reserve, spectacular coastal walks and beaches, good pubs and restaurants. An excellent base for exploring the quiet, unspoilt world of the South Hams, historic Plymouth or rugged Dartmoor.
Brochure available on request.

# EAST HOOK COTTAGES

### Okehampton, Devon

#### MEMBER OF THE DARTMOOR TOURIST ASSOCIATION

In the heart of Devon, on the fringe of Dartmoor, with woodland surroundings, two comfortably furnished Holiday cottages. One mile north of the A30 at Okehampton, quiet and peaceful, fifty yards in from the country road. Ample car parking space. The accommodation comprises a pleasant sitting room, with a television and log fire. Kitchen with electric cooker and refrigerator. Children welcome. Dogs allowed. Modern bathroom with shaver point. Three bedrooms. Visitors are requested to supply their own bed linen. Electricity by 50p meter.

**Prices range from £95 - £175**

Please write for further details to:
**Mrs. M.E. Stevens, West Hook Farm, Okehampton, Devon EX20 1RL.**
**Tel: (01837) 52305**

# GRANARY FARM COTTAGES

**Granary Farm Cottages, Yeo Lane, North Tawton, Devon EX20 2DD.**
**Write or telephone for a brochure on (01837) 82252**

#### ON THE FRINGE OF DARTMOOR NATIONAL PARK

Luxury accommodation in stone walled cottages, situated between Okehampton and Exeter. Tastefully converted from original Granary barns. Completely surrounded by idyllic country scenery and lovely river walks along the Tarka Trail just 5 miles from the Dartmoor National Park. All cottages have spacious oak beamed living rooms with wood burning stoves, central heating, fully equipped kitchens, bathrooms and showers etc. Within six private acres you will find an indoor heated pool, orchard, paddock, games room, laundry room and gardens. Nearby facilities include superb restaurants, pubs, shops, riding, fishing, golf, cycling routes, tennis and many accessible tourist attractions. Children and well behaved pets welcome. Cottages with 2 and 3 bedrooms. Sleeps 4-7.

**From £230 per week.** Short breaks available.

# SNAPDOWN FARM CARAVANS

**Mrs. M. Bowen, Snapdown, Chittlehamholt, Umberleigh, North Devon EX37 9PF.
Tel: (01769) 540708.**

12 only, 6 berth caravans, in two sheltered adjoining paddocks, in lovely unspoilt countryside, backing onto trees down quiet lane on farm. Well spread out, each with hard standing for car. Flush toilet, shower, colour TV, fridge, gas cooker and fire. Laundry room with washing machine, tumble dryer, iron etc. Outside seats, picnic tables, barbeque. Table tennis. Field and woodland walks. Children's play area in small wood adjoining. Easy reach sea and moors. Well behaved pets welcome.

**Prices from £85 - £225 (includes gas and electricity in caravans)**

**DISCOUNT FOR COUPLES, EARLY AND LATE SEASON.**

Contact above address for an illustrated brochure.

# MANOR FARM HOLIDAY CENTRE

**Mr. R. A. Loosmore, Charmouth, Bridport, Dorset DT6 6QL.
Tel: (01297) 560226.**

Situated in a rural valley 10 mins. level walk to beach. Two and Three bedroom houses and bungalow sleep 4-6. Colour TV, fully fitted kitchens, gardens and parking space.

Also luxury 6 berth caravans with shower toilet, colour TV, gas fire. Full centre facilities include swimming pool, shop, take-away, laundrette and Bar with family room.
Children welcome. Facilities for the disabled. Shop nearby. Linen provided. Dogs allowed.

**Prices from £100 - £450**

S.A.E. for colour brochure

# LANCOMBES HOUSE HOLIDAY COTTAGES

**Carol & Karl Mansfield, Lancombes House, West Milton, Bridport, Dorset DT6 3TN.
Tel: (01308) 485375.**

Four cosy fully equipped cottages in converted barn with panoramic views to the sea four miles away. Set in 10 acres and surrounded by wonderful walking country. We have many pet animals, including horses, ponies, goats, sheep, ducks and chickens. Children and pets are very welcome.

**Prices range from £220 -£460**

**ETB 4 Keys Commended**

*Dorset*

# THE NUTSHELL

**Mrs. S. Hansford, New Road, Hardley, Hythe, Southampton, Hampshire SO45 3NL.**
**Tel: (01703) 842268.**

The accommodation consists of a mobile home in our large wooded garden in the South-East area of the New Forest. Sleeps 2-4, double bedroom and sofa-bed in lounge. Children welcome. All-electric, £1 coin meter. Colour TV, radiators, Kitchenette with cooker and refrigerator, bathroom with bath, basin, WC. Off-road parking. Bed-linen included.
**£80 - £130 per week.** Out of season breaks, fuel for Park-Ray fire included.
*WE REGRET NO SMOKERS OR PETS.*

We are 2 miles from the attractive village of Hythe on Southampton Water with its pier and train, passenger ferry and marina. From the mobile home, walkers can enjoy heathland and woodland walks on adjacent Beaulieu Heath. We are within easy reach of several activity centres, offering a variety of sports and leisure pursuits, including swimming.

Lyndhurst in the heart of the New Forest is only twenty minutes distant by car. Notable local attractions include Beaulieu Motor Museum and Exbury Gardens. Our 2 local beaches are Lepe and Calshot, on the Solent, and there are regular ferry services to the Isle of Wight from Lymington and Southampton. We are well placed for visits further afield, eg. Bournmemouth and the Dorset coast, historic Winchester and the Hampshire Downs, and naval heritage Portsmouth. **Brochure on request.**

# BRIMSTONE COTTAGE

**Mrs. J. Brooke, Nicholson Farm, Docklow, nr. Leominster, Herefordshire HR6 0SL.**
**Tel: (01568) 760346.**

Delightful cottage and bungalow's at this 17th century Working Dairy Farm in the lovely county of Herefordshire. Well equipped units including colour TV, linen hire. Two take wheelchairs, sleeps 2-5. Carp fishing on the farm. Golf course, 2 heated swimming pools, tennis, horse riding and wonderful walking all within 15 mins drive. This is a peaceful valley with lovely views of England as it used to be. Ideal for touring Welsh border, Wye and Severn Valley, Ludow, Malverns and Brecon Beacons. Two theatres and Stratford 90 mins. Pets Welcome.

Send for brochure, stamp appreciated.

# COUNTRY LOVERS RETREAT

### Leominster

Cosy stone cottages for 2-6 people surrounded by large rambling Victorian gardens and woodland. Linen, colour TV and logs. Outdoor swimming pool, croquet, lawn tennis. Glorious unspoilt countryside, black and white market towns, castles, museums. Base for Ludlow, Malverns, Brecons, Wye Valley. **Three night breaks available.** Open all year.

**For colour brochure & tourist map contact:**
Mrs. Ormerode, DOCKLOW MANOR, Docklow, Leominster, Herefordshire. Tel: (01568) 760643.

# WOODCROFT

### Shalloak Road, Broad Oak, Canterbury, Kent.

Situated on the edge of the village, the accommodation comprises 3 bedrooms. Sleeps 6. Gas C/H and cooking. Woodstove. Big garden, orchard, wood adjoining. No pets. No smoking. Well equipped. Parking space. Shop nearby. Children welcome. Gas cooker.

**Prices range from £110 - £125**

**Contact:**
**Mr. R.L.O. Jackson, Cedar Cottage, 50 Shalloak Road, Broad Oak,**
**Canterbury, Kent CT2 0QE.**
**Tel: (01227) 710284**

# 98 COAST DRIVE
### Lydd-on-Sea, Romney Marsh, Kent.

This is a compact family bungalow with uninterrupted sea-views from the front sun lounge along the front of the property. The accommodation can sleep 6 in 3 bedrooms (duvets and linen are provided). The property also comprises an inner lounge with colour television, bathroom, toilet and a fitted kitchen with electric cooker and fridge. The utility area houses a washing machine, freezer and ironing facilities. There are lawns front and rear with garden furniture for relaxing in the sun. Children welcome. Shop nearby.

**Prices from £120 - £255**

Contact: Mrs. F. I. Smith, Holts Farm House, off Coopers lane, Fordcombe, Tunbridge Wells, Kent TN3 0RN. Tel/Fax: (01892) 740338.

# KIRKSTEAD OLD MILL COTTAGE HODGE'S LODGES
**Woodhall Spa, Lincolnshire.**

We offer quality facilities and comfort to ***non-smoking*** families seeking a home from home and a warm welcome for their holiday. Hodge's Lodges properties have every modern convenience including telephone, automatic washer, dishwasher, cot, highchair and free on-site parking. Linen hire available. Open all year. Short breaks available.
This detached, sunny, isolated house is set in farmland beside a quiet river, noted for its fishing. Membership of local leisure club is included. Pets welcome.
**The weekly rates are from £120 - £480**

Please apply to:
**Mrs. Barbara Hodgkinson, Hodge's Lodges, 52 Kelso Close, Worth, Crawley, Sussex RH10 7XH.**
**Tel: (01293) 882008. Fax: (01293) 883352. E-mail: tonyh@sfhg.org.uk**

**ETB 4 Keys Highly Commended**

Norfolk

## NORFOLK
# WINTERTON-ON-SEA

Self-contained ground floor of cottage in centre of quiet seaside village near Great Yarmouth. Fully equipped for self-catering family holiday. One double, one twin and one single bedroom. Sleeps 5 plus cot. Bed linen provided. Pets welcome. Parking space. Beamed sitting room with colour TV. Electric cooker and metered electricity. Secluded garden. Broad sandy beach, good walks along coastal dunes (nature reserve) and close to Norfolk Broads.

**Weekly lettings from Saturdays, May to September from £150 - £310 per week.**

**Please write for details to:**
**Mr. M. J. Isherwood, 79 Oakleigh Avenue, London N20 9JG.  Tel: 0181-445 2192.**

# ALNMOUTH
### Northumberland

This 375 acre mixed arable land and livestock farm has 3 delightful cottages in a quiet setting overlooking the coast and the picturesque village of Alnmouth. Great area for walking, visiting historic castles and towns. Each cottage has 3 bedrooms and can sleep up to 7 people. Log fires, cooking electric cooking and heating, large gardens and ample parking. Dogs by arrangement.

For further details Contact:
**Mr. W.G. Farr, Wooden Farm, Alnmouth, Alnwick, Northumberland NE66 2TW.**
**Tel: (01665) 830342.**

**Prices from £165 - £190**

### ETB 1 Key Approved

# TITLINGTON HALL FARM
**Mrs V. Purves, Alnwick, Northumberland NE66 2EB.**
**Tel: (01665) 578253.**

Three lovely country cottages available for long lets or short breaks. Situated in a quiet and beautiful area with interesting places close by. The cottages can sleep parties of 10 people. They are spacious and very well equipped with central heating, TV, fridge, electric cooker, microwave, washing machine, tumble drier and all linen. Facilities for the disabled. Children welcome. Pets by arrangement.

**Prices from £165 - £295.**

For more information or a brochure please contact the above address.

# WITHYCOMBE FARM

**Mrs. E. M. Stanbury, Winsford, Minehead, Somerset TA24 7AB.**
**Tel/Fax: (01643) 851287.**

Self contained wing of farmhouse, with private lawn. Sleeps 2-6 + cot. Linen provided. Fully centrally heated. Quiet secluded position on a working beef and sheep farm, joining open moorland. Post Office, shop, pub, garage and church in the beautiful village of Winsford. Good central location for touring, walking or riding around Exmoor. Tarr Steps 4 miles. Wimbleball Lake for fishing or sailing 7 miles. Ample parking.

**Terms from £165 including electricity.**

# PANBOROUGH BATCH FARM

**Mrs. Pamela Borthwick, Panborough, nr. Wells, Somerset BA5 1PN.**
**Tel: (01934) 712882.**

Spacious, self contained apartment for 2, part of Grade II 320 year old farmhouse.
Centrally heated and beautifully furnished and decorated.
Attractive kitchen, well fitted, microwave, washing machine. Lounge/Diner. TV/large bedroom,
Inglenook, half tester. Shower room. Garden, wonderful views, complete peace.
Central for Cathedral, Wookey, Cheddar, Bath,
Bristol, riding, fishing, walking and the sea.

**Prices from £155 per week.**

Open all year.

# KNOWLE FARM COTTAGES LTD

**Mrs. Boyce, Knowle Farm, West Compton, Shepton Mallet, Somerset BA4 4PD.**
**Tel: (01749) 890482  Fax: (01749) 890405.**

Four charming cottages. Superbly converted from old barns and furnished to a high standard. Pretty garden with garden furniture to relax in and separate play area for children.
Situated in quiet countryside yet close to Wells, Glastonbury, Bath etc. Good Golf Courses and plenty of interesting family attractions to visit. Regret no pets.

Please telephone for brochure or more information.

**Prices from £150 - £400**

**4 Keys Commended**

# PEKES

## Chiddingly, Halisham, Sussex BN27 4AD.

In grounds of Tudor manor house, up drive of 350 yards with unspoilt views, Pekes offers unique self-catering with exceptional facilities: indoor heated swimming pool, sauna/jacuzzi, solarium, hard tennis. All very well equipped. Children welcome, pets by arrangement.

**Fabulous large Oast House sleeps 7/11, £825 - £1100 per week. Breaks £525 - £675. 3 period cottages sleep 4 to 6, £325 - £630 per week. Breaks £195 - £320.**

Contact: **Eva Morris on 0171-352 8088 or Fax: 0171-352 8125. 124 Elm Park Mansions, Park Walk, London SW10 0AR.**

**Tourist Board Grading 4 to 5 Keys Commended**

# COPES FLAT

## Brook Street, Warwick, Warwickshire.

In Warwick town centre, a peaceful secluded first floor flat with its own entrance and high level garden which is ideal for meals al fresco. Close to Warwick Castle, shops and restaurants in the town. Timber framed sitting/dining room; bathroom with bath and shower; kitchen, electric cooker, washing machine and drier; central heating. Linen provided. Ideal location for Stratford-Upon-Avon, Cotswold villages, Oxford and Worcester. 2 miles from Junction 15 off M40. Parking space.

**Prices range from £150 - £275**

S.A.E. for further details to:
**Mrs. H. Elizabeth Draisey, Forth House, 44 High Street, Warwick CV34 4AX.
Tel: (01926) 401512  Fax: (01926) 490809.**

# "EMBERTON"

## Hunton, Bedale, North Yorkshire.

"Emberton" is a 2 bedroom stone built cottage midway between Bedale & Leyburn. It is conveniently situated for touring both the Yorkshire Dales and North York Moors.

Fully fitted kitchen, electric cooker, microwave, washer/dryer, refrigerator and radio cassette player. Colour television and log fire in lounge. 1 double bedroom, 1 single bedroom including folding bed. Central Heating and electricity included. All linen is provided. Ordinance Survey Maps and walks in the dales are included for your use. Well behaved pets are also welcomed. Open April to October.

**Charges from £175 to £275 per week. For brochure please telephone (01702) 78846.
Contact: Trevor and Wendy Mills, 131 Glendale Gardens, Leigh-on-Sea, Essex SS9 2BE**

---

# BAILE GATE HOUSE HODGE'S LODGES
## The city of York

We offer quality facilities and comfort to ***non-smoking*** families seeking a home from home and a warm welcome for their holiday. Hodge's Lodges properties have every modern convenience including telephone, automatic washer, dishwasher, cot, highchair and free on-site parking. Linen hire available. Open all year.
Short breaks available.
This new semi-detached, luxury town house, with a south-facing balcony, has views of the medieval wall and River Ouse. Walk to all the historic sites and shops.

**The weekly rates are from £250 - £660**

Please apply to:
**Mrs. Barabara Hodgkinson, Hodge's Lodges, 52 Kelso Close, Worth, Crawley, Sussex RH10 7XH.
Tel: (01293) 882008. Fax: (01293) 883352. E-mail:tonyh@sfhg.org.uk**

## ETB 5 Keys De Luxe

---

GREEN GABLES HOTEL

### Scarborough, North Yorkshire

Good quality self contained flats within Green Gables Hotel, adjoining Falsgrave Park. Well equipped and fitted throughout. Terms include bed linen, towels, all electricity/gas, also table tennis and use of our own *heated indoor swimming pool.* Colour TV in each unit. Full size snooker table. Clothes washing facilities are available and assistance with washing up and cleaning is offered high season. Licensed lounge bar.

**Prices from £129 - £375 per week.**

Please write or phone for brochure.
**Mr. M. Hopper, Green Gables, West Bank, Scarborough, North Yorkshire YO12 4DX.
Tel: (01723) 361005.**

## ORILLIA COTTAGES

**Mr. Mike Cundall, 89 The Village, Stockton on the Forest, York, Yorkshire YO3 9UP. Tel: (01904) 400600.**

Orillia Cottages have been completely renovated to provide comfortable accommodation, full of character and charm. These delightful period cottages retain many of their original features, yet contain all modern conveniences and facilities. Situated in the centre of Stockton on the Forest, a picturesque village set in peaceful countryside, they are just three miles from the historic city of York. Each cottage is well equipped, decorated to a high standard and centrally heated. Linen provided. electric cooker. Shop nearby. Children welcome. Dogs allowed. Parking space.

**Prices range from £150 - £350 per week**

# HARROGATE
## HOLIDAY COTTAGES

**Mrs. Angela Durance, The Old Post Office, Kettlesing, Harrogate, Yorkshire HG3 2LB.**
**Tel: (01423) 772700  Fax: (01423) 772359  E mail: hhc@dial.pipex.com**
**Web Address: http://dspace.dial.pipex.com/hhc/**

Come walking in the Dales, visit York, Lightwater Valley Theme Park, Betty's Cafe and a host of other delightful places in which you may enjoy Yorkshire hospitality to the full. Stay in our personally inspected cottages and apartments in Harrogate, York, the Yorkshire Dales, Thirsk and Herriot country, sleeping 2-12 people.

* Open all year round
* Dogs and children welcome
* Free colour brochure

*EXCELLENT VALUE FROM £147 - £555 PER PROPERTY PER WEEK*

# SWALLOW APARTMENTS

# Self Catering
## *Accommodation*
### Scotland

## SCOTLAND

Carefully selected cottages in quiet locations throughout Scotland. Small family-run business providing a personal service.

For a **free brochure** please write or telephone us at —

### Hamster Cottages

**(PP)**
**BIGGAR**
**Scotland**
**ML12 6ND**

telephone —
**(01899) 308 543**

*Aberdeenshire*

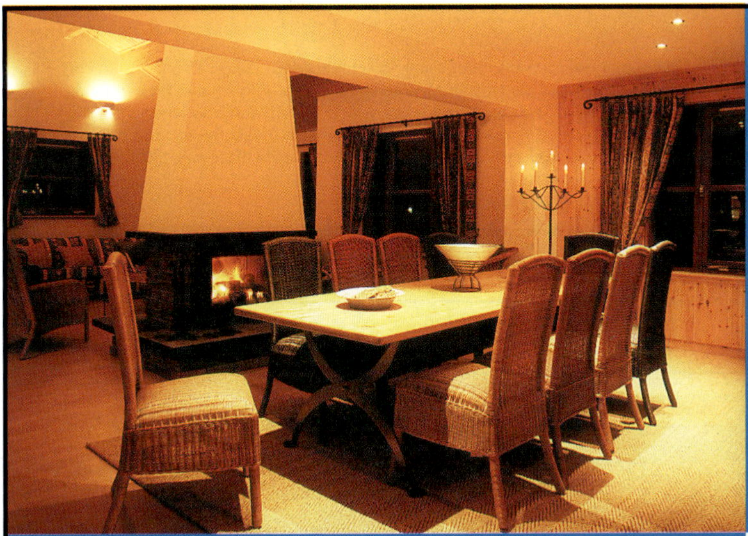

# Aviemore
## 01479 810165

▼ ALL YEAR ROUND ▼ 1-4 BED LUXURY BUNGALOWS SLEEPING 2-10 ▼ GREAT LOCATION FOR ALL ACTIVITIES AT FOOT OF MAJESTIC CAIRNGORMS ▼ SOME EVEN HAVE NORDIC SAUNAS AND WOOD BURNING STOVES ▼ ON SITE SERVICE

QUALITY STREET
HOLIDAY HOMES



# STRONTIAN SCOTLOCH LODGES
## Argyll

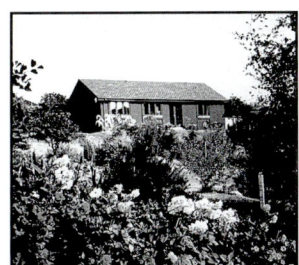

Quality, scenic value. S.T.B. 4 Crowns Highly Commended. 3 Scandinavian cottages very well appointed to accommodate 2-6 persons. Facilities for the disabled, electric cooking, children welcome, shop nearby, linen provided and parking available. Beach nearby and pets welcome. Magnificent views over Loch Sunart. These cottages would be an ideal base from which to explore Lochaber, Mull and Iona.

**Attractive rates, discounts for 2 week stays.**

For your colour brochure contact:
**Mr. Charles Wright, Scotloch Lodges, Monument Park, Strontian, by Fort William, Inverness-shire PH36 4HZ. Tel: (01967) 402004.**

## ELMBANK BUNGALOW AND CARAVANS

**Mrs Christine Cain, Utopia, Acharacle, Argyll PH36 4JL.**
**Tel: (01967) 431717.**

Self contained modern bungalow and two caravans. Scenic and peaceful highland village 45 miles from Fort William on the banks of Loch Shiel. Views of the Hills of Moidart and the Isles of Rhum and Eigg. Walking, fishing and many local places of interest. Shop nearby. Children welcome. Fully furnished and very well equipped and up-to-date i.e. fastext colour TV, video, microwave, gas cooker, fridge, freezer, dishwasher, washing machine. CD Stereo, telephone, fax, ansaphone etc. Close to shops and village pub. Sleeps 2 - 8.

**For further information contact:**
**Mr. C. Omand, The Braes, Acharacle, Argyll PH36 4JL. Tel: (01967) 431317.**

## APPIN HOLIDAY HOMES

**Mr. & Mrs. P. Weir, Appin, Argyll PA38 4BQ.**
**Tel: (01631) 730287.**

An excellent choice of self catering chalet bungalows, traditional cottages and superior holiday residential caravans, set apart in this area of outstanding beauty, midway between Oban and Fort William. Sleeps 2-5. Each fully self-contained. Very private. Ideal for families, also honeymoons...very romantic! A nature lovers' paradise. Hill and shoreline walks. Free fishing (salt & freshwater). Boats available. Play area. Launderette. Baby sitting service. Pony trekking, sailing and licensed inn nearby. Good touring centre. Special early and late terms with extra discount to a couple. Free colour brochure (SAE please).

**Price guide: £155 - £345 per unit weekly.** *Personal attention from resident proprietors.*

**STB 4 Crowns Commended**

## GALLANACH

**Major J. W. MacDougall, Gallanach, Oban, Argyll PA34 4QL.**
**Tel: (01631) 562176.**

Self contained cottage attached to mansion house on an estate near Oban, sitting in own grounds overlooking the Sound of Kerrera and one mile from public road, five miles from Oban. Beautiful situation by the sea with one or secluded places suitable for bathing and plenty of hill ground for walkers close at hand. Oban is the starting point for steamers and trips to the Islands. The cottage has accommodation for eight persons and is fully furnished with electric cooker and colour TV. Please bring your own linen. Children welcome, also well behaved pets. Four miles from shops and public transport. Car essential, parking. S.A.E. for details.

Open May to October.

## 5 PARK CIRCUS

**Mrs. I. McLellan, 5 Park Circus, Ayr, Ayrshire KA7 2DJ.
Tel: (01292) 287065/260057.**

Spacious first floor apartment in attractive Victorian town house. 2 public rooms, 3 bedrooms, sleeps 6. Situated in quiet tree-lined street close to beach, within walking distance from bus and train stations. Ideal base for golfing, fishing, racing, island hopping and exploring Ayrshire and Arran. Open July - September.

**£300 - £360 per week**

**4 Crowns Commended**

---

## BALNOWLART LODGE

### Ballantrae, Ayrshire

Balnowlart Lodge is a tastefully furnished country house offering "home from home" comfortable accommodation consisting of 1 twin and 2 double bedrooms. (cot available) All linen including towels are supplied. Fully equipped electric kitchen with microwave, automatic washing machine and tumble dryer. Electric shower. Payphone. Electric heating throughout. Located in the Stinchar Valley the lodge enjoys panoramic scenery and is ideally located to enjoy beautiful Galloway and Ayrshire "Burns" country. Many top golf courses nearby. Lots of peaceful walks, 2 miles from local shops, hotels and beach.

**Write to: Mrs. M Drummond, Ardstinchar Cottage, Main Street, Ballantrae, Girvan, Ayrshire KA26 0NA. Tel: (01465) 831343.**

**Prices from £130 - £240**

---

## NEWMILNS, NR. KILMARNOCK
## LOUDOUN MAINS COUNTRY HOLIDAYS

**Mrs. Minnie K. Hodge, Loudoun Mains, Newmilns, Ayrshire KA16 9LG.
Tel/Fax: (01560) 321246.**

Relax in our superb self-catering cottages in an Ayrshire country setting, rich with wildlife and panoramic views of the Rabbie Burns countryside. The Firth of Clyde and the Isle of Arran, which is ideal for touring, fishing, golf, bird watching and seaside resorts. Shop nearby, parking available and pets welcome. The cottages are fully equipped with TV, telephone, baths and linen is also supplied. Facilities for the disabled. Children welcome. Indoor pool and garden furniture (seasonal) with laundry facilities on site. Sleeps 2-10 weekly and short stays available.

**Prices from £145 - £585.**
**For further information please contact Mrs. Hodge at the above address.**

*Fife*

*Inverness-shire*

*Inverness-shire*

*Kirkcudbrightshire*

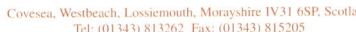

Lanarkshire

Morayshire

Peebleshire

## LOCH TAY LODGES

**Mrs. P. Duncan Millar, Remony, Acharn, Aberfeldy, Perthshire PH15 2HR.**
**Tel: (01887) 830209.  Fax: (01887) 830802.**

These top quality modern self catering units in picturesque Highland village are completely equipped, including linen and towels. There are six units sleeping 4,6 or 8. Log fires and colour TV. Ideally situated for touring the highlands, hillwalking, birdwatching, fishing and special facilities for sailing are available. Not forgeting many golf courses within 30 minutes drive including Gleneagles (1hour) and 18 holes at Taymouth (1.5 miles). For further information please contact us and we will be happy to help you.

**STB 4 Crowns Highly Commended**

## ULVA, STRATHPEFFER

**Mrs. MacQuarrie, Lochussie, Conon Bridge, Ross-shire IV7 8HJ.**
**Tel: (01349) 861561.**

Superior Stone built house equipped to high standard situated in picturesque Victorian spa village amidst beautiful scenery. 3 en-suite bedrooms (1 downstairs) sleeping 8. Large enclosed garden, ample parking. Close to shops, hotels/restaurants. Ideal base for touring. Golf (5 mins), fishing, hillwalking. Inverness 18 miles. Dingwall 4 miles. Ullapool 47 miles.

**STB 5 Crowns Commended**

UNIVERSITY OF STIRLING
**CONFERENCE AND
VACATION CAMPUS**

Holiday apartments, chalets and flats are located in the beautiful parkland grounds of the University of Stirling. In addition, we have town houses available nearby to the historic town of Stirling. Excellent leisure and recreational amenities include theatre/cinema, small shopping complex, bars, indoor swimming pool, squash courts, indoor/outdoor tennis courts, sauna, solarium, sports hall and even our very own 9-hole golf course.

**Tel: (01786) 467141.**

**Prices from £130 - £350**

# COTTAGES

**Loch Shin, by Lairg, Sutherland IV27 4NY.**

**Tel: (015494) 31210.**

Situated 200m from Loch Shin amid spectacular scenery in picturesque countryside of Sutherland on the A838 trans Country route from Lairg to Durness.

Ideally located close to the Overscaig Hotel which is named on most road maps, it makes an excellent base for touring, fishing, bird watching and hill walking.

Each cottage consists of lounge/diner with colour TV two twin bedrooms, bathroom with bath and shower, fitted kitchen with fridge and microwave.

# TWO HOLIDAY HOUSES

**7-9 Harbour Street, Creetown, Wigtownshire.**

Two holiday houses, situated in a small village with panoramic views. Renowned for walks, golf and birdwatching. There is a lawn at the rear of the premises and a museum nearby. Modern facilities, shower, washer dryer. Continental quilts with linen provided.

**Price £190 - £260.**

**Write to: Mrs. M. Dawson, 70 Coach Road, Brotton, Saltburn-By-The-Sea, Cleveland TS12 2RP. Tel: (01287) 676991.**

**3 Crowns Approved**

# COCK INN CARAVAN PARK

**Auchenmalg, Newton Stewart, Wigtownshire DG8 0JT.**
**Tel: (01581) 500227.**

Peaceful, select caravan park adjacent to pleasant little beach and small country Inn. Panoramic view across Luce Bay. Bathing, sailing and sea angling etc. Also bungalow all year round. Golf, fishing and pony trekking.

Modern toilet block, showers, freezing facilities, shaver points and all facilities, shop on site and bar meals available at the Inn. Fully serviced holiday caravans for hire tourers welcome. Sauna and sunbed for hire. Please send for brochure or telephone the above number.

**British Graded Holiday Parks 4 Ticks     Thistle Award**

# PROSPECT HOUSE

**Mrs. A. Shaw, Morningside, Mount Pleasant, Rothesay Isle of Bute PA20 9HQ.
Tel/Fax: (01700) 503526.**

Two delightful complexes of superior self contained apartments: "Morningside" minutes to pier, golf course, town centre: "Prospect House" & cottage, own grounds, sea-front, private parking. Both complexes with magnificent views. Heating, hot-water, linen, towels included. Electricity by the meter. Private parking.

Open all year. 8 Units, sleep 2-5.

**Price (weekly): £159.00 - £335.00**

**4 Crowns Commended**

# ARDROIL

## Western Isles, Lewis

Member of
THE ASSOCIATION OF
SCOTLAND'S
SELF CATERERS

Comfortable cottage in scenic area near hills and beaches. This is where you come if you like hill-walking, bird watching, beach-combing or an 'away from it all' holiday. You can bring your car up to the cottage. Cottage is fully equipped with all linen. Electricity on meter payable as used. Payphone and microwave. Open all year. No pets.

**Charges £150 - £200 a week.**

Booking to:
**Mrs. D. N. MacKay, 2 Melbost, Point, Isle of Lewis HS2 0BG.
Tel: (01851) 704594**

# CREAGON BREAC

## Roag, Dunvegan, Isle of Skye.

Creagan Breac is a byre converted into two spacious semi-detached cottages each fully equipped for six persons. Plenty of parking. Part of Loch Bracadale - Roag Pool is 200 metres from the cottages. There are fine views of The Cuillin Mountains, McLeods Tables and moors. Especially suitable for fishing, diving, walking, bird watching. Good Hotels/restaurants for eating out within a short distance.

**Mrs. J. Robinson, Bridge Cottage, Broughton Mills-In-Furness, Cumbria LA20 6AY.
Tel: (01229) 716402.**

## BRAEVALLA CHALETS

**Mr. J. Cox, Varkasaig, Orbost, Dunvegan, Isle of Skye IV55 8ZB.**
**Tel/Fax: (01470) 521231.**

The three chalets are located on the banks of a burn at the foot of MacLeod's Table North, a flat-topped mountain in the north-west of the island. They lie at the end of a private track on the edge of an uninhabited wilderness of hills and moorland, half a mile from the sea. Each chalet is completely self-contained and can accommodate up to four people. There are two bedrooms (one double, one twin), living/dining room, kitchen and bathroom (with bath and shower). Open all year. Bed linen provided.

**From £100 to £205 per week.**

# BORRERAIG

**Mr. J. Cox, Varkasaig, Orbost, Dunvegan, Isle of Skye IV55 8ZB.**
**Tel/Fax: (01470) 521231.**

This traditional Highland crofter's cottage occupies an idyllic, private location on the shores of Loch Dunvegan. There are uninterrupted sea views over the loch and across the Minch to the outer Hebrides. The cottage has been sympathetically restored and is furnished mainly with antiques. Open fire.
Two bedrooms (one double, one twin), sleeping up to four.
Bed linen and towels provided.

**Prices range from £170 to £320 per week.**

### Mrs. M. MacDonald, 20 Borve, by Portree, Isle of Skye IV51 9PE. Tel: (01470) 532301.

The cottages are family run and on a small working croft. They have their own garden area with picnic tables, and lovely views of surrounding hills and countryside. There is ample parking space available at the cottages. There is also a wide range of river, sea and loch fishing at the nearby Skeabost Hotel and a pleasant 9-hole golf course. A regularbus service is available 200 yards from the cottages. Each cottage has 1 double and 1 twin bedroom, shower room, large comfortable lounge with colour TV, electric fire and extra sofa/bed. There is also a kitchen/diner with electric cooker, fridge, toaster, washer/dryer and dishwasher. The cottages have panel and storage heaters throughout, and all linen is also provided. Cot and high chair available on request. Pets are welcome, but must be kept under control.

## HOLIDAY COTTAGES

Come to Skye and enjoy a peaceful holiday in our cottages which are generously equipped to a very high standard being awarded 4 Crowns Commended by the Scottish Tourist Board. The cottages enjoy a spectacular site with views of the Cuillins and Snizort Loch. Ideal for the holidaymaker who wants to unwind in peace and quiet. Washer/dryer, microwave oven provided. No pets allowed.

For brochures etc. contact:
**Mrs. K.C, MacKinnon, Daldon, Bernisdale, by Portree, Skye IV51 9NS.
Tel: (01470) 532331.**

# Self Catering
# *Accommodation*

**Wales**

---

# WALES'S WEST COAST

## SELF-CATERING APARTMENTS
## ABERYSTWYTH – OVERLOOKING CARDIGAN BAY

- Flats & houses for 7–10 persons ■ Convenient campus location
- Sports centre, squash, badminton and heated indoor pool
- 5 minutes town centre ■ Arts Centre complex
- Fully equipped – cutlery, crockery, microwave, bedlinen, towels
- 24 hour security ■ Free parking
- Mountains, beaches, slate mines, steam trains and *much, much more!*

Prifysgol Cymru
**Aberystwyth**
The University of Wales

Further information:
Conference Office, The University of Wales
Penbryn, Penglais, Aberystwyth SY23 3BY
Tel (01970) 621960/621961
Fax (01970) 622899

# PEN ISAF CARAVAN PARK

**Mr. & Mrs. T. P. Williams, Llangernyw, Abergele, Conwy, North Wales LL22 8RN.
Tel: (01745) 860276.**

This small caravan site is in beautiful unspoilt countryside ideal for touring North Wales and situated 10 miles from the coast and 12 miles from Betws-y-Coed. Caravans have shower, flush toilets, H & C, calor gas cooker, electric light and fridge. Fresh eggs and milk can be obtained from the farm on which this 20 caravan site is situated. Children especially enjoy a holiday here, there being ample space. Facilities for fishing. Pets are allowed but must be kept under control. Parking available.

Open March to October.

*Terms on application with S. A. E. to above address.*

# "BRON DERW"

**Mrs. B. A. Edwards, "Bron Derw", Llanrwst, Conwy LL26 0YT.
Tel: (01492) 640494.**

"Bron Derw" is an attractive stone-built farmhouse situated on the outskirts of the market town of Llanrwst. It is also within easy reach of many popular seaside resorts as well as the Snowdonia range. A comfortable well furnished and self-contained part of the farmhouse is available with accommodation for up to 4 persons. Electric heating cooking facilities. Bed linen provided and car parking available. Children welcome and child minding upon request. Sorry no pets. Shops, swimming pool and other amenities nearby Beach 15 miles. Cleanliness assured. Reasonable terms.

**Prices from £120 - £175 per week.**

Please send an S. A. E. to the above address for further details.

# BRYN BRAS —CASTLE—

**Llanrug, Nr. Caernarfon, Gwynedd LL55 4RE.
Tel/Fax: (01286) 870210**

Welcome to beautiful Bryn Bras Castle - romantic apartments, elegant tower house, mini-cottage, for 2 to 4, within distinctive Romanesque castle, enjoying breathtaking scenery amid gentle Snowdonia foothills. Easy reach mountains, beaches, heritage, local restaurants/inns. Each apartment is fully self-contained, spacious, peaceful with individual character. Generously equipped from dishwasher.....flowers. Central heating, hot water, and linen provided free. All highest grade (ex. one). 32 acre gardens, woodlands, panoramic walks. Warmth, convenience, comfort in serene surroundings. No young children.

Short breaks all year from e.g. £120.00 for 2 persons for 2 nights. Weeks £300-£600

**W.T.B. GRADE 5**

# CRICCIETH COUNTRY COTTAGES

**B. Jones, Rhandir, Boduan, Pwllheli, Gwynedd LL53 8UA.**
**Tel/Fax: (01758) 720047 or Tel: (01766) 8102195**

A truly romantic, memorable and special place to stay and relax in comfort. Open all year. Sleep 2-6 plus cot. Warm and inviting with log fires, ingle-nook and oak beams. Washing/drying machines, dishwasher, microwave, freezer and electric cooker. Some with jacuzzi, four poster, sauna or snooker table. Fishing, riding, wonderful walks, peace and quiet with Snowdonia and unspoilt beaches on the doorstep. Children and dogs welcome. Parking available.
Further enquiries to the above address.

**Prices start from £150 per week.**

# NOLTON HAVEN

**Mr. Jim Canton, Haverfordwest, Pembrokeshire SA62 9NH.**
**Tel/Fax: (01437) 710263.**

The farmhouse is beside the beach on a 200 acre mixed farm, with cattle, calves and many Show ponies! It has a large lounge which is open to guests all day as are all the bedrooms. Single, double and family rooms, two family rooms en-suite, 4 other bathrooms. Pets and children most welcome, baby sitting free of charge. 50 yards to the beach, 75 yards to the local Inn/restaurant. Pony trekking, surfing, fishing, excellent cliff walks, boating and canoeing are all nearby. Riding holidays and short breaks all year, a speciality.

**Colour brochure on request.**

# LLANDDINOG FARM COTTAGES
Solva, Haverfordwest.

Delightful luxury cottages grouped around farm courtyard, only 3 miles from sandy beaches, coastal paths and local shops. Fully equipped, centrally heated. Fishing, riding, watersports, golf, island trips, bird watching, seals and puffins. Colour TV, barbecue, large flowery garden, swings, small animals. Cot, high-chair, linen. Short breaks. Children welcome. Pets allowed. Linen provided. Parking.

**Prices per week from £130 - £430.**

**Contact:**
**Mrs. Sarah Griffiths, Llanddinog Old Farmhouse, Solva, Haverfordwest, Pembrokeshire SA62 6NA. Tel: (01348) 831224.**

# FISHGUARD BAY CARAVAN AND CAMPING PARK

**Mr. N. Harries, Dinas Cross, Newport, Pembrokeshire SA42 0YD.**
**Tel: (01348) 811415  Fax: (01348) 811425.**

Beautiful views and walks available from this secluded site on Pembrokeshire's 'Heritage' coast. Modern, full service caravans for hire. Tourers, tents, motor caravans welcome.

Children welcome, Parking space. Dogs allowed.

Ideal centre for exploring the delights of the Pembrokeshire Coast National park.
**Please contact the above address for more information.**

# Severn Arms Hotel

**Mr. G. Lloyd, Penybont,, Llandrindod Wells, Powys LD1 5UA.**
**Tel: (01597) 851224. Fax: (01597) 851693.**

### MOBILE HOMES

6 - 8 berth luxury mobile homes on quiet riverside site within hotel grounds in small village. All mains facilities including colour TV. Private fishing on River Ithon (6 miles). Concessionary rates on two golf courses. Ideally situated for touring the heart of Wales. Dogs and children welcome. Parking available. Shop nearby.

**Prices range from £120 - £200.**

For further details write to the above address.

# BRECON BEACONS
### 1 Caerfannell Place, Talybont-on-Usk, Powys.

This traditional Welsh Cottage is set on the edge of the Brecon Beacons National Park. The small garden is laid to lawn with bordering shrubs leading down to the river and there is garden furniture for relaxing in the sun. The accommodation comprises a double, family and twin bedded rooms, bathroom and separate shower room. Facilities include a fully fitted kitchen/diner, fridge, freezer, microwave, oven and hot plates. Also provided are washing machine, tumble dryer, iron and ironing board and a hair dryer. Linen and duvets provided. **Prices from £130 - £320.**

Contact: **Mrs. F. I. Smith, Holts Farm House, Fordcombe, Tunbridge Wells, Kent TN 3 0RN.**
**Tel/Fax: (01892) 740338**

# Self Catering
## *Accommodation*

---

### ALT-NA-CRAIG

**Mrs. Lindsay, 65 Beach Road, Portballintrae, Co. Antrim, Northern Ireland BT57 8RT.
Tel: (01442) 825870.**

A six bedroomed house, facing the sea, with the road and the bank between the house and the beach. At the back, up some steps, there is a small attractive garden. The large kitchen/dining room, with an Aga to cook on, opens onto a patio. The sitting room faces north to the sea, the TV room, with a balcony, and ping pong room face south. Many golf courses within easy reach and fishing available locally. Near Giants Causeway with beautiful cliff walks.
**Phone for details.**

---

### THE CHALET

**Mrs. Armstrong, Dean's Hill, 34 College Hill, Armagh, Co. Armagh,
Northern Ireland BT61 9DF.
Tel: (01861) 522099.**

2 bedroom bungalow within the courtyard of a Georgian family home with farm and tennis court yet inside city boundary of historic and ecclesiastical interest. Easy to walk to shops, Planetarium, Museums and Leisure Centre. Linen for hire. Parking available. Handicapped/Disabled facilities. Gas cooking facilities. Shop nearby.

**Prices from £90 per week. Phone for details.**

# JIRAH

**Write to: Bertie Henderson, "The Causeway", 59 Drumsnade Road, Ballynahinch, Co. Down, Northern Ireland. Tel: (01238) 561885.**

The bungalow has 5 en-suite bedrooms, 2 livingrooms, a large kitchen with electric cooking facilities and dining area. There is also a large play area and large garden.
Children are welcome and there is parking available. It is on a private site on the main Cranfield resort road, overlooking Mourne Mountains and Irish Sea 10 minutes walk.
Shops, 100 yards and hotel 2 miles. It is 2 miles from the fishing village,
Kilkeel with golf and horse riding within 2 miles. Newcastle Seaside resort 9 miles,
Warren Point Harbour 9 miles.

# CRANFIELD CHALETS

**Write to: 125 Harbour Road, Kilkeel, Co. Down, Northern Ireland BT34 4AT. Tel: (016937) 62745.**

Cranfield Chalets are the ideal place to spend a relaxing holiday amidst the scenery of the beautiful Mourne countryside situated just a few yards from the clean, sandy Cranfield Beach which is ideal for wind surfing and water skiing. Golf course, fishing, hotel and shops nearby.
6 chalets - 1 living, 1 dining, 1 kitchen, 2 bedrooms. Sleeps 5.
Children welcome. Facilities for the disabled. Electric hob and oven provided.
Linen for hire. Parking available. Phone for details.

**Prices from: £115 per week Low Season .
£225 per week High Season**

# Trade Description Act

The accommodation mentioned in this guide has not been inspected, and the publishers rely on information provided.

The publishers have every confidence in their advertisers but cannot be held responsible for the accuracy of the descriptions published.

# *Farm and Country*

Accommodation

Photograph: Fluxton Farm Hotel, Ottery St. Mary, Devon.

# Our World by the Sea

Map Ref. H8

## FOR INEXPENSIVE QUALITY

FEATURED BY **BBC**

Q EXCELLENT

### BEACH MODERN LUXURY HOLIDAY HOME *or Caravan*

With the beach moments from your door. Top Grade 5 Award Park, in an area of outstanding natural beauty. This is a quiet secluded cove and Park with sub-tropical plants confirming Gulf Stream mild climate. Safe bathing, water sports, sea & river fishing. Ramble along the flat coastal strip. The local post office & shop is only 3 min. walk. Nearby restaurants, Bar Snacks, Take Aways, golf, pony trekking, three modern leisure centres, Nature Trails in the Historic Glynllifon Country Park. Tour **beautiful Snowdonia** and the famous Llŷn peninsula, beaches & Portmeirion. Featured by the BBC, Wales Tourist Board & British Holiday Home Parks. Families return to us year after year with the new Dual expressway making the journey so easy. Come & view anytime. All our Accommodation comprises Shower, W/basin & Toilet, 2 or 3 Bedrooms, Remote Control Colour TV, Well Heated, **Free Electric & Gas,** Fridge/Freezer, Cooker, Electric Blanket, Kettle, Hoover, Blankets, Pillows, Crockery, Cutlery, Cooking Utensils. Bring your own sheets, pillow cases & towels or own duvet. Most have **Heated Bedroom,** Microwave & Toaster. **Full Central Heating to 65°** on Request. Some are double glazed. Try a **"Super 12"** Home which is 20% more spacious. Park next to your Accommodation. Try a £12 Minibreak Special. Holiday Home Caravans for sale on Park. Phone for our detailed Brochure.

| SUPER 12 20% more spacious | 1998 | Model Type | Sleeps | Bed rooms | MARCH 21/28 | APRIL GF 4 | BH 11 | 18 | 25 | MAY 2 | 9 | BH 16 | BH 23 | 30 | JUNE 6 | 13 | 20 | 27 | JULY 4 | 11 | 18 | 25 | AUGUST 1/8 | BH 15/22 | 29 | SEPTEMBER 5 | 12 | 19 | 26 | OCTOBER 3 | 10/17 | 24 | Model Type |
|---|---|---|---|---|---|---|---|---|---|---|---|---|---|---|---|---|---|---|---|---|---|---|---|---|---|---|---|---|---|---|---|---|---|
| | Week Commencing | | | | | | | | | | | | | | | | | | | | | | | | | | | | | | | | | |
| | Economy older Caravan | A | 4-6 | 2 | 35 | 45 | 65 | 39 | 45 | 49 | 45 | 45 | 99 | 69 | 79 | 89 | 95 | 105 | 119 | 129 | 179 | 189 | 189 | 139 | 89 | 79 | 65 | 55 | 49 | 39 | 49 | A |
| | Economy Standard older Caravan | B | 4-8 | 2 | 45 | 59 | 85 | 55 | 49 | 59 | 55 | 55 | 149 | 89 | 95 | 105 | 115 | 125 | 149 | 155 | 219 | 229 | 229 | 229 | 199 | 119 | 89 | 75 | 65 | 59 | 49 | 69 | B |
| | Economy Standard older Caravan | C | 6-10 | 3 | 49 | 69 | 99 | 59 | 49 | 69 | 59 | 59 | 159 | 99 | 105 | 109 | 125 | 139 | 159 | 159 | 229 | 239 | 239 | 249 | 239 | 209 | 139 | 95 | 79 | 69 | 65 | 55 | 79 | C |
| | Superior Holiday Home | D | 4-8 | 2 | 65 | 89 | 119 | 69 | 69 | 89 | 89 | 95 | 189 | 125 | 139 | 145 | 155 | 165 | 179 | 179 | 259 | 259 | 279 | 279 | 239 | 149 | 119 | 99 | 85 | 75 | 69 | 99 | D |
| | Superior Holiday Home | E | 6-10 | 3 | 69 | 115 | 129 | 79 | 75 | 99 | 95 | 99 | 199 | 139 | 149 | 159 | 169 | 179 | 199 | 199 | 279 | 299 | 309 | 309 | 279 | 169 | 139 | 115 | 99 | 89 | 75 | 119 | E |
| | Superior Plus Holiday Home | F | 4-8 | 2 | 69 | 99 | 129 | 79 | 75 | 95 | 95 | 99 | 199 | 139 | 139 | 149 | 169 | 179 | 199 | 199 | 279 | 299 | 299 | 299 | 249 | 169 | 139 | 109 | 99 | 85 | 75 | 109 | F |
| | Superior Plus Holiday Home | G | 6-10 | 3 | 75 | 119 | 159 | 85 | 79 | 129 | 99 | 119 | 239 | 159 | 169 | 189 | 199 | 219 | 239 | 299 | 319 | 329 | 329 | 299 | 179 | 159 | 129 | 109 | 95 | 85 | 129 | G |
| | UP MARKET PLUS Holiday Home | H | 4-6 | 2 | 75 | 119 | 159 | 85 | 89 | 119 | 109 | 129 | 229 | 159 | 169 | 179 | 199 | 219 | 239 | 289 | 319 | 329 | 319 | 319 | 289 | 189 | 149 | 129 | 119 | 99 | 89 | 119 | H |
| SUPER 12 | Superior Holiday Home | I | 4-8 | 2 | 69 | 115 | 169 | 89 | 89 | 129 | 109 | 119 | 249 | 159 | 169 | 179 | 199 | 219 | 239 | 299 | 329 | 329 | 329 | 289 | 189 | 159 | 129 | 119 | 95 | 89 | 129 | I |
| SUPER 12 | Superior Holiday Home | L | 6-10 | 3 | 85 | 159 | 219 | 119 | 89 | 159 | 129 | 159 | 279 | 205 | 219 | 229 | 249 | 259 | 279 | 289 | 349 | 369 | 375 | 369 | 339 | 229 | 179 | 159 | 139 | 119 | 109 | 169 | L |

**SUPER SHORT BREAKS – ANYTIME**
**3** nights weekend. **4/3** nights midweek, **HALF** weekly price to next £ and add →
*Other dates/nights by arrangement. Phone for quotation.*
**ANY DATES TO SUIT YOU**

**NO HIDDEN EXTRAS. COME AND INSPECT ANYTIME & CHOOSE**

| 10 | 20 | 45 | 20 | 15 | 25 | 20 | 20 | 45 | 25 | 25 | 25 | 30 | 30 | 40 | 45 | 45 | 50 | 40 | 30 | 25 | 20 | 15 | 15 | 30 |

*Deposit £33 P.W., and Insurance £1 Nightly for caravan. Cots & High Chairs £2 Nightly each. Dogs £2 Nightly.
Full Central Heating to 65° Request. Over 6 persons £5 per night each. All prices inc. VAT @ 17½%.*

### INSTANT HOLIDAYS – ANYTIME

Should you be able to take a last minute break, please ring **01286 660400,** and we will do our best to accommodate you – the same day if you wish.

**MINIBREAK – A few days, week-end or mid-week**
4-6 Berth FROM **£10** per night per Holiday Home, Caravan **A Type**
4-8 Berth FROM **£12** per night per Holiday Home, Caravan **B Type**
6-10 Berth FROM **£14** per night per Holiday Home, Caravan **C Type**

**ANY 4 DAYS** – BEACH MODERN LUXURY HOLIDAY HOME, ANY 3 NIGHTS. Extra nights available. Model A, B or C. FROM

| | MARCH | APRIL | MAY | JUNE | JULY | AUGUST | SEPTEMBER | OCTOBER |
|---|---|---|---|---|---|---|---|---|
| | BERTH | BERTH | BERTH | BERTH | BERTH | BERTH | BERTH | BERTH |
| | 4-6 4-8 6-10 | 4-6 4-8 6-10 | 4-6 4-8 6-10 | 4-6 4-8 6-10 | 4-6 4-8 6-10 | 4-6 4-8 6-10 | 4-6 4-8 6-10 | 4-6 4-8 6-10 |
| 21 | 28 35 35 | 4th 43 49 55 | 2nd 49 55 59 | 6 65 73 78 | 4 89 104 109 | 1 139 159 169 | 5 79 99 109 | 3 39 45 48 |
| 28 | 33 33 35 | 11th 69 79 95 | 9 43 48 49 | 13 69 78 83 | 11 95 108 109 | 8 139 159 169 | 12 59 70 74 | 10 34 39 43 |
| | | 18 38 48 49 | 16 43 48 49 | 20 73 83 88 | 18 124 145 149 | 15 139 159 169 | 19 53 65 69 | 17 34 39 43 |
| | | 25 29 39 39 | 23rd 59 119 125 | 27 78 88 95 | 25 139 159 165 | 22 159 169 189 | 26 48 53 55 | 24 55 69 73 |
| | | | 30 55 65 69 | | | 29th 125 155 159 | | |

### EASTER WEEK-END
8th April to 15th April
| | 4-6 | 4-8 | 6-10 |
|---|---|---|---|
| From | Berth | Berth | Berth |
| 2 nights | £39 | £75 | £79 |
| 3 nights | £69 | £79 | £95 |
| 4 nights | £75 | £89 | £99 |
Also *"Super 12" 20% more spacious. Villa chalets & Executive Bungalows.*

### MAY DAY BANK HOLIDAY WEEK-END
1-8 MAY  4-6 Berth  4-8 Berth  6-10 Berth
Any 3 nights F  £49  £55  £59

### WHIT BANK HOLIDAY WEEK-END
21-28 MAY  4-6 Berth  4-8 Berth  6-10 Berth
Any 3 nights F  £89  £119  £125

### AUGUST BANK HOLIDAY WEEK-END
28 AUG-2 SEPT  4-6 Berth  4-8 Berth  6-10 Berth
Any 3 nights F  £149  £149  £155
Also *"Super 12" 20% more spacious. Villa chalets & Executive Bungalows.*

**ALSO VILLA CHALET**

## *Also* FOR SALE

New & one owner Villa Chalets, Holiday Homes & Caravans for sale on the Park.

*Come and inspect anytime*

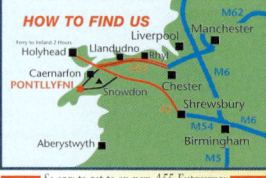

**HOW TO FIND US**

M62 · Liverpool · Manchester · Holyhead · Llandudno · Caernarfon · PONTLLYFNI · Snowdon · Chester · M6 · Shrewsbury · M54 · Aberystwyth · Birmingham · M5

**So easy to get to on new A55 Expressway**

BEACH HOLIDAY, WEST POINT, THE BEACH, PONTLLYFNI, CAERNARFON, NORTH WALES, LL54 5ET

## PERSONAL ATTENTION, BROCHURE & RESERVATIONS – TEL. 01286 660400

# Farm and Country
## Accommodation
### England

## DINNABROAD FARM

**Mrs. M. A. Adcock, St. Teath, Bodmin, Cornwall PL30 3LR.**
**Tel: (01208) 880342.**

Self catering cottage stands at the head of a picturesque valley looking towards the sea with extensive views of North Cornish Coast and Atlantic. It is in a secluded position from the farmhouse and buildings. Visitors are welcome to roam the 150 acres of mixed farmland, valleys and its own 1/2 mile of cliffs in this designated area of Outstanding Natural Beauty and its wild life. Sandy beaches are at Polzeath and Trebarwith, the picturesque fishing village of Port Issaac is three miles away. The cottage sleeps 4-6 plus cot. All electric: cooker, fridge, colour TV, bathroom with toilet. Ample parking space, car essential.

**Terms from £90 - £140 weekly. Pets welcome.**

## BOSKENSOE FARM

**Mrs. G. Matthews, Mawnan Smith, Falmouth, Cornwall TR11 5JP.**
**Tel/Fax: (01326) 250257.**

Bungalow overlooks the farm on the edge of the village. Sleeps 6/8 with colour TV, electric cooker, fridge/freezer, washing machine and microwave. Fitted with storage heaters and electric fires. Children welcome. Spacious garden and ample parking for cars and boats. Dogs permitted. Situated in the picturesque village of Mawnan Smith. Falmouth 5 miles, 1.5 miles from lovely Helford River famous for beautiful coastal walks, gardens and scenery. Several quite safe beaches for bathing. Also excellent sailing and fishing facilities. Apply for a brochure.

Prices from £130 - £375

**Tourist Board Registered**

## LOWER DUTSON FARM

**Kathryn Broad, Launceston, Cornwall PL15 9SP.**
**Tel: (01566) 776456.**

Enjoy a holiday on our traditional working farm. A warm welcome awaits you at our 17th century farmhouse. Central for touring both coasts, Devon and Cornwall. Guests are welcome to walk around the wooded coarse fishing lake and along the River Tamar which borders three of our fields. You may even see Kingfishers, buzzards, herons, wild deer etc. **Bed and Breakfast from £16.00 per person per night.** Reductions for children, en-suite. Colour television lounge. Tea/coffee making facilities.

**Self catering £120 - £320 per week.** Fitted kitchen, automatic washing machine, tumble dryer, microwave, colour television and video. Storage heaters. Bathroom and extra toilet and shower in separate room.

**4 Keys Commended - Self Catering     2 Crowns Commended - B & B**

## MULFRA FARM

**Mrs. Monica Olds, Newmill, Penzance, Cornwall TR20 8XP.**
**Tel: (01736) 363940.**

Superb accommodation on this hill farm high on the edge of the Penwith Moors. The 17th century stonebuilt, beamed farmhouse has far reaching views; is attractively decorated and furnished and offers two double en-suite bedrooms with tea/coffee trays, TV, shaver points and heated towel rails. The comfortable lounge has an inglenook fire place and Cornish stone oven. Dining room with separate tables, sun lounge. Car essential, ample parking. Warm friendly atmosphere, good food. Beautiful walking country. Ideal centre for exploring West Cornwall. We have our own Iron age village as well as cows calves and horses. Further details with pleasure.

**Bed and Breakfast and Evening Meal £130 per week. Bed and Breakfast £16.00.**

## CONSOLS FARM

**Messrs. J. Husband & Sons, St. Ives, Cornwall TR26 2HN.**
**Tel: (01736) 796151.**

Several properties sleeping 4/6/8. A selection of 4 properties are available. Large cottage set in garden in quiet surroundings, sleeps 8 people. Sitting room with TV, fully fitted kitchen (fridge, electric cooker etc.); bathroom; 5 bedrooms. Also annexe flat in garden grounds. 1 double bed, 1 set bunk beds in family room; kitchen; lounge; bathroom; toilet etc.; small garden and patio; ample parking. Situated 1 mile from St. Ives; cottage flat sleeping 4 at end of farmhouse on working farm. Sitting room with TV; 2 bedrooms; kitchen; bathroom; toilet etc. Flat in St. Ives town, sleeps 4/6. 3 bedrooms, lounge, kitchen and bathroom. Parking in town car park, 100 yards away. Full details on request.

**Terms from £120**

# TREWEY FARM

**Mrs. N. I. Mann, Zennor, St. Ives, Cornwall TR26 3DA.
Tel: (01736) 796936**

On the main St. Ives to Land's End road, this attractive granite-built farmhouse stands among gorse and heather-clad hills, half-a-mile from the sea and five miles from St. Ives. The mixed farm covers 300 acres with Guernsey cattle and fine views of the sea; lovely cliff and hill walks. Guests will be warmly welcomed and find a friendly atmosphere. Five double, one single and three family bedrooms (all with wash basins); bathrooms, toilets, sitting room, dining room. Cot, high chair and baby sitting available. Pets allowed. Car essential - parking. Open all year. Electric heating. Evening Dinner, Bed and Breakfast or Bed and Breakfast only.

**S.A.E. for terms, please.**

# CROFT HOUSE

**Mrs E. A. Stockdale, Bolton, Appleby-in-Westmorland, Cumbria CA16 6AW.
Tel: (017683) 61264.**

Croft House is situated in Bolton, an unspoilt village of Sandstone houses and farms on the banks of the River Eden, 3 miles north of Appleby off A66. Excellent base for exploring Eden Valley, Lakes, Dales and Border Country. The historic town of Appleby welcomes visitors to its ancient castles and churches and to the country's oldest Gypsy fair, held annually in June. Local attractions include pony trekking, golf, fishing and swimming. The comfortable farmhouse offers traditional farmhouse breakfast and comprises sitting room with colour TV, dining room, 1 twin and 2 double bedrooms with wash basins; separate bathroom and shower. Children welcome; cots and babysitting. Pets welcome by arrangement. 5 minutes drive away from new Oasis Holiday Village. **Self catering Barn conversions sleeps 2-10.** Stabling provided for anyone bringing pony on holiday.

# DENTON HOUSE GUEST HOUSE

**Mrs M. Monkhouse, Caldbeck, Cumbria CA7 8JC. Tel (016974) 78415**

# NORMAN CRAGG FARM BED & BREAKFAST

**Caldbeck, Cumbria CA7 8HX. Tel (017684) 84376**

Denton House is a large 17th century House with new extension, modernised to 20th century standards but still retaining character. We are an ideal base when travelling to or from Scotland, walking the Northern Fells or touring the Lakes. Norman Cragg farmhouse also has lots of character. Log fires welcome everyone in both places. Marvellous views from rooms. Denton House has en-suite facilities. We offer all home cooking. Children and pets welcome, ample parking. **Bed & Breakfast. Evening Meal optional.** S.A.E. for brochure.

# DUCKINTREE HOUSE

**Sylvia Capstick, Kaber, Kirkby Stephen, Cumbria CA17 4ER.**
**Tel: (017683) 71073.**

Duckintree is a working family farm set in the quiet Eden Valley countryside just off the A685 Kirkby Stephen to Brough road. Easy access from M6 and A66, plus the Lakes and Yorkshire Dales or ideal for breaking your journey from the South of England/Midlands to Scotland. Car essential, ample parking. The rooms overlook a large garden and countryside. **Bed and Breakfast from £15. Evening Meal can be provided. Reductions for children under 12 years.** Pets welcome by arrangement. Open March to October.
**Also six berth static caravan.**

**Write or phone for details.**

# BASSENTHWAITE HALL FARM

**Mrs. A. M. Trafford, nr Keswick, Cumbria CA12 4QP.**
**Tel: (017687) 76393.**

By a stream with ducks and an old wooden bridge stand three immaculate high standard cottages of charm and character on the farm in the quiet and delightful village of Bassenthwaite, 6 miles north of Keswick, 2 miles to Bassenthwaite Lake, Skiddaw also 2 miles. Ideal walking area. Children can spend many happy hours in the nearby stream or play on the swings in the wood. They may also feed the ducks and hens and roam freely. Excellent inn nearby, serving good food. The cottages contain two, three and four bedrooms respectively. Colour television, showers, storage heaters, open fires. Open all year, weekend and mid week breaks available. **Also small stable flat for two and farmhouse Bed & Breakfast. 1 large cottage, suitable for disabled available. S.A.E. for colour brochure.**

# GILL HEAD FARM

**Mrs. Janis Wilson, Troutbeck, Penrith, Cumbria.**
**Tel: (017687) 79652.**

Enjoy a pleasant stay at Gill Head Farmhouse, dated 17th century. Lovely character with old beams and log fire. Situated in the Lake District National Park; ideal for walkers in glorious countryside. Lake fishing and golf courses nearby. Also boating. riding and climbing. All rooms en-suite with central heating and tea/coffee making facilities. There is also a kitchen for guests. uses.

**Bed, Breakfast and Evening Meal available.**
**An apartment sleeps 2/4 with mod cons. Children and dogs welcome.**

# SWALEDALE WATCH

**Mr. & Mrs. Savage, Whelpo, Caldbeck, Wigton, Cumbria CA7 8HQ.**
**Tel: (016974) 78409.**

Swaledale Watch is a working sheep farm within Lake District National Park where guests are very welcome to browse around or walk in the fields. Caldbeck is well situated for walking and touring. The village itself offers shops, pub, petrol, restaurants etc. Equidistant are Carlisle, Penrith, Cockermouth, Keswick or visit Hadrians Wall or the beautiful Eden Valley. Enjoy the village walks on well marked footpaths, including the limestone gorge with its waterfall or retrace Caldbeck's history on mining and milling industries long since gone. The accommodation is warm and comfortable, all rooms tastefully decorated and open fires when there is a chill in the air. All bedrooms are en-suite with tea tray, colour TV, clock radio and central heating. **Full English breakfast. Optional Evening Meal 4 nights each week with imaginative menus.** Everyone is made very welcome. No smoking. No pets in the house.

**AA QQQQ Selected**                                   **ETB 2 Crowns Highly Commended**

# NEW HOUSE FARM

**Longrose Lane, Kniveton, Ashbourne, Derbyshire DE6 1JL.**
**Tel: (01335) 342429.**

Organically managed, New House Farm is a traditional family farm in the South Peak District. Carsington water is 2 miles, Ashbourne 3, Alton Towers 10, Dove Dale is a lovely 5 mile walk. There is a bus service and village pub serving family meals. There are pets, free range livestock and a Permaculture nursury selling plants and produce. Guided farm-walks feature Bronze-Age burials, Lime Kiln, Lead-mines, quarry, wild flower area and Ley-line. We serve organic, free-range and fair - Traided foods. Vegetarians/other diets welcome. An enclosed play-area, children's teas, light suppers and baby sitting available. **£8.00 - £15.00 for Bed & Breakfast.** We also arrange free working holidays. Individual/group camping and a venue for study courses. Please telephone for details.

# PARKERS FARM HOLIDAY PARK

**Mr. & Mrs. Parker and family, Ashburton, Devon TQ13 7LJ.**
**Tel: (01364) 652598  Fax: (01364) 654004.**

A friendly, family run farm site, set in 400 acres and surrounded by beautiful countryside. 12 miles to Torbay, overlooking Dartmoor National Park.
Ideal for touring Devon/Cornwall. Perfect for children and pets, with all farm animals, play area and plenty of space to roam. Also large area for dogs. Holidays cottages and caravans fully equipped except for linen. Level touring site with some hard standings. Free showers in very clean, fully tiled block. Laundry room and games room. Small family bar, restaurant, shop and phone.

**GOOD DISCOUNTS FOR COUPLES.**

# BUCKLAND FARM

**Mrs. S.G. Taylor. Raymond Hill, nr. Axminster, Devon EX13 5ZS.
Tel: (01297) 33222.**

A warm welcome and comfortable accommodation awaits you, 3 miles from Lyme Regis and Charmouth. We are situated back off A35 in 5 acres of quiet and unspoilt surroundings for you to sit or wander in. Accommodation on ground floor in 2 family bedrooms, 1 double with en-suite shower and 1 twin bedded room, all with colour TV, washbasins, electric blankets and tea/coffee making facilities. Bathroom, shower in bath, WC, separate WC. Lounge with colour TV/video log fire if needed. Dining room with separate tables. Plenty of good food with free range eggs. Cot and high chair available. Access to rooms at all reasonable times. Friendly pub two minutes walk for evening meals. No smoking. Payphones. **Bed and Breakfast from £13.00.** Children at reduced rates. Also self-catering caravan available. Details and terms on request.

# STONE FARM

**Mrs. L. P. A. Joslin, Brayford, Barnstaple, Devon EX32 7PJ.
Tel: (01271) 830473.**

Charming 16th century character farmhouse on 180 acres working farm. 7 acres woods, well situated in peaceful countryside. Six miles between market town of Barnstaple and Exmoor. Ideal touring centre for moors and North Devon's sandy beaches. Accommodation is spacious and comfortable in family, double and twin en-suite rooms, with colour TV, tea/coffe facilities, heaters and shaving points; dining room; 2 lounges; toys for children. Exposed beams and inglenook fireplaces. Plentiful fresh food of the highest quality provided for full English breakfast. A friendly relaxed holiday with no restrictions. **Bed and Breakfast from £19.00**. Optional Evening Meal. Reductions for children. No pets. Please write or telephone for brochure and colour photo.

# WEST TITCHBERRY FARM

**Mrs. Yvonne Heard, (F.C.H), Hartland, Bideford, Devon EX39 6AU.
Tel: (01237) 441287.**

Completely renovated 18th Century farmhouse, comfortably furnished and well appointed. One family room with washhand basin, one double with washhand basin and one twin bedded room. Shared bathroom and separate shower room. Lounge with log fire and colour television. Hot drink making facilities, dining room with separate tables where excellent home cooking is served using farm produced meat and fresh vegetables, wherever possible. A games room and walled garden are available for guests use. The coastal footpath winds its way around this 150 acre mixed farm situated between Hartland Lighthouse and The National Trust beauty spot of Shipload Bay. Hartland Village 3 miles, Clovelly 6 miles, Bideford, Westward Ho! and Bude approximately 17 miles. Children welcome at reduced rates; cot, high chair and babysitting.
**S.A.E for terms. Bed and Breakfast or Evening meal.** Sorry, no pets.
**Also self catering cottage available from £90 - £320.**

# FOSFELLE COUNTRY HOUSE HOTEL

**Mrs. E. D. Underhill, Hartland, Bideford, Devon EX39 6EF.
Tel: (01237) 441273.**

17th century manor house set in six acres of grounds in peaceful surroundings with large ornamental gardens and lawns. Fosfelle offers a friendly atmosphere with excellent food, licensed bar, TV lounge with log fires on chilly evenings. Games room for children. Comfortable en-suite bedrooms with H. & C. and tea making facilities. Family room and cots available. Centrally heated throughout. Within easy reach of local beaches and touring Devon and Cornwall. Trout and coarse fishing and also clay shooting available at the hotel. Riding and golf also nearby. Open all year. Reductions for children. Dogs welcome. Details on request.

# HIGHER COWNHAYNE FARM

**Mrs. E. Pady, Cownhayne Lane, Colyton, Devon EX13 6HD.
Tel: (01297) 552267.**

Higher Cownhayne is a family working farm with milking cows, beef cattle, breeding horses, children's ponies and farm dogs and cats. Private trout fishing. Private aircraft landing strip, 400 yards long, suitable for Cessna Piper, Rally Club or helicopter. Also Model Air craft flying. Within easy reach of seaside resorts. 3 farmhouse S/C apartments, camping and caravan site on farm (all sleep 4 to 8 persons). All fully equipped including colour TV, fridge. electric cooker. Linen not supplied. Cot available. Sorry, no pets. Parking space. Shops half mile.

S.A.E., please for all replies.

# LOWER FUGE FARM

**Mrs. Brenda Wall, Strete, nr. Dartmouth, South Devon TQ6 0LL.
Tel/Fax: (01803) 770541.**

Nicely furnished holiday house on working farm close to Slapton and Blackpool Sands, near to a leisure park and golf course. This accommodation sleeps 8 plus cots, comprises of one double room and two family rooms, some en-suite facilities and a separate bathroom, bed linen provided, beds ready made. Spacious sitting room with colour TV and video. Large kitchen/diner with electric cooker, microwave, dishwasher, washing machine, tumble dryer, fridge/freezer. Large garden with lawn. Parking, car essential.

**Contact for terms.**

# WELSFORD FARM

### Mrs. C. Colwill, Hartland, Devon EX39 6EQ.
### Tel: (01237) 441296.

Relax and enjoy the peaceful countryside, yet still be within east reach of town,
interesting places and sandy beaches with miles of scenic cliff walks. This 400 acre dairy
farm is 2 miles from Hartland village and 4 miles from cobbled
Clovelly and rugged Hartland coastline. Comfortably furnished farmhouse with colour TV lounge
and H. & C. in bedrooms. Children welcome at reduced rates and they can wander
around the farm and pets corner. Babysitting always available.
Good country food using home-grown produce. Car essential. Warm welcome. Regret no pets.
Open April to October.

**Bed and Breakfast and 4-course Evening Meal from £140 per week. Bed and Breakfast £15 per night.**

# LOWER CAMPSCOTT FARM

### Mrs. M. K. Cowell, Lee, nr. Ilfracombe, Devon EX34 8LS.
### Tel: (01271) 863479.

Placed in the beautiful Fuchsia Valley, Lower Campscott Farm offers guests a warm welcome and happy
holiday atmosphere. We have **4 self catering cottages; 2 Keys Approved** smallest sleeps 4 persons;
largest sleeps 10 persons. The cottages are newly converted farm buildings and are all furnished.
Linen supplied. Communal laundry room.
**Also available, one 6 berth caravan** with gas cooking and heating, shower and flush toilet.

**The farmhouse,** set on a 91 acre dairy farm, offers guests accommodation comprising two double and one
twin bedded room, bathroom, toilet, sittingroom and diningroom. Bed and Breakfast. Ideal base for touring the
various beauty spots in the area and the unspoilt village of Lee. Children will love the many rock pools at Lee
Bay. Ilfracombe three miles. Delightful walking country.

**Send S.A.E. for details or telephone above number.**

# THE BUNGALOW, HIGHER COARSEWELL FARM

Mrs. S. Winzer, Ugborough, nr. Ivybridge, Devon PL21 0HP.
Tel: (01548) 821560.

Part of a traditional family run dairy farm. Situated in the heart of the
peaceful South Hams countryside, near Dartmoor and local unspoilt sandy
beaches. A very spacious bungalow with beautiful garden and meadow
views. One double with bathroom en-suite and one en-suite family room.
Linen provided. Good home cooked food, full English breakfast provided.
Children welcome - cot, high chair and babysitting available. Access for the
disabled. Open all year. A379 turn off from main A38 Exeter to
Plymouth road. Parking space. Dogs permitted.

**Bed and Breakfast from £14 daily, optional Evening Meal extra.**

# MARSH MILLS

**Mrs. M. Newsham, Aveton Gifford, Kingsbridge, South Devon TQ7 4JW.**
**Tel/Fax: (01548) 550549.**

Georgian Mill House, overlooking the River Avon, with mill pond, mill leat and duck pond. Small farm with friendly animals. Peaceful and secluded, just off the A379, Kingsbridge 4 miles, Plymouth 17 miles. Bigbury and Bantham with their beautiful sandy beaches are nearby, or enjoy a walk along our unspoilt river estuary, or the miles of beautiful South Devon Coastal Paths. We are only 8 miles from Dartmoor. One double and one double/twin room, both en-suite with colour TV; other rooms have washbasins, and there is a guest bathroom with additional separate W.C. All bedrooms have tea/coffee making facilities, and room heaters. Guests have their own lounge/dining room with colour TV. Beautiful gardens, ample car parking. Well controlled dogs by arrangement.

**Bed and Breakfast from £16 per night. Telephone, Fax or SAE for brochure or enquiries.**

# BLACKWELL PARK

**Mrs B. Kelly, Loddiswell, Kingsbridge, Devon TQ7 4EA.**
**Tel: (01548) 821230.**

Blackwell Park is a 17th century farmhouse situated five miles from Kingsbridge and two miles from Loddiswell. Many beaches within easy reach, also Dartmoor, Plymouth, Torbay and Dartmouth. Adjoining 54 acres of nature reserve woodland managed by the Devon Wildlife Trust. The farmhouse has seven bedrooms for guests, all with H.& C., Tea/Coffee facilities, some en-suite. Separate tables in dining room; lounge with colour TV. Large games room with darts, snooker, table tennis, skittles, etc. Garden with plenty of grass area, for games, and large car parking area. Ample food with choice of menu. Help yourself to tea or coffee any time. Fire certificate. **CHILDREN AND PETS ESPECIALLY WELCOME.** Babysitting. **Bed, Breakfast and Evening Meal or Bed and Breakfast only.** **English Tourist Board 2 Crowns**

# CROSS FARM HOLIDAYS

**Mr. & Mrs. M. Turner, East Allington, Kingsbridge, Devon TQ9 7RW.**
**Tel: (01548) 521327.**

Lovely old part of farmhouse and beautifully converted barn. Both sleep 11. Equipped to a very high standard with dishwasher, microwave, washing machine, dryer, fridge freezer, duvets, linen. Cleanliness guaranteed. Play area, recreation barn. This working farm is in an area of outstanding natural beauty close to coast, Salcombe and Dartmouth. Baby minding available. Children most welcome to help feed animals. Parking space. Dogs allowed. A truly family holiday. Brochure available.

**Prices from £225 - £700**

# BURTON FARM

**2 Crowns Highly Commended**

**Anne Rossiter, Galmpton, Kingsbridge, Devon TQ7 3EY.**
**Tel: (01548) 561210.**

Working farm in South Huish Valley, one mile from the fishing village of Hope Cove, three miles from famous sailing haunt of Salcombe. Walking, beaches, sailing, windsurfing, bathing, diving, fishing, horse-riding - facilities for all in this area. There is a dairy herd and three flocks of pedigree sheep. Guests are welcome to take part in farm activities when appropriate. Traditional farmhouse cooking and home produce. Four course Dinner, Bed and Breakfast. Access to rooms at all times. Tea/coffee making facilities, TV, some en-suite. Games room. No smoking. Open all year, except Christmas. Warm welcome assured. Small functions catered for. 2 self-catering cottages recently renovated retaining original features. 5 mins. walk from farm. Well equipped, comfortably furnished. 1 mile from 2 beaches. 3 miles Salcombe. Dogs by arrangement. Details and terms on request. **Bed and Breakfast from £21 - £25.**
**2 Self Catering Cottages, 5 minutes walk from the farm, also available from £30 per day - £450 per week.**

# GREAT SLONCOMBE FARM

**Mrs. Trudie Merchant, Moretonhampstead, Devon TQ13 8QF.**
**Tel/Fax: (01647) 440595.**

Share the magic of Dartmoor all year round while staying in our lovely 13th century farmhouse full of interesting historical features. A working dairy farm set amongst peaceful meadows and woodland abundant in wild flowers and animals including badgers, foxes, deer and buzzards. A welcoming and informal place to relax and explore the moors and Devon countryside. Comfortable double and twin rooms with en-suite, central heating, TV's and coffee/tea making. Delicious Devonshire suppers and Breakfasts with new baked bread. Open all year. No smoking.

**ETB 3 Crowns Highly Commended**

# FLUXTON FARM HOTEL

*Cat Lovers Paradise*

Lovely 16th century farmhouse in beautiful Otter Valley, 4 miles from sea at Sidmouth, 2 acre garden with trout pond, stream and garden railway. Licensed. Two lounges (one non-smoking) both with colour television.

Bar. Beamed candlelit dining room, superb food using all local fresh produce. All bedrooms en-suite with TV and central heating. 'Teasmades'. Parking. Children and pets welcome.

**Terms from: Dinner, Bed and Breakfast £30.00 per person per night.**
**Bed and Breakfast £23.00.**

Contact:
**Mrs Ann Forth, Ottery St. Mary, Devon EX11 1RJ.**
**Tel: (01404) 812818.**

**AA Listed**                    **STB 3 Crowns**

# GRANARY FARM COTTAGES

**Yeo Lane, North Tawton, Devon EX20 2DD**
**Tel: (01837) 82252**

Luxury accomodation in stone walled cottages, situated between Okehampton and Exeter. Tastefully converted from Granary barns. Completely surrounded by idyllic country scenery and lovely river walks along the Tarka Trail just 5 miles from Dartmoor National Park. All cottages have spacious oak beamed living rooms with wood burning stoves, central heating, fully equipped kitchens, bathrooms and showers etc. Within six private acres you will find an indoor heated pool sauna, orchard, paddock, games room, laundry room and gardens. Nearby facilities include superb restaurants, pubs, shops, riding, fishing, golf, cycling routes, tennis and many accesible tourist attractions. Children and well behaved pets welcome. Cottages with 2 and 3 bedrooms. Sleeps 4-7. **From £230 per week.** Short breaks available. Write or telephone for a brochure.

# HATCHLANDS FARM

**Mrs. Sheree Palmer, Blue Post, Avonwick, nr. Totnes, Devon TQ9 7LR.**
**Tel/Fax: (01364) 72224.**

A very warm welcome awaits you at Hatchlands, a luxury farmhouse set on a working farm amist Devon's most beautiful scenery, offering tranquility, magnificent views and unique walks. There are 2 guest bedrooms, both en-suite with colour TV and tea making facilities; one has a four poster bed. In the sun lounge there is a snooker table with fabulous views over the landscaped gardens and 20ft pond stocked with Koi Carp. Breakfast is a scrumptious 4 courses served at a time to suit you. Hatchlands is a 355 acre dairy, arable and beef farm, situated in the South Hams; close to many award winning beaches and near to Dartmoor which must not be missed!

**Bed & Breakfast is very reasonably priced £14.00 - £20.00**
*with further reductions for children and weekly bookings.*

# SNAPDOWN FARM CARAVANS

**Mrs. M. Bowen, Snapdown, Chittlehamholt, Umberleigh, North Devon EX37 9PF.**
**Tel: (01769) 540708.**

12 only, 6 berth caravans, in two sheltered adjoining paddocks, in lovely unspoilt countryside, backing onto trees down quiet lane on farm. Well spread out, each with hard standing for car. Flush toilet, shower, colour TV, fridge, gas cooker and fire. Laundry room with washing machine, tumble dryer, iron etc. Outside seats, picnic tables, barbeque. Table tennis. Field and woodland walks. Children's play area in small wood adjoining. Easy reach sea and moors. Well behaved pets welcome.

**Prices from £85 - £210 (includes caravans)**

**DISCOUNT FOR COUPLES, EARLY AND LATE SEASON.**

Contact above address for an illustrated brochure.

# KILMORIE HOLDINGS

**S. J. Barnfield, Gloucester Road, Snigs End, Corse, Staunton, nr. Gloucester, Gloucestershire GL19 3RQ. Tel: (01452) 840224.**

Deceptively spacious, yet warm and cosy benefitting from full central heating. Built 1848 Grade II Listed tastefully modernised, extended, all ground floor accommodation. Double, twin, family and single bedrooms all having colour TV, wash basins, radio, tea trays, comfortable guests lounge. Dining room overlooking our large attractive gardens with ample seats, relax and watch birds and butterflies we encourage to visit. Make friends with our goats, ponies, sheep, ducks (children may "help") free range hens provide excellent eggs for breakfast. Discover more Gloucestershire countryside by taking a leisurely walk across farmland on a network of waymarked footpaths which start at Kilmorie. Traditional home cooking, safe ample parking, tents/tourers welcome. Children over 5 years. No dogs.
**Bed and full English Breakfast from £15.00. 3 Course Evening Dinner, Bed and Breakfast from £22.50.**

# EFFORD COTTAGE BED & BREAKFAST

**Mrs. Patricia Elliss, Everton, Lymington, Hants SO41 0JD.
Tel: (01590) 642315 or Mobile 0374 703075 for brochure.**

Our friendly, award winning Guest House is a spacious Georgian cottage, standing in an acre of garden. All rooms have en-suite facilities together with full beverage facilities, CTV, heated towel rail, hair dryer, electric blanket, trouser press and mini fridge. We offer a four course, multi-choice breakfast with homemade bread and preserves. Optional evening meals, by qualified chef, using homegrown vegetables. An excellent centre for exploring both the New Forest and the South Coast with sports facilities, fishing, bird watching and horse riding in the near vicinity. Private parking. Dogs welcome. Sorry no children under 12 years.

**Bed and Breakfast from £21 per person, Evening Meal from £15.**

**AA Selected QQQQ RAC Highly Acclaimed
ETB 3 Crowns Commended STB Member Welcome Host**

# MOOR COURT FARM

**Peter & Elizabeth Godsall, Stretton, Grandison, nr. Ledbury, Herefordshire HR8 2TR.
Tel: (01531) 670408.**

Relax and enjoy our attractive 15 century timber-framed farmhouse with adjoining oast house, whose location will ensure a peaceful break. We are a traditional working Herefordshire hop and livestock farm situated in scenic countryside. Central to the major market towns, easy access to the Malverns, Wye Valley and Welsh borders. Spacious bedrooms, en-suite or private bathroom, tea/coffee making facilities, oak-beamed lounge and dining room. Fishing is available in our own pool and there are stables on the farm.

**Terms from: Bed and Breakfast £17.50. Evening Meal £12.50.**

**ETB Commended**

## WEBTON COURT

**Mrs. R.T. Andrew, Kingstone, Hereford HR2 9NF.**
**Tel: (01981) 250220.**

Webton Court is a Georgian black and white farmhouse situated in the heart of the beautiful Wye Valley. The farm supplies all their own vegetables and fruits and home cooking can be enjoyed each day. There are many places to visit from touring the Forest of Dean to the rugged Welsh mountains where wild ponies naturally graze. Journey through Shakespeare's country. Nearby are the 'Olde Worlde' Herefordshire villages of Weobley, Eardisland and Pembridge with their timbered black and white cottages. Horse riding is available nearby. Guest lounge with colour TV, all rooms. H.&C., tea/coffee making facilities, black & white TV in all bedrooms. Twin/Double en-suite bedrooms. Car parking. Licensed to sell wines and spirits. Please contact us for further information.

**ETB 2 Crowns**

## ROSE FARM

**Mrs. J. Durrant, School Lane, Suton, Wymondham, Norfolk NR18 9JN.**
**Tel: (01953) 603512.**

Rose Farm is situated 2.5 miles from Attleborough, 5 miles from Snetterton Race Course and 2.5 miles from the charming market town of Wymondham. Wymondham is well known for its historic twin-towered Abbey Church and other buildings of great interest. We are 3/4 mile from the A11 trunk road from London to Norwich and therefore within easy reach of all coastal resorts, the Norfolk Broads and the Breckland Forest. On our smallholding of 8 acres we keep geese, ducks, bantams and chickens - offering free range eggs throughout the year. We have donkeys which young children are welcome to ride. All bedrooms are ground floor and have their own TV's. The accommodation is fully centrally heated. Reductions for children. Dogs welcome. Open all year except over Christmas.

**Bed and Breakfast from £19.00.**          **ETB Registered**

## LORBOTTLE WEST STEADS

**Mrs. H. M. Farr, Thropton, Morpeth, Northumberland NE65 7JT.**
**Tel: (01665) 574672.**

This working farm lies in Whittingham Vale surrounded by the rolling hills of the Cheviots and Simonside's charming unspoilt countryside. 4.5 miles away lies the market town of Rothbury. We are very central for visiting all parts of Northumbria which is steeped in historical interest and natural beauty. We offer **Bed and Breakfast from £15.00.** Own lounge/dining room with open fire and colour TV. Full central heating. Guests only bathroom. Bedrooms have colour TV and drinks tray. Also self catering cottage sleeps five, full CH by gas, DG, linen provided, well equipped kitchen and comfortably decorated and furnished.

**ETB Listed Commended          3 Keys Commended**

# GORSELANDS FARMHOUSE

**Mrs. B. Jones, Auberge, Boddington Lane, nr. Long Hanborough,
nr. Woodstock, Oxfordshire OX8 6PU.
Tel: (01993) 881895  Fax: (01993) 882799.**

Gorselands is a beautiful old Cotswold stone farmhouse situated in idyllic countryside with its own grounds of 1 acre. Convenient for Woodstock, Blenheim Palace, North Leigh Roman Villa and Oxford. The house has flagstone floors, exposed beams and a guests lounge. Evening meals are served in the candlelit galleried dining room. Large family/double/twin en-suite rooms available. There is a full size billiards table and tennis court for guests' use (rackets available). Cot and babysitting service. **Bed and Breakfast from £19.75. Evening meal from £10.95.** Drinks licence.

**Elizabeth Gundrey Recommended    RAC Listed    ETB 2 Crowns Commended**

# THE HALL

**Mrs. Christine Price, Bucknell, Shropshire SY7 0AA.
Tel: (01547) 530249.**

Christine and Eddie Price welcome you to their large Georgian farmhouse on a 200 acre sheep/cereal farm. After a substantial breakfast you will be ready to embark upon this captivating Welsh border region, the Central Wales hills, North Herefordshire's black and white villages, and our own South Shropshire historic towns and castles. We have 3 bedrooms; 1 twin en-suite and 2 double with washbasins. All have TV and tea/coffee making facilities.

**Bed and Breakfast from £18.00 per person. Evening Meal £10.00.**

**ETB 2 Crowns Commended**

# FALCONERS FARM

**Mrs. Judith Peach, Milton, Ash, Martock, Somerset TA12 6AL.
Tel: (01935) 823363.**

A Georgian farmhouse set on 320 acres of mixed working farmland on a Duchy of Cornwall farm belonging to the Prince of Wales Estates. All visitors welcome to tour farm and watch. A family farm just off A303. Nearest town Yeovil seven miles. Horse riding and coarse fishing convenient for shopping in Taunton. Local attractions include Montacute House and Cricket St. Thomas Wildlife Park. The coast is three quarter of an hour's drive. Accommodation in three guest rooms (one family), own bathroom. All children welcome, cot, high chair and babysitting available. Car essential. Telephone or write for further details.

**Bed and Breakfast from £14 - £17 per person per night.**

# HUNGERFORD FARM

**Mrs. Sarah Richmond, Washford, Watchet, Somerset TA23 0JZ.**
**Tel: (01984) 640285.**

Hungerford Farm is a comfortable 13th century farmhouse on a 350 acre mixed farm. Situated in beautiful countryside on the edge of the Brendon Hills and Exmoor National park. Within easy reach of the North Devon Coast, 2.5 miles from the Bristol Channel and Quantock Hills. 3/4 mile from Somerset Railway. Open all year. Marvellous country for walking, riding and fishing on the reservoirs. Stabling available for own horses. Family room and twin-bedded room with TV, bathroom, shower, toilet; own lounge with TV and open fire. Children welcome at reduced rates, cot and high chair. Sorry, no pets. Reductions for longer stays. Open March to end of November.

**Bed and Breakfast from £16.00, evening drink included.**

# AGDON FARM

**Mrs. M. Cripps, Brailes, Banbury, Warwickshire OX15 5JJ.**
**Tel: (01608) 685226.**

A warm welcome awaits all our guests on our working farm. Our comfortable Cotswold stone farmhouse is set in 500 acres of mixed farming in an unspoilt part of the countryside, 10 miles from M40. Within walking distance of Compton Wynyates, in close driving range of the Cotswolds, Warwick, Stratford-upon-Avon, Banbury, Oxford and Blenheim Palace. Accommodation with full English Breakfast. Home produced food served. TV room, separate dining room, guests bathroom. Central heating. Pleasant rooms with tea/coffee making facilites. Cot, high chair and baby sitting available. Linen provided. Parking space. Dogs allowed.

**Tourist Board Registered**    **Prices from £17.50 per person per night.**

# CAMP FARM

**Mrs. Sandra Evans, Hob Lane, Balsall Common, nr. Coventry, Warwickshire CV7 7GX.**
**Tel: (01676) 533804.**

Camp Farm is a farmhouse 150 to 200 years old. It is modernised but still retains its old world character. Nestling in the heart of England in Shakespeare country, within easy reach of Stratford-upon-Avon, Warwick, Kenilworth, Coventry with its famous Cathedral and the New National Centre site. Camp Farm offers a warm, homely atmosphere and good English food, service and comfortable beds. Dining room and lounge with colour TV. Bedrooms - 3 double, 2 twin and 2 single rooms. Open all year.

**Bed and Breakfast from £22.00.**

**Tourist Board Listed Commended**

## CHURCH FARM

**Mrs. Marian J. Walters, Dorsington, Stratford-upon-Avon, Warwickshire CV37 8AX.**
**Tel: (01789) 720471  Fax: (01789) 720830  Mobile: 0831 504194**

A warm and friendly welcome awaits you throughout the year at our Georgian farmhouse with open fires and central heating. Stratford-upon-Avon, Warwick, NEC, Royal Showground, Cotswolds and Vale of Evesham are all within easy driving distance. Guests are free to explore the 127 acre mixed working farm. Gliding, ballooning, micro-lighting, boating and fishing are all nearby. Tea/coffee facilities and TV's in all rooms. Most rooms with en-suite. Good places within 2 miles for evening meals. Children welcome at reduced rates. Cot/high chair. Car essential. Full fire certificate held.

**Bed and Breakfast from £17 - £19 per person.**

**Tourist Board Registered 2 Crowns Commended**

## WHITFIELD FARM

**Mrs. J. Wakeham, Ettington, Stratford-upon-Avon, Warwickshire CV37 7PN.**
**Tel: (01789) 740260.**

Situated down its own private drive, off the A429, this 220 acre mixed farm (wheat, cows, sheep, geese, horses, hens) is ideal for a quiet and relaxing holiday. Convenient for visiting the Cotswolds, Warwick, Coventry, Stratford and Worcester. Fully modernised house with separate lounge and colour TV, 2 en-suite bedrooms, two double and one twin bedrooms with washbasins and tea/coffee making facilities; bathroom, two toilets, dining room. Sorry no pets. Reduced rates for children, cot and babysitting by arrangement. Car essential - parking. Open all year (except Christmas) for **Bed and Breakfast from £15.00 per night**. Home produced food served. Full English Breakfast. S.A.E. please.

**AA Recommended**

## DOG KENNEL FARM COTTAGES

**Mrs. Jill Allen, Iford, nr. Bradford-on-Avon, Wiltshire BA15 2BB.**
**Tel: (01225) 723533.**

300 acre beef farm with calves and hens. Children welcome, baby minding, dogs welcome. Thirty miles from sandy beach. Bath 6 miles. The farm cottage is in the grounds of our 300 acre farm, which is situated in the Limpley Stoke Valley, a very quiet spot in beautiful wooded countryside - 1 mile off the A36 Warminster-Bath road. Guests are welcome to look over the farm at any time where we have calves, hens and family pets. About 150 yards distance in front of the cottage is the river Frome, also Iford Manor with its Italian gardens and the Mill House. There are many places of interest within motoring distance of which Longleat House and Lion Reserve, Tropical Bird gardens, Wells Cathedral, Cheddar Gorge and caves, Castle Combe and Bath are just a few examples. We have ample parking facilities. Reductions for children under 10 years. **Bed and Breakfast £15.00 - £16.00.** Homely atmosphere.

# LOWER FIELD FARM

### Mrs. Jane Hill, Willersey, Broadway, Worcestershire WR11 5HF.
### Tel: (01386) 858273/0976 897525  Fax: (01386) 854608.

Lowerfield Farm offers genuine farmhouse comfort and hospitality in a late 17th century stone and brick farmhouse looking out onto the Cotswold hills. Delightful rooms all en-suite with tea and coffee making facilities, hair dryers, clock radio and colour TV. This peaceful location provides an ideal base from which to explore the Cotswolds, Statford-upon-Avon, Warwick and Sudely Castles, Oxford, Cheltenham and beyond. Children welcome. Baby minding available. Parking space. Dogs allowed. Evening meal by arrangement or wealth of good
eating houses nearby. Open all year.

### Bed and full English Breakfast from £20 per head.

## BRICKBARNS FARM

**Mrs. J. L. Morris, Hanley Road, Malvern Wells, Worcestershire WR14 4HY.
Tel: (016845) 61775.**

Brickbarns, a 200 acre mixed working farm is situated two miles from Great Malvern Hills, 300 yards from the bus services and 1.5 miles from the train. The house, which is 300 years old, commands excellent views of the Malvern Hills and guests are accommodated in 1 double, 1 single and 1 family bedroom with washbasins; 2 bathrooms, shower room, 2 toilets; sitting room and dining room. Children welcome and cot and babysitting offered. Central heating. Car essential, parking. **Open Easter to October for Bed and Breakfast from £16 nightly per person, (£15 for longer stays).** Reductions for children and Senior Citizens. Birmingham 40 miles, Hereford 20, Gloucester 17, Stratford 35 and the Wye Valley is just 30 miles.

# ROWANTREE FARM

**Mrs. B. Tindall, Danby, Whitby, Yorkshire YO21 2LE.
Tel: (01287) 660396.**

Rowantree Farm is situated in the heart of the North Yorks Moors. It is a large stone built old farmhouse with panoramic moorland views. It is a working farm comprising 120 acres. It is set in ideal walking country and is also close to the coast. The Moors information centre is close at hand where trained staff are always willing to hand out information on the whole of the North Yorks Moors. There are 3 bedrooms: 1 twin, 1 double and 1 family. There is a spacious residents lounge and separate dining room with colour television. Children are welcome and babysitting can be arranged. Ample car parking space

**Bed and Breakfast from £15.00. Evening Meals provided on request, £7.00.
Discounts for weekly bookings**

# ORILLIA HOUSE

**Mike Cundall, 89 The Village, Stockton-on-Forest, York, Yorkshire YO3 9UP.
Tel: (01904) 400600.**

A warm welcome awaits you at Orillia House, conveniently situated 3 miles north east of York, 1 mile from A64. The house dates back to the 17th century and has been restored to offer a high standard of comfort with modern facilities, yet retaining its original charm and character. All rooms have private facilities, colour TV and tea/coffee making facilities. Our local pub provides excellent evening meals. We also have our own private car park. Telephone for our brochure.

**Bed and Breakfast from £18.00**

**ETB Registered 2 Crowns Commended**

# Trade Description Act

The accommodation mentioned in this
guide has not been inspected, and the publishers rely
on information provided.

The publishers have every confidence in their advertisers but cannot be
held responsible for the accuracy of the descriptions published.

# Farm and Country Accommodation

## Scotland

*Argyll*

## APPIN HOLIDAY HOMES

### Mr. & Mrs. P. Weir, Appin, Argyll PA38 4BQ. Tel: (01631) 730287.

An excellent choice of self catering chalet bungalows, traditional cottages and superior holiday residential caravans, set apart in this area of outstanding beauty, midway between Oban and Fort William. Sleeps 2-5. Each fully self-contained. Very private. Ideal for families, also honeymoons...very romantic! A nature lovers' paradise. Hill and shoreline walks. Free fishing (salt & freshwater). Boats available. Play area. Launderette. Baby sitting service. Pony trekking, sailing and licensed inn nearby. Good touring centre. Special early and late terms with extra discount to a couple. Free colour brochure (SAE please).

**Price guide: £155 - £345 per unit weekly.** *Personal attention from resident proprietors.*

**STB 4 Crowns Commended**

## ROCKHILL FARM COUNTRY HOUSE & SELF CATERING COTTAGES

### Mrs. Whalley, Ardbrecknish, by Dalmally, Argyll PA33 1BH. Tel: (01866) 833218.

Residential Licence, 5 bedrooms all facilities. Dalmally 10 miles. Inverary 13 miles. Ideal spot for those wanting real peace and quiet overlooking the loch to the Cruachan range of mountains. This is a Hanoverian horse's stud farm with lots of mares and foals. Enjoy the comfortable, informal cottage style accommodation and the highly acclaimed home cooking. We have 1100 yards of private lochshore trout and coarse fishing and a private Lochan. A boat can be hired or bring your own. Superb area for birdwatching, walking, climbing and touring many castles and gardens. Also available on the farm for weekly hire are **two Self Catering units - 1 bungalow and 1 traditional stone cottage** both overlooking the loch, well equipped to sleep 6. Everything provided except linen, which can be hired. Electricity by meter reading. Established 1960. **AA/RAC Recommended**

# BUSBIEHILL GUEST HOUSE

**Mr. & Mrs. P. Gibson, Knockentiber, Kilmarnock, Ayrshire KA2 0DJ.**
**Tel: (01563) 532985.**

Busbiehill is the oldest guest house in the area with many recommendations from home and abroad. This homely county guest house with panoramic views, overlooks Irvine to the Arran hills. Very central for overnight stays to Erskine Bridge A52 or ferry to Arran. Kilmarnock is one of the best planned towns with every facility for tourists and homely friendly people, also suitable for a relaxed holiday for golfers with 22 courses within easy reach. We are 1 mile from A71, Glasgow 22, Largs 22, Edinburgh 63. Nearest station Kilmaurs. 5 double with 2 en-suite, 3 twin bedded, 5 bathrooms with toilet upstairs. Ladies, gents toilet downstairs. No pets. Children welcome over 5 years. Tea making facilities.

**Bed and Breakfast from £15.00**

# NINEWELLS FARMHOUSE

**Barbara Baird, Woodriffe Road, Newburgh (nr. Perth), Fife KY14 6EY.**
**Tel: (01337) 840307.**

Situated in a quiet elevated position overlooking the River Tay, with magnificient views which can be enjoyed from the lounge. Close proximity Junction 9 - M90.
An ideal situation for your golfing holiday with very many courses within easy reach. Central for St. Andrews, Carnoustie, Rosemount & Ladybank.
A warm welcome is assured in this very comfortable farmhouse on a fully operational stock/arable farm, by Gavin & Barbara Baird. Parking available. Non Smoking.

**STB Highly Commended**

# SPINKSTOWN FARMHOUSE

**Mrs. Anne Duncan, St. Andrews, Fife KY16 8PN.**
**Tel: (01334) 473475.**

Only 2 miles from St. Andrews on the A917 coast road to Crail, Spinkstown is a uniquely designed farmhouse. Bright and spacious it is furnished to a high standard with accommodation in double and twin rooms, all with en-suite facilities. Dining room and lounge with colour TV. Substantial farmhouse breakfast to set you up for the day, evening meals by arrangement only. The famous Old Course, historical St. Andrews and several National Trust properties are all within easy reach, as well as swimming, tennis, putting, bowls, horse riding, country parks, nature reserves, beaches and coastal walks. Plenty of parking available.

**Bed and Breakfast from £18.50 - £20.00. Evening Meal £12.00.**

**AA Selected QQQQ          STB Highly Commended**

# GLEN LOY LODGE HOTEL

**Mr. and Mrs. A. G. Ward, Banavie, nr. Fort William, Inverness-shire PH33 7PD.
Tel: (01397) 712700.**

Glen Loy Lodge is a well-appointed, comfortable country house providing good food and wine in a warm, friendly, relaxed atmosphere. Situated in its own grounds by the River Loy amid deer forest, river, loch and mountains. Close to Fort William and Ben Nevis. Ideal base for walking, climbing, fishing and motoring. Central heating. Seven double and two single bedrooms all en-suite, two bathrooms, three toilets; two sitting rooms; dining room. Children welcome, cot available; car essential, ample parking; residential licence. The Lodge has a boat on Loch Arkaig, fishing free for guests.

**Evening Dinner, Bed and Breakfast or Bed and Breakfast. Rates from £18.00 - £26.00, reduced for children.**

**STB 3 Crowns Commended**

# HIGH PARK FARM

**Mrs. J. E. Shaw, Balmaclellan, Castle Douglas, Kirkcudbrightshire DG7 3PT.
Tel: (01644) 420298.**

A warm welcome awaits guests at High Park. This 171 acre family-run farm is situated by Loch Ken, popular for fishing and boating. 12 miles from Catle Douglas and 2 miles from New Galloway. All bedrooms have washbasins, shaver points, tea/coffee making facilities plus central heating. Our comfortable sitting/dining room has colour TV and an on colder nights an inviting log fire. Contact for further details.

**Bed and Breakfast from £15.00**

**STB 1 Crown Commended**

# CRAIGHALL FARMHOUSE

**Mrs. Mary Fotheringham, Forgandenny, Bridge of Earn, Perthshire PH2 9DF.
Tel: (01738) 812415.**

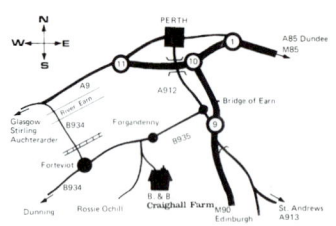

Situated in the lovely Earn Valley we offer true Highland hospitality in our farmhouse only 6 miles south of Perth and half a mile west from Forgandenny on the B935. The farm is within easy reach of Edinburgh, St Andrews, Glasgow and Pitlochry. Golf, tennis and swimming nearby, hill walking and lovely scenery. Accommodation includes rooms with private facilities and en-suite; tea/coffee making facilities; guest lounge with colour TV. Children welcome. Sorry no pets.

**Bed and Breakfast from £16.50**

**STB 3 Crowns     AA & RAC Highly Acclaimed**

# Farm and Country
## Accommodation

### Wales

## LLORAN GANOL FARM

**Mrs. G. Jones, Llansillin, nr. Oswestry, Clwyd SY10 7OX.
Tel: (01691) 791287.**

A friendly welcome is assured at this modern farm set in 300 acres of Welsh valley. A busy working farm of dairy, sheep and cattle, it has surrounding garden and lawns. Fly fishing and rough shooting. Tastefully furnished farmhouse has two double bedrooms (one double, one twin), each with washbasin and tea/coffee making facilities: modern bathroom. Large lounge and dining room; colour TV. English Breakfast and Evening Meal by prior arrangement. Self Catering cottage also available.

**Bed and Breakfast from £15; Dinner, Bed and Breakfast from £30. Weekly Self Catering from £80.**

**WTB 1 Crown**

## GLANDWR

**Mrs. B. Cole, Trefriw, nr. Llanrwst, North Wales LL27 0JP.
Tel: (01492) 640431.**

Glandwr is a large Country House on the outskirts of Trefriw village and overlooking the Conway River and its Valley. With beautiful views towards the Clwydian Hills. 3 miles away is the market town of Llanrwst and Betws-y-Coed and Swallows Falls lies 5 miles away. Good touring area as all North Wales coastal and mountain areas are within easy reach of Trefriw. Just above the village lies Crafnant Lake offering fishing and walking. There is golfing and pony trekking close by. Comfortable rooms, lounge with TV, dining room, all bedrooms fitted with washbasins. Good home cooking using local produce whenever possible. Parking space. Guide dogs and hearing dogs for deaf especially welcome.

**Bed and Breakfast from £16.**

# GLYN UCHAF

**Mrs. Baxter, Conwy Old Road, Dwygsylchi, Penmaenmawr, Conwy LL34 6YS.**
**Tel: (01492) 623737.**
**WTB 3 Crowns**

This is an old mill house, set in 11 acres of National Parkland, beautifully situated in mountainous countryside. Quiet, peaceful, holiday. Three minute walk to village with its pubs. 2.5 miles historic Conway, 5 miles to Llandudno and Colwyn Bay. An ideal touring centre for Snowdonia. Accommodation for guests in 3 bedrooms, all en-suite, with tea & coffee making facilities and views over Anglesey. Dining room, residents' lounge with colour TV. Children welcome and pets allowed. Also stabling available for those wishing to bring their own horses. Pony trekking and fishing available locally. Golf. Good home cooking using home grown products (soups, pates, roasts, etc.). Ample parking. Guests have access to house at all times. **Bed and Breakfast, Evening Meal optional. Reductions for children under 12. Further details on request - S.A.E. or phone please.**

# PORTHMADOG

**Mrs. E. A. J. Williams, Tyddyn Deucwm Isaf, Penmorfa, Porthmadog,**
**Gwynedd, North Wales LL49 9SD.**
**Tel: (01766) 513683.**

Luxurious 6 berth leisure home, between Porthmadog and Criccieth, just off the Caernarfon Road. Boasts magnificent views of Cardigan Bay, Porthmadog Estuary and Criccieth Castle. Only 1 on quiet, sunny, sheltered working farm. Approximately 7 minutes from beach (Black Rock Sands - 2 miles from Golden Sands), 2 minutes from shops, 5 minutes from "Little Trains" and Porthmadog. Fishing nearby. Excellent area for walking and climbing. 3 separate bedrooms, velour seating in lounge. Electricity and gas, fridge, stove, shower room and toilet. Power plugs. Colour TV. Barbecue on request. Dogs by arrangement.

S.A.E. for details.

# THE GREEN LANTERN GUEST HOUSE

**Mrs. M. Brown, Hawdref Ganol Farm, Cimla, Neath, Glamorgan SA12 9SL.**
**Tel: (01639) 631884.**

For those wishing to sample Welsh hospitality at its best, then a visit to this luxury 18th century farmhouse is a must. Set in its own grounds, perched on a hillside overlooking the Vale of Neath, just a mile from the birthplace of Richard Burton. If you require a peaceful and relaxing break, and home cooking at its best, please give us a call.

**Bed and Breakfast from £20 - £23 per person. Evening Meal £10.**

**AA Premier Selected QQQQQ**
**WTB 3 Crowns Highly Commended**

## CUCKOO MILL FARM

**Mrs. D. D. Davies, Pelcomb Bridge, St. David's Road,
Haverfordwest, Pembrokeshire.
Tel: (01437) 762139.**

Cuckoo Mill Farm is a 320 acres mixed farm in central Pembrokeshire.
Plenty of country walks
on and around the farm and a small trout stream.
Six miles from the beach. Meal times to suit guests.
H. & C. & tea making facilities.
Pets allowed.

**Reductions for children and senior citizens.**

Open all year.

# NOLTON HAVEN

## Mr. Jim Canton, Haverfordwest, Pembrokeshire SA62 9NH.
## Tel/Fax: (01437) 710263.

St. David's, Nolton Haven Farmhouse and Cottages, in the Pembrokeshire
National Park is situated beside Nolton Havens' sandy beach which they
overlook. The farm guest house offers Bed and Breakfast and is open to
guests all day, with free babysitting.

The six stone slate and pine cottages offer discerning guests the ideal
situation to enjoy the superb Pembrokeshire coastline. The cottages are fully
equipped with colour TV, fridge/freezer and microwave.

75 yards to the local Inn restaurant.

### Colour brochure on request.

### Prices range from £130 - £400 per week

| | Aberdeen | Birmingham | Bristol | Cardiff | Carlisle | Dover | Edinburgh | Fort William | Glasgow | Holyhead | Hull | Inverness | Leeds | Liverpool | London | Manchester | Newcastle | Norwich | Nottingham | Plymouth |
|---|---|---|---|---|---|---|---|---|---|---|---|---|---|---|---|---|---|---|---|---|
| Aberdeen | - | 698 | 830 | 864 | 377 | 942 | 203 | 254 | 238 | 745 | 579 | 171 | 528 | 579 | 882 | 568 | 381 | 789 | 637 | 1017 |
| Birmingham | 434 | - | 142 | 174 | 319 | 328 | 480 | 657 | 478 | 245 | 225 | 737 | 195 | 163 | 193 | 143 | 333 | 283 | 85 | 327 |
| Bristol | 516 | 88 | - | 76 | 454 | 336 | 613 | 792 | 613 | 380 | 373 | 872 | 354 | 298 | 193 | 277 | 481 | 375 | 232 | 201 |
| Cardiff | 537 | 108 | 47 | - | 486 | 393 | 645 | 824 | 645 | 330 | 406 | 904 | 386 | 330 | 249 | 311 | 513 | 430 | 266 | 262 |
| Carlisle | 234 | 198 | 282 | 302 | - | 639 | 158 | 336 | 158 | 367 | 275 | 417 | 195 | 201 | 504 | 192 | 93 | 457 | 303 | 639 |
| Dover | 585 | 204 | 209 | 244 | 397 | - | 735 | 977 | 800 | 566 | 420 | 1059 | 435 | 484 | 127 | 463 | 566 | 274 | 348 | 468 |
| Edinburgh | 126 | 298 | 381 | 401 | 98 | 457 | - | 214 | 74 | 526 | 373 | 254 | 320 | 360 | 665 | 352 | 174 | 581 | 428 | 798 |
| Fort William | 158 | 408 | 492 | 512 | 209 | 607 | 133 | - | 164 | 705 | 613 | 105 | 533 | 539 | 842 | 529 | 388 | 795 | 641 | 977 |
| Glasgow | 148 | 297 | 381 | 401 | 98 | 497 | 46 | 102 | - | 526 | 435 | 278 | 356 | 360 | 665 | 352 | 248 | 616 | 462 | 798 |
| Holyhead | 463 | 152 | 236 | 205 | 228 | 352 | 327 | 438 | 327 | - | 356 | 785 | 267 | 166 | 430 | 198 | 428 | 494 | 283 | 565 |
| Hull | 360 | 140 | 232 | 252 | 171 | 261 | 232 | 381 | 270 | 221 | - | 694 | 98 | 209 | 303 | 159 | 230 | 243 | 150 | 558 |
| Inverness | 106 | 458 | 542 | 562 | 259 | 658 | 158 | 65 | 173 | 488 | 431 | - | 615 | 620 | 922 | 608 | 431 | 875 | 723 | 1057 |
| Leeds | 328 | 121 | 220 | 240 | 121 | 270 | 199 | 331 | 221 | 166 | 61 | 382 | - | 121 | 319 | 71 | 150 | 280 | 117 | 539 |
| Liverpool | 360 | 101 | 185 | 205 | 125 | 301 | 224 | 335 | 224 | 103 | 130 | 385 | 75 | - | 348 | 56 | 282 | 389 | 175 | 483 |
| London | 548 | 120 | 120 | 155 | 313 | 79 | 413 | 523 | 413 | 267 | 188 | 573 | 198 | 216 | - | 328 | 460 | 185 | 209 | 388 |
| Manchester | 353 | 89 | 172 | 193 | 119 | 288 | 219 | 329 | 219 | 123 | 99 | 379 | 44 | 35 | 204 | - | 232 | 299 | 113 | 463 |
| Newcastle | 237 | 207 | 299 | 319 | 58 | 352 | 108 | 241 | 154 | 266 | 143 | 268 | 93 | 175 | 286 | 144 | - | 410 | 257 | 666 |
| Norwich | 490 | 176 | 233 | 267 | 284 | 170 | 361 | 494 | 383 | 307 | 151 | 544 | 174 | 242 | 115 | 186 | 255 | - | 193 | 570 |
| Nottingham | 396 | 53 | 144 | 165 | 188 | 216 | 266 | 398 | 287 | 176 | 93 | 449 | 73 | 109 | 130 | 70 | 160 | 120 | - | 418 |
| Plymouth | 632 | 203 | 125 | 163 | 397 | 291 | 496 | 607 | 496 | 351 | 347 | 657 | 335 | 300 | 241 | 288 | 414 | 354 | 260 | - |

**Roman Figures = Miles;  Italic Figures = Kilometres**

# KEY TO MAPS

1

2

WESTERN
ISLES

Stornoway
Ullapool

SKYE

Mallaig

Fort
William

Oban

3

Campbeltown

Stranraer

Belfast

Dublin

11

Wick

A836

Inverness

Aberdeen

Dundee

M90
M80
M9
EDINBURGH
GLASGOW
M8
M74

A1

4

Carlisle

A69

Newcastle

A1(M)

M6

5

Leeds

Hull

M62

Manchester

M1

M180

M66

M6

6

A5

M54

Birmingham

M42

M50

M5

Cardiff

M4

M4

M3

M5

Plymouth

7

9

10

M1

M40

M25

LONDON

M20

M23

Harwich

M11

Dover

Calais

8

Oostende

Dunkerque

All maps on pages 1-11 are 20 miles to 1 inch

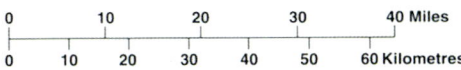

© Baynefield Carto-Graphics Ltd. 1995

ISLES OF SCILLY

Bryher
Samson
Annet
St. Agnes
Tresco
Gugh
St. Martin's
St. Mary's
Hugh Town

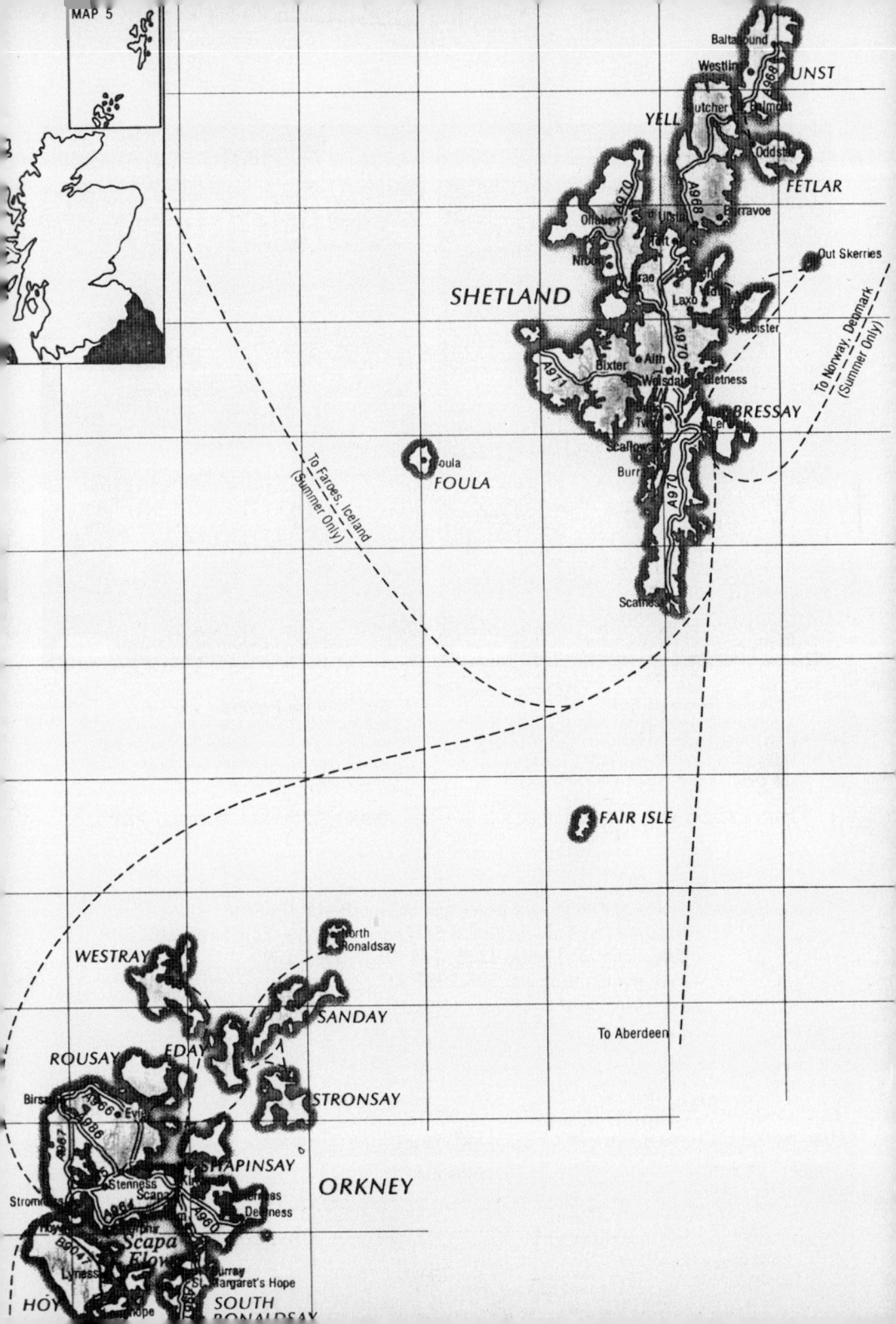

MAP 5

BALTASOUND
Westling
UNST
YELL
utcher Belmont
Oddsta
FETLAR
Ollaberry
Ulsta
Burravoe
Nibon
Toft
Brae
SHETLAND
Laxo
Out Skerries
Symbister
To Norway, Denmark
(Summer Only)
Bixter
Aith
A970
Wellsdale
Gletness
To Faroes, Iceland
(Summer Only)
BRESSAY
Tving
Ler
Foula
Scalloway
FOULA
Burra
A970
Scatness

FAIR ISLE

WESTRAY
Lorth
Ronaldsay
SANDAY
ROUSAY
EDAY
STRONSAY
To Aberdeen
Birsa
A966
Evie
SHAPINSAY
Stenness
Scapa
ORKNEY
Stromness
Deerness
A964
A960
Scapa Flow
Lyness
Burray
St. Margaret's Hope
HOY
SOUTH
RONALDSAY

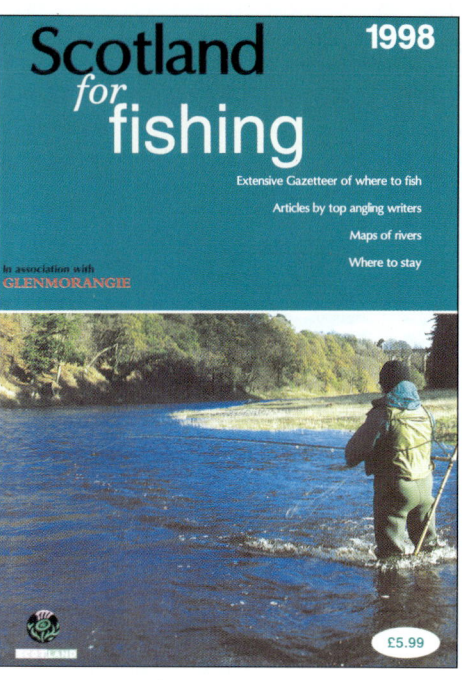

## Scotland Home of Golf

A directory of more than 400 prestigious golf courses, with 50 of the most challenging selected and assessed, all photographed by a well known golf writer. Organised trips and places to stay.

**ISBN 1 873163 60 6  £6.50 incl. P&P**

## Scotland for Fishing

Permits, fishing rights, boat hire, season/dates, rod hire, fly fishing and spinning. Articles and photography by well known contributors. Places to stay; organised packages.

**ISBN 1 873163 59 2  £6.50 incl. P&P**

Please tick your choice and send your order and cheque/Postal Order to:
Pastime Publications Ltd, 8 St. Andrew Square, Edinburgh EH2 2PP.
Telephone: 0131-556 1105  Fax: 0131-556 1129.
VAT Registration No. 593 1987 91.

Name

Address

Tel. No                    Fax No

Date                       Signature